TO FIGHT
AND LEARN

TO FIGHT AND LEARN

THE PRAXIS AND PROMISE OF LITERACY IN ERITREA'S INDEPENDENCE WAR

LES GOTTESMAN

The Red Sea Press, Inc.
Publishers & Distributors of Third World Books

11-D Princess Road
Lawrenceville, NJ 08648

P. O. Box 48
Asmara, ERITREA

The Red Sea Press, Inc.

Publishers & Distributors of Third World Books

11-D Princess Road   P. O. Box 48
Lawrenceville, NJ 08648   Asmara, ERITREA

Copyright © 1998 Les Gottesman

First Printing 1998

Cover Design: Jonathan Gullery
Cover photgraph from *Eritrea: Revolution at Dusk* (p. 95) by Robert Papstein
    (Red Sea Press, 1991) copyright © Robert Papstein, 1991

Library of Congress Cataloging- in-Publication Data

Gottesman, Leslie.
      To Fight and learn : the praxis and promise of literacy in
   Eritrea's independence war / by Les Gottesman.
         p. cm.
      Includes bibliographical references (p.) and index.
      ISBN 1-56902-067-1 (hardcover). -- ISBN 1-56902-068-X (pbk.)
      1. Education--Eritrea--History. 2. Education--Social aspects-
 -Eritrea. 3. Politics and education--Eritrea. 4. Eritrea--Politics
and governments. 5. Literacy--Eritrea. 6. Critical theory.
 I. Title
LA1521.G68   1998
370'.9635--dc21

                           97-51628
                             CIP

Thanks to Wolde Mesghinna, Karen A. Hauser,
Paul Highfield, Annie Herda, Frank Duhl,
Megan Lehmer, Caroline Harrover,
Elias Amare Gebrezgheir, and Lisa Roth.

This book is dedicated to the martyrs of the
Eritrean National Literacy Campaign, 1983–1987

[S]tories are at the heart of what explorers and novelists say about strange regions of the world; they also become the method colonized people use to assert their own identity and the existence of their own history. The main battle in imperialism is over land, of course; but when it came to who owned the land, who had the right to settle and work on it, who kept it going, who won it back, and who now plans its future—these issues were reflected, contested, and even for a time decided in narrative. As one critic has suggested, nations themselves *are* narrations. The power to narrate, or to block other narratives from forming and emerging, is very important to culture and imperialism, and constitutes one of the main connections between them. Most important, the grand narratives of emancipation and enlightenment mobilized people in the colonial world to rise up and throw off imperial subjection; in the process, many Europeans and Americans were also stirred by these stories and their protagonists, and they too fought for new narratives of equality and human community.

Edward W. Said, 1993

The problems of Eritrea, whether of its past, its present, or its future, are extraordinarily interesting for a whole number of reasons, and whether or not one is especially concerned with African questions. These problems are interesting for their human reference: the Eritreans with all their distinctive character and style, their ecology, their ethnic composition, their record of suffering oppression and of resisting oppression, their country and what (in spite of large and lengthy invasions) they have been able to make of their country. These problems, again, are interesting to the historian because they draw much of their substance from the very depths of the development of nationalism in the colonial and postcolonial world. They are interesting to the political scientist for their intractability, but also for their possible solutions that now stand to be examined. They are interesting to linguists, soil scientists, agronomists, and, not least on the list, plain observers of the drama of the human scene. They are old problems, not new ones; all that is new today are their possible solutions.

Basil Davidson, 1980

TABLE OF CONTENTS

Introduction 1
The Research Process 4
    Research Participants 5
    Non-Eritreans Living in Eritrea 5
    Educational Administrators 6
    Literacy Teachers 7
    Women 7
    Government Officials 8
    Others 8
  The Research Problem, Themes, and Questions 8
    Questions for Students 9
    Questions for Teachers 9
    Questions for Administrators 10
  Conceptual Framework of the Research
    Method 12
  Conceptual Framework of the Research
    Problem, Themes, and Questions 17
    Narrative and Self 18
    Narrative and Legitimation 22
    Notes 23

I War and Beyond 27
  Country and People 30
  A Model of Development 30
  Education and Transformation 32
  Notes 35

II History of Eritrea 39
  Claims and Counter Claims 39
  The Colonial Period 40
  Development Under the Italians 41

British Administration. 44
Federation and Annexation 45
The Eritrean Liberation Front 47
The Dergue. 48
Eritrea in World Politics 50
Self-Reliance in War 53
From War to Peace 56
The Provisional Government of Eritrea 56
Notes 61

III Education, Precolonial to Postliberation. 67
The Tradition of Exemplary Practice 68
Education in Italian Eritrea 75
Educational Development in the British Decade . . . 78
Education in the Federal Period, 1952-1962 80
Imperial Education 81
Education Under the Dergue 83
EPLF Education Programs. 86
    Development of Country-wide Schooling 87
    The National Literacy Campaign 89
    Educational Objectives 91
    Education After Liberation 95
Notes 105

IV Education and Development: Two models 111
The Weak Basic Needs Approach. 112
Empowerment, or The Strong BNA 117
Self Reliance: Trial and Trend 118
Notes 122

V Hermeneutic and Critical Problems 125
Legitimation 127
Ricoeur's "Political Educator" 130
Fusion of Horizons 135

Philosophical Hermeneutics and Critical Theory . . 140
Misunderstanding 142
Ideology as Distortion 143
Ricoeur's Reconciliation of Hermeneutics
    and Critical Theory 144
Ideology and Narrative 147
Constraints on Praxis 149
Constraints on Women 153
The Hermeneutic Project 155
Communities of Memory 157
Narrative and Nationalism 158
Construction of Memory 159
Effective History 162
Notes 165

VI **Legitimation of Literacy** 173
A Decade's Difference 174
The Literacy Campaign: Plan and Practice 175
Communicative Praxis 179
Negotiation 184
    Validity Claims 186
    Intelligibility and Truth 188
    Rightness 193
    The EPLF Subculture 199
    Truthfulness 204
    Behavior Change 205
    Work and Risk 206
    Innovation 207
    Coercion 211
    *The Praxis of Negotiation and the
        Promise of Literacy* 213
    Students as Teachers, Teachers as Students . . 222

Postliberation Negotiation:
Language of Instruction 225
Legitimation 230
Notes 245

Conclusion: Return to the Source 251
Notes 262

Index 267

ILLUSTRATIONS

Senait Lijam and Leteyesus Negassi. 7

A boy's sweater celebrates independence
after 30 years of war. 27

Eritrea in the Horn of Africa. 31

A graffitist's tribute to Mussolini near Decamhare 43

Formerly blind woman cured by EPLF surgeons. 55

Haile Selassie's Red Sea palace, destroyed
by aerial bombing. 57

Sister Mary Thomas Johnston. 85

Classroom at Sembel Elementary School, Asmara 96

Beraki Ghebreselassie 100

Kaleab Haile. 176

Texture of communicative praxis. 181

Zecarias Tedros 190

Bilen household containers
(watercolor by Zecarias Tedros) 191

Young Tigre woman
(watercolor by Zecarias Tedros). 191

Tigre mother from Nacfa
(watercolor by Zecarias Tedros). 192

Woldemichael Ghebretensae 198

Berhane Demoz. 210

Saleh Mahmud 214

Ayn Alem "Joe" Marcos 236

INTRODUCTION

R esearch is a continuation of dialogue by other means."[1] Hans-Georg Gadamer's statement is true in at least two senses. The process of research is a conversational practice. And the reporting of research furthers conversation within the community of scholars, and, in some cases, in the public sphere too.

The research I report on here, on wartime education in Eritrea, participates in three dialogical processes: *(a)* the confrontation between tradition and social innovation, *(b)* discussion and debate among proponents and practitioners of differing models of social transformation for national development in Africa, and *(c)* colloquy across the increasingly "blurred" boundaries that nominally separate "schools" of theory and practice in the humanities and human sciences.[2] I have assembled a dialogue from these diverse scholarly sources, in which they question and answer each other, build on each other's theories and arguments, and even finish each other's sentences.

In addition, my research and this report include actual dialogue, as it is commonly thought of, that is, face-to-face conversations. In 1993, from February through April, I lived in Asmara, working as a volunteer with curriculum designers and teacher trainers of the Department of Education of the Provisional Government of Eritrea;[3] teaching at the University of Asmara; and leading workshops for journalists for what was to be the country's first independent newspaper. In April 1993, I witnessed Eritrea's historic, United Nations-supervised referendum in which an astonishing 99.805

percent of voters cast ballots for independence. In the course of these activities, I met the educators and adult students with whom I recorded conversations for this study.

Early in the process of conducting these interviews, I began to meet the men and women, now in their twenties, who had spent their teenage years as literacy teachers in far-flung villages in areas liberated by the Eritrean People's Liberation Front (EPLF). Some of these rural areas had been only semi-liberated, still vulnerable to incursions by Ethiopian troops, and the teachers had been threatened with capture and death. However, rather than highlighting the dangers and their narrow escapes, the stories they told me focused more on the learning process they themselves had gone through as they encountered and worked within the various Eritrean cultures. The transcriptions of their memories of and reflections on the mid-1980s literacy campaign form the primary data of this study, and appear herein at length.

My interest in Eritrea dates from the early 1980s when I worked on a relief drive for Eritrean refugees, the Eritrea Material Aid Campaign. EMAC raised money to support subsistence industries and training at the Solomuna refugee camp in liberated Eritrea, and collected school supplies to be sent to the Revolution School (also called the Zero School) in Eritrea. The campaign was mounted by a small number of Eritreans—members of the San Francisco Bay Area chapter of the National Union of Eritrean Students in North America, an organization of the EPLF—and Americans.

As well as collect money and school materials, EMAC tried to increase public awareness of the Eritrean independence cause. As part of the campaign, the EMAC members developed educational literature and slide shows, and presented films, speakers, and classes on Eritrea at libraries and community centers. In the course of the campaign, we had the opportunity to meet with and present public programs featuring EPLF leaders, some of whom have since become government officials. I became familiar with Eritrean history, politics, and the conduct of the war. In my reading and in conversations with Eritreans, I was impressed by the EPLF's approach to social problems and their programs in education, health, and agriculture, and in organizing grass roots democracy.

In the mid-1980s, with the Horn of Africa stricken by drought and famine, Eritreans in the United States refocused their organizational efforts toward collecting famine relief. Political questions of the war and support for Eritrean independence were downplayed. In truth, there had been little interest in or support for Eritrea forthcoming from Americans. Although EMAC had raised a few thousand dollars, and the Eritreans expressed appreciation for our work, we were unable to overcome Eritrea's political isolation; although fighting an avowedly socialist enemy backed by the Soviet Union, the EPLF *(a)* was denounced by the United States as secessionist and Marxist, and *(b)* was determined—and confident of their ability—to conduct a self-reliant war and end up victorious, independent, and beholden to no one. On these accounts, the Eritrean cause alienated Americans of all political persuasions. In 1985, EMAC was discontinued.

With the end of the war in 1991, supporters of the Eritrean cause were overjoyed. Although I had done no work on behalf of Eritrea for several years, I had maintained contact with Wolde Mesghinna, a northern California representative of the EPLF who had worked closely with EMAC. Wolde had, many years before, issued an open invitation to EMAC members to celebrate Eritrean independence in Eritrea at the war's end. In 1991 I was working on my doctorate in education at the University of San Francisco, in a program which encouraged international research. Eritrea was the obvious choice for me, and I contacted Wolde to explore the possibility of going there. He was enthusiastic, suggested people in Eritrea I might contact, and was kind enough to convey my letters to the Department of Education and to the University of Asmara on his trip to Eritrea in December, 1991 (at that time mail to Eritrea had to be hand-carried).

I desired not only to learn of but also to contribute to educational efforts. In contacting Eritrean educators regarding my research, I also volunteered my services in any capacity they might find useful, outlining my background in educational administration and in teaching English-as-a-second-language, literature, composition, and public speaking at Golden Gate University. My letters were mostly unanswered, owing no doubt to the lack of international mail service. Upon arriving in Asmara in early February, 1993, however, I found all of the educational institutions I had contacted ready to assign me some work. I happily obliged, and spent three months engaged in educational projects: I taught an

English composition class at the University of Asmara; conducted twice-weekly writing workshops for the Curriculum Development Institute of the Department of Education; edited curriculum materials, textbooks, and proposals; presented weekend workshops to teacher trainers at the Teacher Training Institute; and co-presented twice-weekly journalism workshops to the prospective staff of a newspaper under development by the Regional Centre for Human Rights and Development.[4] Through these projects, I met many of the educators who became participants in my research.

The Research Process

The research method I have used is based on philosophical hermeneutics as an interpretive framework for texts[5] "taken away" from Eritrea. The bulk of these texts consists of transcriptions of recorded conversations with Eritrean educational administrators, teachers, and students. Additional texts are in three forms: *(a)* notebooks of personal reflections on these conversations and of general observations on Eritrean society, *(b)* official and unofficial documents on education by Eritrean educators, Eritrean government departments, and non-governmental, non-Eritrean agencies working in Eritrea, and *(c)* memories ("among those 'texts' taken away we can include memories—events patterned, simplified, stripped of immediate context in order to be interpreted in later reconstruction and portrayal"[6]). This data was recorded and collected in Eritrea from February through April 1993.

The research process followed the pattern characterized by Robert N. Bellah as action-reflection-universality.[7] The process recognizes "that social science is a moral as well as a cognitive enterprise and that the relations between the social scientist and those who are studied must be moral rather than manipulative." "Moral regard" for the participants in the study and a collaborative approach to the process "involves ... sharing of research findings ... and reciprocal self-interpretation between the social scientist and the society that is studied."[8]

> [W]e start from where we are, in the midst of society, observing persons and actions that are deemed good or bad, right or wrong. We attempt to clarify our ideas

about action by rational reflection and discussion, but action itself is rooted in established practice (*hexis, habitus*) that is not caused by nor fully amenable to theory or theoretical reconstruction. This is one reason why interpretation (of potentially inexhaustible meanings) takes precedence over explanation (in principle without remainder) in the human studies.[9]

Bellah cautions against a view of this process as merely mirroring social reality; social scientists "have commitments not only to the people they study but also to the tradition in which they stand, a tradition that has theoretical and methodological content" that informs the researcher's role in the conversations and in the interpretive process. However, the "substantive moral content"[10] of the process derives not from sociological theory and methodology, but from the ethical tradition of the discipline: "the paradigmatic example of the ethically mature person can never be transcended by a rationally constructed theory."[11]

Research Participants

Including those conducted before and after the period I spent in Eritrea, thirty-eight conversations comprised the "data" for this study. Of these, thirty-six were electronically recorded, and thirty-one of those have been transcribed, amounting to over 186,000 words. Participants fall into six groups, with some individuals appearing in two categories. I spoke with five non-Eritreans living in Eritrea; twelve administrators of the Department of Education of the Provisional Government of Eritrea; four individuals who had been young teachers in the mid-1980s national literacy campaign; eight women, four of whom were staff members of the National Union of Eritrean Women; three officials of non-educational departments of the Provisional Government of Eritrea; and four other individuals.

Non-Eritreans Living in Eritrea
All of my participants were Eritreans except for Scott Jones, Karen A. Hauser, Paul Highfield, Sister Mary Thomas Johnston, and Sherry Phillips. I recorded three telephone conversations with Scott

Jones, a forest scientist working on major reforestation projects in Eritrea. I did not record, but took notes on, a telephone conversation with Karen A. Hauser, who was Development and Outreach Director of the Eritrean Relief Committee. (Jones and Hauser were in Eritrea at the same time as I was, Hauser in a new position with the Regional Centre for Human Rights and Development. However, my conversations with them were conducted earlier, in the United States in 1991 and 1992.) Paul Highfield is British, has lived in Eritrea for eight years, teaching English and developing English curriculum for the Department of Education. He is an EPLF member. My conversations with Highfield were the first I recorded in Eritrea, on March 2, 1993, and the last I recorded, on January 18, 1994, when Highfield visited California. Sister Thomas is Scottish and a member of the Comboni Sisters, the order that founded the University of Asmara in 1958; she has lived in Eritrea since 1964 and in 1993 was the Chair of the English Department of the University. Sherry Phillips is Trinidadian, has lived in Canada, and was residing in Asmara where she was a staff member and researcher of the National Union of Eritrean Women.

Educational Administrators

The largest category of participants, a total of twelve, were administrators of the Department of Education: Kaleab Haile, head of the Adult Education Division; Ayn Alem "Joe" Marcos, in charge of teacher training; Tesfamicael Gerahtu, head of the Curriculum Development Institute; Yacob Tewelde, member of the English Panel of the Curriculum Development Institute; Mohammedin Jassir, a member of the Saho Panel of the Curriculum Development Institute; Semere Solomon, head, and Berhane Demoz and Girmay Haile, members, of the Planning and Program Division; Woldemichael Ghebretensae, head of the Provincial Office of Education, Senhit Province, in the city of Keren; Solomon Ghebremariam, an administrator of the Provincial Office of Education, Seraye Province, in the town of Mendefera; and Beraki Ghebreselassie, head of the Department of Education. Paul Highfield, whom I included in the non-Eritreans group, is also a member of the educational administrators group.

Literacy Teachers

In my first few conversations with educational administrators Kaleab Haile and Ayn Alem Marcos, they emphasized the historical and experiential importance of the national literacy campaign of 1983 to 1987—both in the development of pedagogy and curriculum for adults, and in the formative development of a group of educators, the teachers of the literacy campaign. With the help of Ayn Alem Marcos, I began to seek out teachers who had participated in the literacy campaign. Many of them were still involved in education, as teachers, administrators, or university students. The literacy teachers with whom I spoke were Solomon Woldmichel, Abraham Bahre, Zecarias Tedros, and Saleh Mahmud, all of them presently students at the University of Asmara, where former combatants were allowed to enroll for the first time in Fall 1992. Finding them was a slow process conducted through word of mouth. Fortunately, over time, I was able to meet all the literacy workers whose names I had who lived in Asmara. I was not given the names of any of the women who taught in the campaign.

Senait Lijam, Education Coordinator, and Leteyesus Negassi, head of the Project Department of the National Union of Eritrean Women. They have been EPLF members since the early 1970s.

Women

I had hoped that women would appear in all categories. Sadly, I came in contact with few women educators.[12] I sought women for interviews. I spoke with Abeba Tesfagiorgis, a founder and director of the Regional Centre for Human Rights and Development and author of *A Painful Season and a Stubborn Hope: The Odyssey of an Eritrean Mother* (1992). I interviewed four members of the National Union of Eritrean Women, Leteyesus Negassi, Senait Lijam, Elsa Gebreyesus, and Sherry Phillips. Finally, I spoke with Salome Iyob, an adult high school student and computer operator for the Department of

Education. This category, of course, also includes Karen A. Hauser and Sister Mary Thomas Johnston, non-Eritrean women living in Eritrea.

Government Officials
In addition to educational administrators, I spoke with Saleh Meki, Secretary of Marine Resources and Inland Fisheries, and Yemane Ghebreab, Deputy Secretary of the Department of External Affairs. These conversations dealt with the overall political, economic, and development situation in the country.

Others
Four individuals are not accounted for the in the above groups. Wolde Mesghinna is an engineer who, at the time of our conversation, was working in Berkeley, California. Wolde was my regular contact with the Eritrean struggle from the late 1970s to the present, and he made the initial contact with the Department of Education on my behalf which allowed me to conduct my research in Eritrea. Issayas Tesfamariam is a historian working at the Hoover Institute at Stanford University, Palo Alto, California. Conversations with Wolde and Issayas were the earliest I recorded, in 1991 and 1992. I met Alula Mesfun in Asmara, where he had returned after a long absence. He was an EPLF fighter in the late 1970s before he went to Europe where he has lived since. Kiflemariam Zerom is an English instructor who generously shared his office with me at the University of Asmara.

The Research Problem, Themes, and Questions
In conversations in Eritrea I sought not just information on the educational policies and programs available and under development. In addition, I attempted to elicit (and record) narrative accounts of students', teachers', and administrators' educational experiences, and speculation (that is, a narrative of their expectations) on the effects of their past, present, and future educational experiences on themselves, their communities, and Eritrean national life. Using hermeneutic analysis of plots, metaphors, narrative selectivity, representations of time, characterizations of self and community, etc., I have examined two principle themes—negotiation (appeals to traditions

and to the idea of modernization in introducing education to the population, and individual and popular reactions of resistance and accommodation to such appeals) and legitimation (acceptance and rejection of change-oriented educational experiences)—and I have drawn conclusions regarding the efficacy of specific educational practices in effecting change. This study provides support for the general proposition that those educational policies which are based on or incorporate customary social practices and traditional knowledge and thought are the more effective in bringing about changes in social practices.

The research conversations were aimed at eliciting narratives of two types: *(a)* accounts of past and present educational experiences, and *(b)* speculations about the future effects of education on the individual, community, and Eritrean society. The following prompts and questions were used in conversations.

Questions for Students

1. Tell me your educational history.

2. How does/did your family and/or community feel about your getting an education?

3. How has education fitted in with your life so far? How has it fitted in with your family? Your community?

4. What is going to happen to you? How will education change your life? How will it change your family? Your community?

5. What is going to happen in Eritrea? How is education changing Eritrea? What do you think of that?

Questions for Teachers

1. Where, when, and whom did you teach?

2. What was the cultural, social, and educational background of your students and their community? How did the community feel about education prior to your coming?

3. How did the students respond to schooling? How did the community respond? Were there conflicts? What happened?

4. What did you learn from the students? Did your teaching change because of this? Did the curriculum change? Did the students make demands or insist that education address certain issues of importance to them? Or stay away from some issues?

5. How did schooling help students accomplish projects and goals they already had? How did it introduce new projects and goals? What happened?

6. What personal changes did students experience? How did they express these changes?

7. How do the results of your educational practice fit in with the nationalist struggle and development of Eritrea? How do students see this?

Questions for Administrators

1. How have educational demands changed since liberation? What do people want? What do they expect from the government?

2. How well can the government respond to people's needs and wants for education? Are there issues where the government disagrees with people's ideas regarding educational policies and programs?

3. What does the government want from the people? What will be compulsory in education? How much will communities be expected to be involved in making decisions and in running the educational programs?

4. What lessons from the period of providing education in the field[13]—to fighters and to the population—seem most useful in the present and future programs and policies?

I attempted continually to encourage narrative responses in the conversations; this was not, however, always necessary: as Elliot G. Mishler has observed,

> "answers" to questions often display the features of narratives. . . . Clearly, they may be elicited by direct questions to "tell a story," but they also appear as responses to narrow questions about specific topics and individuals' reports in in-depth interviews of significant life experiences and events. When interviewers allow respondents to speak and when investigators are alert to the possibility and look for narratives, their ubiquity is evident.[14]

"Provided investigators can give up control over the research process and approach interviews as conversations, almost any question can generate a narrative," notes Catherine Kohler Riessman. "[E]ven questions that could be answered by a yes or no can generate extended accounts."[15] However, I found that two topics evoked avoidance and resistance to narration. Participants avoided giving information on combat deaths and injuries (requests for which I did not press). The formula I heard most often was that a family member or comrade-in-arms "was martyred." The second resistance I encountered was the reluctance of (especially senior) government administrators, including those in education, to speak to me of personal experiences. I asked Beraki Ghebreselassie, the head of the Department of Education, if he would "tell me a little bit" about his background. "I'm not ready to," he replied, "because it doesn't seem to be relevant to tell you my background." I similarly began my conversation with Tesfamicael Gerahtu, head of the Curriculum Development Institute:

> LES GOTTESMAN: Mainly I'm going to ask you about curriculum, of course. But before I do, I would like to know a little bit about your background in education, what you've done through the years, because I don't know.
>
> TESFAMICAEL GERAHTU: You mean me personally?
>
> LG: Personally, yes. Whatever you want to say. Just briefly.
>
> TG: I don't think I have too much to say.

These responses were in keeping with the often-noted self-effacing political style of EPLF members.[16] An exception to this was Ayn Alem Marcos, the head of teacher training; he expressed great regret that so little documentation of the EPLF's experiences had survived the war and was, himself, a source of many stories relating his own experiences or those he knew of. Younger Department officials such as Berhane Demoz were more willing to speak of their experiences, but it was the youngest educators, who as teenage Zero School students fanned out "behind enemy lines" (Ayn Alem Marcos' phrase) in the mid-1980s to spread literacy to rural Eritreans, whose stories were most personal and autobiographical. The lingering amazement with which they looked back on their moral and intellectual growth, in those dangerous days, became the *bildungsroman* of my research.

Conceptual Framework of the Research Method

Philosophical hermeneutics informs the conceptual framework of both the research methodology (analysis of a text created through the transcription of dialogues), which is discussed in this section, and the terms of analysis and interpretation of the text thus created, which is discussed in the next section of this chapter, *Conceptual Framework of the Research Problem, Themes, and Questions.*

In my study, I, a North American white male urban university professor, have attempted to understand how (that is, when) education can bring about social change among African peasants and pastoralists (and when not). Further, I suggest how educational policies in general can be designed to increase the likelihood of this result. This is an ambitious, seemingly audacious, claim, based as it is on three dozen conversations in which I was, as Clifford Geertz characterizes the problem of cross-cultural analysis and interpretation,

> seeking, in the widened sense of the term in which it encompasses very much more than talk, to converse with [people of another culture], a matter a great deal more difficult, and not only with strangers, than is commonly recognized.[17]

The possibility of success in this endeavor lies in *(a)* the potential of conversation to create understanding and *(b)* the meaning of interpretation. In an essay on Geertz, Paul Ricoeur links conversation to interpretation:

> In conversation we have an interpretive attitude. . . . If
> . . . we want to recognize a group's values on the basis
> of its self-understanding of these values, then we must
> welcome these values in a positive way, and this is to
> converse.[18]

Gadamer characterizes conversation as

> a process of coming to an understanding. Thus it belongs
> to every true conversation that each person opens himself
> to the other, truly accepts his point of view as valid and
> transposes himself into the other to such an extent that
> he understands not the particular individual but what he
> says. What is to be grasped is the substantive rightness of
> his opinion, so that we can be at one with each other on
> the subject. Thus we do not relate the other's opinion to
> him but to our own opinions and views.[19]

Conversational understanding is not a presumptuous shaping by one participant of the symbolic property of another:

> To conduct a conversation means to allow oneself to be
> conducted by the subject matter to which the partners in
> the dialogue are orientated. . . . [T]o question means to
> lay open, to place in the open. As against the fixity of
> opinions, questioning makes the object and all its possi-
> bilities fluid.[20]

Such a conversation is beyond manipulation because it is out of the individual's control:

> a genuine conversation is never the one that we wanted
> to conduct. Rather, it is generally more correct to say
> that we fall into conversation or even that we become
> involved in it. The way one word follows another, with
> the conversation taking its own twists and reaching its
> own conclusion, may well be conducted in some way,
> but the partners conversing are far less the leaders than
> the led. No one knows in advance what will "come out"

of a conversation. Understanding or its failure is like an event that happens to us.[21]

A second stage of interpretation is the appropriation by one conversant of the collective symbolic product. This, it is important to state, is not "appropriation as taking possession; rather, it consists in subordinating ourselves to the text's claim to dominate our minds."[22] This interpretive "event"[23] allows cross-cultural understanding:

> the miracle of understanding consists in the fact that no like-mindedness is necessary to recognize what is really significant and fundamentally meaningful in tradition. We have the ability to open ourselves to the superior claim the text makes and to respond to what it has to tell us.[24]

In explaining what anthropologists do, Geertz writes, "we begin with our own interpretations of what our informants are up to, or think they are up to, and then systematize those."[25] This is interpretation at another "remove" from the conversational moment—which Geertz acknowledges:

> the object of study is one thing and the study of it another. . . . [A]nthropological writings are themselves interpretations, and second and third order ones to boot. (By definition, only a "native" makes first order ones: it's *his* [*sic*] culture.) They are, thus, fictions; fictions in the sense that they are "something made," "something fashioned."[26]

Yet the interpretive fictions or removes, at whatever order, do not falsify, diminish, or deny the force of the original object over the meaning which interpretation aims at. "The meaning to be understood is concretized and fully realized only in interpretation, but the interpretive activity considers itself wholly bound by the meaning of the text."[27] These are the conditions, then, and the guarantee, of the interpretive task of making meaning, in North America, of the text of conversations recorded in Eritrea. Confronting those texts and the task of interpretation, I have had the memory of the face-to-face conversations, my initiating questions, probing questions, and requests for clarification, and my interpretations *in situ*, spoken or unspoken, during and immediately after each conversation (notebook entries made after each conversation have aided me in re-claiming its physical, emotional, and interpretive context). Never-theless, interpretation is always *now*, always here. Whereas, as James Clifford points out, "To understand discourse you 'had to have been there' in the presence of the discoursing subject," inter-pretation, on the other hand, "is not interlocution. It does not depend on being in the presence of a speaker."[28] Gadamer, howev-er, sees interpretation as *modeled* on discursive interlocution:

> in dialogue spoken language—in the process of question and answer, giving and taking, talking at cross purposes and seeing each other's point—performs the communi-cation of meaning that, with respect to the written tra-dition, is the task of hermeneutics. Hence it is more than a metaphor; it is a memory of what originally was the case, to describe the task of hermeneutics as entering into dialogue with the text.[29]

Nevertheless, the meaning of the transcribed conversations, the con-versations as text, will have changed and grown, in response to new questions: "the meaning of a sentence is relative to the question to which it is a reply, but that implies that its meaning necessarily exceeds what is said in it."[30] These new questions will have sprung from the categories of interpretation, "using nomological principles that are the contribution of the [interpretive] discipline and that must not, consequently, be confused with those categories by which a cul-ture understands itself."[31] The interpretive disciplines, in Edward Said's account, can fairly be said to display a culture of their own:

> we must be prepared to accept the fact that a representa-tion is *eo ipso* implicated, intertwined, embedded, inter-woven with a great many other things besides the "truth," which is itself a representation. What this must lead us to methodologically is to view representations (or misrepresentations—the distinction is at best a matter of degree) as inhabiting a common field of play defined for them, not by some inherent common subject matter alone, but by some common history, tradition, universe of discourse. Within this field, which no single scholar can create but which each scholar receives and in which

he then finds a place for himself, the individual researcher makes his contribution. Such contributions, even for the exceptional genius, are strategies for redisposing material within the field; even the scholar who unearths a once-lost manuscript produces the "found" text in a context already prepared for it, for that is the real meaning of *finding* a new text. Thus each individual contribution first causes changes within the field and then promotes a new stability, in the way that on a surface covered with twenty compasses the introduction of a twenty-first will cause all the others to quiver, then to settle into a new accommodating configuration.[32]

In Ricoeur's account, interpretation of a text involves two processes: distanciation and appropriation.

The moment of distanciation is implied by fixation in writing and by all comparable phenomena in the sphere of the transmission of discourse. Writing is not simply a matter of the material fixation of discourse; for fixation is the condition of a much more fundamental phenomenon, that of the autonomy of the text.[33]

This autonomy is analogous to the differentiations met earlier: Gadamer's differentiation of the sentence and what it says, and Geertz's distinction between object of study and the study itself.[34] Ricoeur points to the prior distanciation "already present in discourse itself . . . the distanciation of the said from the saying." Distanciation Ricoeur identifies as the "condition" of interpretation and appropriation as its moment of: "What is sought is [not] an intention hidden behind the text, but a world unfolded in front of it. . . . To understand is not to project oneself into the text but to expose oneself to it; it is to receive a self enlarged by the appropriation of the proposed world which interpretation unfolds."[35] Appropriation overcomes the seeming audacity (or impossibility) of cross-cultural understanding:

One of the aims of all hermeneutics is to struggle against cultural distance. This struggle can be understood in . . . . genuinely hermeneutical terms as a struggle against the estrangement from meaning itself, that is, from the system of values upon which the text is based. In this sense, interpretation "brings together," "equalises," renders "contemporary and similar," thus making one's *own* what was initially *alien.*[36]

My act of understanding how education changes Eritreans is also intended to be an act of generalization, of understanding how educational policies, in general, can be designed to effect social change in adult populations in underdeveloped countries. This task is not a later stage of analysis, a "recommendations" section of the report. This intention cannot be separated from who I am, an educator, a fact always already present in my conversations, reflections, and analyses. This fact, and the exigencies of my research, bring forth that aspect of appropriation which can be designated as application, the third element in Gadamer's hermeneutic triad of understanding, interpretation, and application. I am pointing here to a specific instance of application. In fact, all parties to all conversations always apply understanding because in the use of language "concepts are constantly in the process of being formed."[37] In Gadamer's account, "understanding always involves something like applying the text to be understood to the interpreter's present situation. . . . [A]pplication [is] just as integral a part of the hermeneutical process as are understanding and interpretation."[38] The immediacy of understanding "proves to be an event" because the text makes a claim on us as we (already) are, that is, "at every moment, in every concrete situation, in a new and different way."[39] Application is the act of (and proof of) hermeneutics overcoming "the alienation of meaning that the text has undergone" due to time, culture, or situation.[40]

Conceptual Framework of the Research Problem, Themes, and Questions

The research problem, themes of inquiry, and conversation questions are based on a theoretical relationship between narrativity and legitimation. This study essentially asks: How can adult education effect social change? How will education overcome problems of the legitimation of policies which seek to change social practices? The conversation questions are meant to prompt narratives of Eritreans' educational experiences and expectations. I must explain, then, the link between change, legitimation, and narrative.

Narrative and Self

Education has been crucial in social transformations which have already begun in Eritrea, for example in programs for settling pastoralists into agricultural communities; in reforestation; in changing health habits and sanitation practices; in changing marriage customs; in bringing women into politics, the military, community development, and professional careers. Social changes such as these necessitate, for individuals and communities, new self-understandings within livable narratives. "Narrative," says Donald E. Polkinghorne, "is the form of hermeneutic expression in which human action is understood and made meaningful."[41] Philip Lewin explains:

> We come to comprehend the world and our place in it by embedding the events of everyday life in larger structures. These narrative threads orient our immediate sense of who we are.... From time to time, these narratives are reconstructed, not only incorporating new experience but reconceptualizing old.[42]

In the process of education, individuals encounter new narratives in which, according to Ricoeur, "[w]hat is to be interpreted ... is a proposed world which I could inhabit and in which I could project my ownmost possibilities."[43] These possibilities, Kevin J. Vanhoozer explains, are possibilities for action: "The world projected by the work allows one to explore possibilities of action and so have 'fictive experiences.' By 'fictive experience' Ricoeur understands a virtual manner of inhabiting the proposed world."[44] They are also possibilities for "imaginative variations of the *ego*."[45] In other words, education provides the opportunity for adults to inhabit new stories and new selves. But for a narrative to be taken up, it must be one which

> retrospectively revises, selects, and orders past details in such a way as to create a self-narrative that is coherent and satisfying and that will serve as a justification for one's present condition and situation.... It also includes the construction of a future story that continues the "I" of the person.[46]

Selection and ordering also operate in the projection of a future story. The themes I pursued—*(a)* specific notions of tradition or modernization to which education as a formal process makes appeal, *(b)* the range of responses to such appeals, and *(c)* the final acceptance or rejection of the educational process—are designed to elicit narrative accounts which will answer specific questions about education and social change. These themes center on the question of whether, and a description of how, promise unfolds within educational praxis.[47] Promise is a key concept because promise underwrites the risk of a refashioned self-narrative.

> There needs to be some continuity between past and future stories. A problem may arise, however, because the past story is a recollection of what has already been, and the future story, although it needs to be a continuation of the past, requires an open and adaptive character."[48]

Stephen Crites speaks of two types of "unhappiness" arising from the misapplication of narrative strategies, for

> there is a crucial formal difference between images and stories recollected and those projected. Those recollected are capable of high definition, a large measure of completeness. An image of the future is vague and sketchy, a story incomplete and thin.[49]

I take "unhappiness" as a present condition resulting from the inability to legitimate a narrative account of either the past or the future.

> The first type of unhappiness consists in the failure to appropriate my personal past by making a connected, coherent story of it. Of course I cannot fail to have a past, but I can let it be forgotten, or I can actively suppress it, or I can be so intent on my future project that I let my roots in the past grow weak. In either case I lose my identity, having no more of a story than the bare chronicle that appears on my curriculum vitae. . . .
>
> The second type of unhappiness consists in the failure to pro-ject [*sic*] myself hopefully into the future. I cannot, short of death, fail to have a future, but I can ignore or actively resist its claim and live from day to day without any projective scenario, or I can devote all my energy to protecting and reiterating the identity I

have recollected out of the past. In either case, I live without risk and without hope, doing only what is necessary to subsist more or less in the manner to which I am accustomed.[50]

Education, in proposing new narratives, must navigate between the Scylla of a dictatorial past and Charybdis of a lotus-eating future. Education, offering objects for consideration and projects for adoption, promises that traditional notions of the good life will be fulfilled while avoiding the constriction of the good to the repetition of the past. "The effort to narrate the future in the same detail as the past commits the formal error of treating it as if it were past," says Crites, a vain act of control, but understandable in some individuals or communities because the future "can be profoundly threatening" to those who want to "shore up the [selves they have] come to own: who want[their] past to be [their] future."[51] But when education does this it's not merely a "formal error," a narrative overreach—it's a deception, a lie, and a trick. Past forms must serve new goals, and about this there must be no sleight of hand, no surprise ending. In land reform in Eritrea, the return to traditional land redistribution schemes is aimed not at a recreation of the past but at an opening of new possibilities, for example the innovations of land being allotted to women, landlord power being challenged, and democracy being practiced in the distribution process.

At the same time, appeals to modernization have to avoid the displacement from the past which renders identity indistinct. Modernization, says Ricoeur, "while being an advancement of mankind, at the same time constitutes a sort of subtle destruction" of traditional cultures and, more importantly, of the "creative nucleus" of culture.[52] "To become a self," according to Crites, "is to appropriate a past, and that takes digging."[53] Nevertheless, it's the future which is vague and unformed, not the past. The

> very indeterminacy of the future, which perils the passage from cup to lip, also permits hope to spread its wings, with its wild dreams: a hope that only in a proximate sense is directed to some definite goal of a definite self, while ultimately it is directed to the very boundlessness of possibility.[54]

Possibility is the space of hope. "Hope is precisely that openness of the present toward the boundless horizon of possibility."[55] Education, in proposing a narrative, a specific possible future, transforms hope to promise: hope engaged. Then,

> [l]ife-span events are parts of an ongoing process which culminates in the "effect" to be explained. Although the reason why the life event has occurred does not flow from a deduction of formal logic, the perception of the patterned totality described by narrative brings with it the experience of causal "power."[56]

The end of the war in Eritrea has opened up possibilities which can occasion a range of future-oriented thinking, from highly imaginative to concrete and technical. While the structural changes now occurring in Eritrean society, politics, the economy, and so on, are experienced differently by individual Eritreans depending on region, ethnic identity, and recent history, all Eritreans are sharing a collective revisioning of the future in which diverse hopes are recast as promise. Promise defines causal power, individual and community responsibility, meaningful action, and signs of failure and success: "each fulfillment is perceived as confirmation, pledge, and repetition of the promise."[57]

Negotiation, accommodation, and resistance are processes in the appropriation of new stories. Within the "imaginative variations of the *ego*" which Ricoeur characterizes as appropriation,[58] some variations are more successful, more credible, more integrative, more *me* than others. There is the accustoming of oneself to the new form of one's identity, as one does to bold new clothes. There is the gathering of experience and information which puts flesh and features on identity, that one may find in it the contours of one's own personality. That is why education is a process and teaching is an art, why political strategies for change exist, and why strategies which unfold in calculated steps need not be manipulative, for they are interpretive circles, with temperature-takings, remedies, steps forward and back: negotiations, and accommodations too.

Acceptance or rejection identify the fork in "the narrative path"[59] where one or another narrative is chosen. Of course, the words *acceptance* and *rejection* only make sense from the point of view of an individual, group, or institution that is not identical with the people to whom it appeals, because rejection of one narrative means that another is taken up. Indeed the institution, if unable to lead the community, may need to turn around and follow the community into the future; but at such turns institutions are always slow-moving.

Narrative and Legitimation

Because this narrative path is such a narrow one, new narratives and new roles that might be encouraged by teachers and educational administrators—those most likely to be impatient in desiring change—may not be credible to the students or their communities. In this case, the educational institution—even education itself—may lose the loyalty of the students.

On the other hand, education which does not propose change will not serve community needs, for the economy and politics of Eritrea and the population's relationships to its leaders, to production and technology, and to the rest of the world, are all changing. Even a purely functional approach to education—developing technical skills without attempting to raise issues of the community's relation to technology and production—will only temporarily disguise the forces impelling and benefiting from material change, while withholding from the population the skills and understanding to confront social and economic stratification, centralization of political power and decision making, and disruption of traditions, and in consequence will only forestall—but at the same time strengthen the tendency toward—legitimation crisis.

Legitimation implies a point of choice, that fork in "the narrative path"[60] at which the individual or the collective must accept or reject the logic or the desirability of the proffered narrative. "An interpretation must not only be probable, but more probable than another."[61] That alternatives (hence choice) are inherent in narrative is shown by Ricoeur's "minimal narrative sentence": "X did A in such and such circumstances, taking into account the fact that Y does B in identical or different circumstances."[62] Legitimation becomes an issue when alternatives diverge on points viewed by the participants as ethical considerations.

> [T]he narrative can impose itself as an *ethical model*, i.e.,
> as a paradigm which in practice orients life; and it is by
> this institution of a narrative as a model of the good life

that the ethical understanding and orientation of daily action begins. One judges, acts and projects in the life of the narrative in which one lives.[63]

The choice, then, is an ethical act:

That all our acts possess a certain narrative form is certainly a necessary condition, but not a sufficient one, for constituting an ethical vision. What more is required is a true narrative, that is, a mimetic configuration where the middle between the beginning and the end is not only an occurrence, but the figuration of a *point* which, like "mimesis," *reveals* more than reflects a difference between the good and the bad, and, more fundamentally, creates the vision of the good life, as distinct from a wasted and frustrated life.[64]

The necessity of ethical choice defines the tasks faced by the educator—whom Ricoeur calls the "political educator."[65] First, the political educator "should make apparent the ethical significance of every choice appearing to be purely economic. Secondly, he ought to struggle for the erection of a democratic society." This requires "integrat[ing] the universal technical civilization with the cultural personality . . . with the historical singularity of each human group."[66]

Using a framework of hermeneutic social sciences to analyze teachers' and students' narratives of their educational experiences within personal and communal social histories and social expectations, I have tried to discover educational policies and practices which successfully mediate traditional social life and social transformation for national development.

Notes

1   Hans-Georg Gadamer, "The Expressive Power of Language: On the Function of Rhetoric for Knowledge," trans. Richard Heinemann and Bruce Krawjewski, *PMLA* 107 (1992): 350.

2   See Clifford Geertz, "Blurred Genres: The Refiguration of Social Thought," in *Local Knowledge: Further Essays in Interpretive Anthropology* (n.p.: Basic Books, 1983), 19-35.

3   In May 1993 the government was reorganized and renamed the Government of Eritrea, and the government Departments, including Education, were

renamed as Ministries.

4   The Regional Centre for Human Rights and Development was shut down by the Provisional Government of Eritrea on March 17, 1993. See Dan Connell, "New Challenges in Postwar Eritrea," *Eritrean Studies Review* 2, no. 1 (1997): 152.

5   Expressions, including actions, which have become fixed in any symbolic or mimetic form. See Josef Bleicher, *Contemporary Hermeneutics: Hermeneutics as Method, Philosophy and Critique* (London: Routledge and Kegan Paul, 1980), 231; James Clifford, "On Ethnographic Authority," *Representations* 2 (1983): 118-146; Clifford Geertz, *The Interpretation of Cultures* (n.p.: Basic Books, 1973); Donald E. Polkinghorne, *Narrative Knowing and the Human Sciences* (Albany, NY: State University of New York Press, 1988), 144; Paul Ricoeur, *Hermeneutics and the Human Sciences*, ed. and trans. John B. Thompson (Cambridge, England: Cambridge University Press, 1981); Calvin O. Schrag, *Communicative Praxis and the Space of Subjectivity* (Bloomington, IN: Indiana University Press, 1986).

6   Clifford, "On Ethnographic Authority," 131. Memories are abetted by photographs, art objects, and souvenirs—really an additional set of "documents" or "texts."

7   Robert N. Bellah, "Social Sciences as Practical Reason," in *Ethics, the Social Sciences, and Policy* Analysis, ed. Daniel Callahan and Bruce Jennings (New York: Plenum Press, 1983), 46.

8   Bellah, "Social Sciences as Practical Reason," 59.

9   Bellah, "Social Sciences as Practical Reason," 46.

10 Bellah, "Social Sciences as Practical Reason," 60.

11 Bellah, "Social Sciences as Practical Reason," 46.

12 See p. 155.

13 The field denotes the liberated and contested areas, mostly rural, where the EPLF operated during the war.

14 Elliot G. Mishler, *Research Interviewing: Context and Narrative* (Cambridge, MA: Harvard University Press, 1986), 105-106.

15 Catherine Kohler Riessman, *Narrative Analysis*, Qualitative Research Methods 30 (Newbury Park, CA: Sage Publications, 1993), 56, 54.

16 For example, see Dan Connell, *Against All Odds: A Chronicle of the Eritrean Revolution* (Trenton, NJ: Red Sea Press, 1993), 120, 172; James Firebrace and Stuart Holland, *Never Kneel Down: Drought, Development, and Liberation in Eritrea*, 2nd printing (Trenton, NJ: Red Sea Press, 1986), 43.

17 Geertz, *Interpretation of Cultures*, 13.

18 Paul Ricoeur, *Lectures on Ideology and Utopia*, ed. George H. Taylor (New York: Columbia University Press, 1986), 255.

19 Hans-Georg Gadamer, *Truth and Method*, trans. Joel Weinsheimer and Donald G. Marshall, 2nd rev. ed. (New York: Crossroad, 1989), 385.

20 Gadamer, *Truth and Method*, 367.

21 Gadamer, *Truth and Method*, 383.

22 Gadamer, *Truth and Method*, 311.

23 Gadamer, *Truth and Method*, 309.

24 Gadamer, *Truth and Method*, 311. Gadamer uses "text" and "tradition" in his context of discussing the interpretation of historical materials.

25 Geertz, *Interpretation of Cultures*, 15.

26 Geertz, *Interpretation of Cultures*, 15, emphasis in original.

27 Gadamer, *Truth and Method*, 332.

28 Clifford, "On Ethnographic Authority," 131.

29 Gadamer, *Truth and Method*, 368.

30 Gadamer, *Truth and Method*, 370.

31 Paul Ricoeur, *Time and Narrative*, vol. 1, trans. Kathleen McLaughlin and David Pellauer (Chicago: University of Chicago Press, 1984), 58.

32 Edward W. Said, *Orientalism* (New York: Vintage, 1978), 272-273, emphasis in original.

33 Ricoeur, *Hermeneutics and the Human Sciences*, 91.

34 Gadamer, *Truth and Method*, 370; Geertz, *Interpretation of Cultures*, 15.

35 Ricoeur, *Hermeneutics and the Human Sciences*, 93-94.

36 Ricoeur, *Hermeneutics and the Human Sciences*, 159, emphasis in original.

37 Gadamer, *Truth and Method*, 403.

38 Gadamer, *Truth and Method*, 308.

39 Gadamer, *Truth and Method*, 309.

40 Gadamer, *Truth and Method*, 311.

41 Polkinghorne, *Narrative Knowing*, 145.

42 Philip Lewin, "Education, Narrative, Character," *Interchange* 21, no. 3 (1990): 26.

43 Ricoeur, *Hermeneutics and the Human Sciences*, 112.

44 Kevin J. Vanhoozer, "Philosophical Antecedents to Ricoeur's *Time and Narrative*," in *On Paul Ricoeur: Narrative and Interpretation*, ed. David Wood (London: Routledge, 1991), 49.

45 Ricoeur, *Hermeneutics and the Human Sciences*, 144.

46 Polkinghorne, *Narrative Knowing*, 106-107.

47 Praxis is the interplay of action, reflection, and knowledge. "Coming to understand a form of cultural life requires competence in moving within that life. Practical involvement is the precondition for reflective clarification, which in turn plays its role in deepening the person's comprehension of how to live" and to act. William M Sullivan, *Reconstructing Public Philosophy* (Berkeley: University of California Press, 1986), 66.

48 Polkinghorne, *Narrative Knowing*, 107.

49 Stephen Crites, "Storytime: Recollecting the Past and Projecting the Future," in *Narrative Psychology: The Storied Nature of Human Conduct* (New York: Praeger, 1986), 164.

50 Crites, "Storytime," 171-172.

51 Crites, "Storytime," 164-165.

52 Paul Ricoeur, *History and Truth*, trans. Charles A. Kelbley (Evanston, IL: Northwestern University Press, 1965), 276.

53 Crites, "Storytime," 164.

54 Crites, "Storytime," 166-167.

55 Crites, "Storytime," 166.

56 Polkinghorne, *Narrative Knowing*, 117.

57 Paul Ricoeur, *The Conflict of Interpretations*, ed. Don Ihde (Evanston, IL: Northwestern University Press, 1974), 405.

58 Ricoeur, *Hermeneutics and the Human Sciences*, 144.

59 Peter T. Kemp and David Rasmussen, eds. *The Narrative Path: The Later Works of Paul Ricoeur* (Cambridge, MA: MIT Press, 1988).

60 Kemp and Rasmussen, *The Narrative Path*.

61 Ricoeur, *Hermeneutics and the Human Sciences*, 213.

62 Ricoeur, *Time and Narrative*, vol. 1, 56.

63 Peter T. Kemp, "Toward a Narrative Ethics: A Bridge Between Ethics and the Narrative Reflection of Ricoeur," in *The Narrative Path: The Later Works of Paul Ricoeur*, ed. Peter T. Kemp and David Rasmussen (Cambridge, MA: MIT Press, 1988), 75, emphasis in original.

64 Kemp, "Toward a Narrative Ethics," 75, emphasis in original.

65 Paul Ricoeur, *Political and Social* Essays, ed. David Stewart and Joseph Bien (Athens, OH: Ohio University Press, 1974), 284-285.

66 Ricoeur, *Political and Social Essays*, 291.

I

WAR AND BEYOND

This boy's sweater celebrates liberation after 30 years of war.

This book investigates the promise of education, as understood by adults, and the practice of educators—teachers, administrators, and educational policy makers—in the newly independent nation of Eritrea. In May 1991, the Eritrean People's Liberation Army "swept 100,000 besieged Ethiopian soldiers out of Asmara, the Eritrean capital,"[1] ending 30 years of Ethiopian occupation and Africa's longest continuous modern war. On May 24, 1993, Eritrea declared itself an independent nation. On May 28, Eritrea joined the United Nations.

The Eritrean independence struggle became synonymous with "self-reliance"—a 30-year war fought from wholly within the country by a politically mobilized population supporting a large, well-trained army using captured weapons. The historical and political necessity of Eritrean self-reliance forced Eritreans to plan and test— while fighting for—the kind of society they wanted.

The Eritrean People's Liberation Front, or EPLF, the leadership of the independence war and subsequently the core of the Provisional Government of Eritrea (from May 1991) and now (since May 1993) of the Government of Eritrea, has had long-standing plans for the redesign of education to meet the country's needs in the era of peace and political independence. In her 1990 film, *Eritrea*, Susan Kalish observed:

> Envisioning a world beyond war, Eritreans give highest priority to education. Children are enrolled in schools inside liberated Eritrea and in neighboring Sudan. Classrooms are camouflaged to avoid detection by Ethiopian bombers. In the upper grades, classes are taught in English. Fluency in English will keep Eritreans current with worldwide developments in science and technology. English will also help an independent Eritrea communicate with her neighbors and the international community. Adult education is also a high priority. In literacy classes, peasants and fighters alike are being retrained and prepared for independence and self-determination.[2]

Also in 1990, Roy Pateman cited as one of his reasons for "predicting the ultimate success" of the EPLF the close relationship between Eritrean peasants and the movement: "Peasants," explained Pateman, "have been as important as technology in transforming societies." However, "peasants are most likely to revolt if faced with a new or sudden imposition which breaks with accepted rules and customs."[3] One such imposition by the Ethiopian regime, of "land reform" and collective farming, swung peasant support decisively to the EPLF in the 1970s.[4] Since then, the EPLF has managed to introduce many reforms, including land redistribution. "Peasant acceptance of the EPLF's land reform policy has been a major reason for the EPLF's continued ability to mobilize popular support," Pateman concluded.[5] The EPLF, Richard Leonard observed in 1988,

> has not only been doing things in a very sensible manner, but doing first things first. Since Eritrea is a peasant society, growth and development must begin with the peasantry. The EPLF has recognised this, and in terms of actions undertaken and results obtained, attention is cent[e]red on the peasantry. First things first means beginning with the creation of local democratic organs of self-government. It means involving peasants in such a way that it is they who are the fundamental actors in developing rural society.[6]

EPLF policy shuns imposition, suddenness, and even, if possible, newness. The EPLF won popular support by working slowly and patiently.[7] The EPLF were never isolationists, but forced isolation perhaps provided the best lessons to be carried into nationhood and international recognition.

The focus of this book is on a short but formative stage of the development of education in Eritrea: the EPLF's national literacy campaign of 1983–1987. In this period, teenage graduates of the Zero School, the boarding school for "EPLF children,"[8] fanned out behind enemy lines to teach reading, writing, arithmetic, health and sanitation, and improved agricultural methods in villages, oases, and rural stations. The teaching of skills was conjoined with political education and was based on the teachers' participation in rural life. The zealous young teachers underwent an experience that severed the distance of their revolutionary idealism from the traditions and culture and adaptive strategies of the Eritrean majority. Today many of those teenagers are still educators—teachers, school principals, administrators—responsible for the policies and practices of the nation's educational system. This book is not a comprehensive overview of Eritrean education, although it brings in a wide range of educational history. Instead, this book focuses on the knowledge that emerged in the literacy campaign that informs the Eritrean approach to education today.

Country and People[9]

Eritrea is a torch-shaped wedge of land, about the size of Britain, along the west coast of the Red Sea in northeast Africa. The Sudan is to the north and west, Djibouti to the southeast, and the Ethiopian province of Tigray to the south. As a former province of Ethiopia, Eritrea formed that country's entire, 750-mile Red Sea coast. The coastal plain, hot, humid, barren and treeless, runs from ten to fifty miles in width along the sea before ascending to the central plateau, 6,000 to 8,000 feet above sea level, arid but cut by fertile valleys. Highland residents are subsistence farmers. West of the highlands are two lowland areas: the semi-desert Barka lowlands stretching toward the Sudan, populated by pastoralists, semi-pastoralists, and recently settled cultivators; and the richer river valleys between the Sudan and Ethiopia, where village peasants are settled. About twenty percent of the 3.5 million Eritreans[10] are urbanized, forming a significant working class. Of the rural population, a 1988 survey showed that sixty-two percent are farmers, thirty-three percent combine farming and herding, and only five percent, in the far northern mountains and southern coastal desert, live a purely nomadic existence. Eritreans comprise nine ethnic groups speaking nine languages. The total population is approximately equally divided between Muslims and Christians, the religious division cutting across some ethnic lines.

A Model of Development

It can be argued that a confluence of regional history and world politics has required and will provide, in Eritrea, a model of self-reliant, innovative development that successfully integrates tradition and social transformation. That model has already accounted for remarkable levels of simultaneous self-reliant warfare; development in education, health, production, and transportation; and political participation by all economic and social sectors and ethnic groups in Eritrea. With independence comes the prospect of peace, prosperity, and democratic government, in a region of the world, the Horn of Africa, largely known for famine, drought, and civil war.[11] Education, including adult education, is a key element in the Eritrean model of development.

The promise of Eritrea was captured in a comment by Dan Connell, an American journalist who has chronicled Eritrea's independence war since 1976:

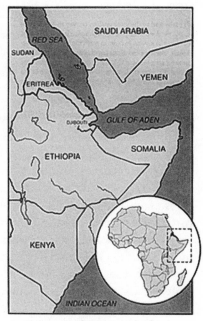

Eritrea in the Horn of Africa.

> So many of us are prisoners of . . . the notion that the fate of the world is determined by an axis that runs between Washington and Moscow. The Eritreans are sending us a far different message, if we choose to hear it: that we can be masters of our own destiny if we are patient and committed enough, if we are willing to endure terrible sacrifices and if we remain in complete and undistracted contact with the reality in which we live, work and struggle.[12]

East-West clientism no longer divides the developing world, but the agony of impoverishment and nationalist wars continues. Post-Cold War commentators continue to point to the absence of strife among Eritrea's ethnic, regional, and religious groups, in contrast to the civil war that seethes in neighboring Sudan, the fratricidal disorder in nearby Somalia, continuing ethnic tensions in Ethiopia, "tribal" wars throughout Africa, and the fracturing of Eastern Europe. Having succeeded in its own nationalist war, which most of the world has come to see as just, Eritrea garners from some quarters unbridled enthusiasm as "a new model for Third World development, based on self-reliance and low-level technology, in a sharing society"[13] and "an encouraging model for development" that is "highly impressive and hope-provoking"[14]—and from more temperate observers earns, in historian Basil Davidson's words, "a reasoned hope."[15]

Education and Transformation

Educational practices and discourses are key sites where traditional and modernizing social forces interact. Adult education is particularly critical in specific social transformations that Eritreans have had—and continue—to tackle, for example pastoralists settling into agricultural communities; land redistribution; and women entering the public political process, community development projects, the military, and professional careers. In later chapters I look at adult education, and adult involvement in the institutions which educate their children, as processes in which adults accept or reject social changes, and in which the legitimation of educational and political leadership takes place. I examine the incorporation of "local" or community-based knowledge[16] into school learning, and the interaction of traditional social practices (on the one hand) and the government's education policies (on the other) in bringing about social change.

Social changes entail, for individuals and communities, new self-understandings which are essentially narrative. Donald E. Polkinghorne's simile is apt: "Acting is like writing a story, and the understanding of action is like arriving at an interpretation of a story."[17] In educational experiences (through conversation and appropriation of texts of many kinds[18]), adults may "write" new stories and roles for themselves, their communities, and nation. But the stories, new or old, they will choose to live embody a promise: a happy ending to their lives, their community's projects, and their people's struggles. These stories constitute a pact between identity, will, and history. Individuals and communities will live *with* dreams, *for* dreams, but not, knowingly, *in* dreams. "To use Coleridge's distinction," says Philip Lewin, "self-narratives are ordinarily works of imagination, not of fantasy. They are composed responsibly, not whimsically, in response to external circumstance." For a narrative to be taken up, it must be "characterized by . . . plausibility, a sense our sensibility has a place in it."[19] Narratives and roles envisioned by change agents such as teachers and educational policy makers must be credible in order for the educational institution and its teachers and administrators—those most likely to be impatient in desiring change and "results"—to be able maintain the loyalty of students or parents. "[G]roup identity," says Kwame Anthony Appiah, "seems to work only—or, at least, to work best—when it is seen by its members as natural, as 'real.'"[20] Speaking politically, and perhaps wryly, Appiah reminds us that "for truths to become the basis of national policy and, more widely, of national life, they must be believed."[21]

On the other hand, education which does not propose transformation will not serve community needs, since the economy and politics of Eritrea and the population's relationships to its leaders, to production and technology, and to the rest of the world, are changing. Even a purely functional approach to education—technical training, say, what Colin Griffin calls "education for adaptation,"[22] which does not attempt to engage the community in questions of their relation to technology, social organization, and economic goals—will merely mask the agenda implicit in material change:

> From a global perspective, the application of science and technology is hardly a neutral process. Rather, it is a process deeply implicated in the exploitation of the poor countries of the world by the rich.[23]

The result might be new forms of economic and social stratification[24]; disruption of traditions brought about by economic opportunity,[25] individual mobility, and the influence of media;[26] increasing political centralization; and possible legitimation crisis.[27]

Using a framework of hermeneutic social sciences, and especially the work of Hans-Georg Gadamer, Paul Ricoeur, and Jürgen Habermas on conversation, narrative, and legitimation, I have analyzed conversations I recorded with educators and students in Eritrea in 1993.[28] In this analysis, I have tried to address the "hermeneutic problem" outlined by Josef Bleicher:

> Hermeneutics can loosely be defined as the theory or philosophy of the interpretation of meaning. . . . The realization that human expressions contain a meaningful component, which has to be recognized as such by a subject and transposed into his own system of values and meanings, has given rise to the "problem of hermeneutics."[29]

The problem has two parts: first, to identify how this process of interpretation "is possible"[30] and takes place, and, second, to satisfy the "aim of understanding," which is "the emergence of practically relevant knowledge in which the subject himself is changed by being made aware of new possibilities of existence and his responsibility for his own future."[31] In the information and narratives I recorded—with Eritrean teachers, educational policy makers and administrators, curriculum designers, and students—I looked for appeals to modernization and to tradition; for examples of conflict, negotiation, and accommodation; and for instances of acceptance and rejection of educational policies and practices. I paid particular attention to the participants' educational experiences as a part of personal life-stories or of community narratives personally experienced, seeing the personal or communal social history as it is demarcated by an individual's life-span, a story whose "ending" therefore relies on speculation and expectation, the projection of the past and present into the future—in a word, "promise." Promise is enacted—that is, it is fulfilled *and* renewed—in the individual's and community's ability and willingness to make decisions and perform actions, to take (returning to Bleicher's "aim of understanding") responsibility for the future.

Analyzing Eritreans' stories revealed educational policies and practices that have successfully mediated traditional life and thought on the one hand, and social transformation for community and national development on the other. Further, formal educational processes and related activities have sometimes offered and at other times pressed communities to decisions and deeds which I interpret as expressing acceptance and approval of the political leadership and policies of the EPLF and the EPLF-led Provisional Government of Eritrea. In and through education *(a)* the EPLF organization has sought legitimation, *(b)* Eritreans have reflected on issues of power and leadership, cultural and national identity, and tradition and social change, and *(c)* communities have acted decisively and unequivocally to embrace or ally themselves with the EPLF's goals, strategies, and membership. These community actions signify a hermeneutic process: new understandings of individual and collective possibility were shared and acted upon.[32] But Eritreans have not only turned to the EPLF as soldiers, savants, and social workers; *(d)* Eritreans have used education to envision their future, to dream responsibly what they will become in a country "beyond war," as Kalish put it in her film,[33] and free of colonialism, drought, famine, and ignorance. Education, they insist, greater than hope, is both a promise and a warrant of the future they have acted to secure.

Notes

1 Roy Pateman, "Eritrea Is Free, While Ethiopia Scrambles for Unity," *Guardian*, 26 June 1991, 14.

2 Susan Kalish, *Eritrea*, prod. Susan Kalish, dir. Susan Kalish, Yasha Aginsky, and John Knoop (Cinema Guild, Inc., *1697* Broadway, Suite *506*, New York, NY *10019-5904*), 1990, film.

3 Roy Pateman, *Eritrea: Even the Stones Are Burning* (Trenton, NJ: Red Sea Press, 1990), 224.

4 Pateman, *Eritrea: Even the Stones Are Burning*, 169, 224.

5 Pateman, *Eritrea: Even the Stones Are Burning*, 225.

6 Richard Leonard, "Popular Participation in Liberation and Revolution," in *The Long Struggle of Eritrea for Independence and Constructive Peace*, ed. Lionel Cliffe and Basil Davidson (Trenton, NJ: Red Sea Press, 1988), 130.

7 Leonard, "Popular Participation," 124.

8 Students at the Zero School were children of fighters, orphans, refugees, or volunteers too young to join the Eritrean People's Liberation Army.

9 This profile is culled from Dan Connell, *Against All Odds: A Chronicle of the Eritrean Revolution* (Trenton, NJ: Red Sea Press, 1993); Edward Paice, *Guide to Eritrea* (Chalfont St Peter, Bucks, England: Bradt Publications, 1994); Pateman, *Eritrea: Even the Stones Are Burning*; David Pool, *Eritrea: Africa's Longest War*, Anti-Slavery Society Human Rights Series Report No. 3 (London: Anti-Slavery Society, 1979); Richard Sherman, *Eritrea: The Unfinished Revolution* (New York: Praeger, 1980).

10 Paice questions this often cited population figure:

> There has yet to be any census of the country post-independence. Official statistics usually quote a figure of 3.5 million, including the half a million or so refugees in Sudan and the 200,000 or so Eritreans living overseas. However, one recent survey carried out by the government using the voters in the referendum as the sample has concluded that the population is more like 2.5 million. Having visited the major population centres, my gut feeling is that this must be more the order of magnitude. *Guide to Eritrea*, 1.

11 Jill Hamburg, "Eritrea Showing a Lot of Promise," *San Francisco Chronicle*, 9 April 1992, A16, A18.

12 Dan Connell, "New Introduction," *Never Kneel Down: Drought, Development and Liberation in Eritrea*, by James Firebrace and Stuart Holland, 2nd printing (Trenton, NJ: Red Sea Press, 1986), 8.

13 Paul Highfield, "A Dangerous Model for the Third World," *New Statesman*, 11 December 1987, 20.

14 Charles F. Laskey, "A Model for Third World Development?" review of *Never Kneel Down: Drought, Development and Liberation in Eritrea*, by James Firebrace and Stuart Holland, *Africa Today* 40, no. 2, (1993): 94-96.

15 Basil Davidson, *The Black Man's Burden: Africa and the Curse of the Nation-State* (New York: Random House, 1992), 319.

16 Clifford Geertz, *Local Knowledge: Further Essays in Interpretive Anthropology* (n.p.: Basic Books, 1983).

17 Donald E. Polkinghorne, *Narrative Knowing and the Human* Sciences (Albany, NY: State University of New York Press, 1988), 142.

18 See p. 24, note 5.

19 Philip Lewin, "Education, Narrative, Character," *Interchange* 21, no. 3 (1990): 27.

20 Kwame Anthony Appiah, *In My Father's House: Africa in the Philosophy of Culture* (New York: Oxford University Press, 1992), 175.

21 Appiah, *In My Father's House*, 5.

22 Colin Griffin, "Ettore Gelpi," in *Twentieth Century Thinkers in Adult Education*, ed. Peter Jarvis (London: Routledge, 1987), 285; Griffin is summarizing and reviewing Ettore Gelpi's work. See also Walter Leirman, "Adult Education: Movement and Discipline Between the Golden Sixties and the Iron Eighties," in *Adult Education and the Challenges of the 1990s*, ed. Walter Leirman and Jindra Kulich (London: Croom Helm, 1987), and Paul Ricoeur, "The Tasks of the Political Educator," in *Political and Social Essays*, ed. David Stewart and Joseph Bien (Athens, OH: Ohio University Press, 1974), 271-293.

23 Griffin, "Ettore Gelpi," 285.

24 Veronica Rentmeesters, for example, finds:

> Overall, women's social position has worsened with their country's integration into the world market and modernization, regardless of whether their [material] condition improved or not.
>
> If we look at formal education, for example, the overall situation is one where initially both sexes lack formal education and have similar positions and low conditions. With development far greater proportions of men are educated than women. The condition of the small group of women who are educated may improve but women's overall position relative to men is worse. As a case in point, in Eritrea it is estimated that 40 percent of men are literate compared to 10 percent of women. "Women and Development Planning," in *Emergent Eritrea: Challenges of Economic Development; Proceedings of a Conference, Asmara, Eritrea, July 22-24, 1991*, ed. Gebre Hiwet Tesfagiorgis (Eritreans for Peace and Democracy, P. O. Box 21632, Washington, DC 20009-0864), 77.

Asseny Muro (1985) examines "sex segmentation" of wage-earners in eastern Africa in "Women Commodity Producers and Proletariats: The Case of African Women," in *Challenging Rural Poverty*, ed. Fassil G. Kiros (Trenton, NJ: Africa World Press, 1985), 61-79. Butch Lee and Red Rover in *Night Vision: Illuminating War and Class on the Neo-Colonial Terrain* (New York: Vagabond Press, 1993) assert that the development of "vertical" class differentiation in "native" societies defines the present post-colonial, "neo-colonial" world capitalist structure, in which the "first and most basic vertical differentiation is for women to become the property of men" (p.105). Ettore Gelpi discusses "segmentation" and "marginalisation" of workers in general in *Lifelong Education and International Relations* (London: Croom Helm, 1985).

25 For example, see Beverly B. Cassara and George N. Reche, "Traditional Adult Education in Kenya: Some Thoughts for Today's World," *Adult Learning* 1, no. 8 (1990): 14-15.

26 See Ettore Gelpi, *Lifelong Education and International Relations*, 10, 18-21.

27 That is, in Ruth Iyob's definition, "active confrontation or a gradual disengagement of the society from its government." In Eritrea, a crisis appeared soon and suddenly. Just one day after the EPLF proclaimed the formation of independent Eritrea's first government, that government was faced with an armed protest by EPLF fighters angered at the announced postponement of the demobilizing of the military. The President, meeting with the protesters, defused the situation, by addressing their grievances. See Iyob, *The Eritrean Struggle for Independence: Domination, Resistance, Nationalism, 1941-1993* (Cambridge, England: Cambridge University Press, 1995), 141-142, 146.

28 Additional conversations were recorded in the United States from November, 1991, to January, 1994.

29 Josef Bleicher, *Contemporary Hermeneutics: Hermeneutics as Method, Philosophy and Critique* (London: Routledge and Kegan Paul, 1980), 1.

30 Bleicher, *Contemporary Hermeneutics*, 1.

31 Bleicher, *Contemporary Hermeneutics*, 3.

32 Bleicher, *Contemporary Hermeneutics*, 3.

33 Kalish, *Eritrea*.

II

HISTORY OF ERITREA

The following is a necessarily brief recounting of Eritrean history. My aim here is to frame an understanding of the new nation's social, political, and economic traditions, resources, problems, and prospects.

Four historical factors led to the EPLF's policy and practice of self-reliance: *(a)* Eritrea's location on the Red Sea led to its having a different history than inland Ethiopia, *(b)* Italian colonization industrialized and modernized Eritrea and educated and politicized Eritreans, in contrast to Ethiopia's feudalism and underdevelopment, *(c)* Eritrea's unsuccessful bid for independence after World War II led to the formation of indigenous political parties and movements, and *(d)* the Cold War neo-scramble for African clients excluded Eritrea from international political and material support.

Claims and Counter Claims

Successive Ethiopian governments have claimed that "the Ethiopian people, of which the people inhabiting the northern part of the country [Eritrea] form an integral part, have had one history, sharing the same fate with the ebb and rise in the country's fortunes."[1] In this account, Ethiopia traces its descent from the Axumite kingdom of the fifth through eighth centuries: the "northern part of Ethiopia, including Eritrea, was in fact the hub of that civilization." This fact, however, in accounts sympathetic to Eritrean independence, suggests "that it is the Eritreans, rather than the Ethiopians, who have a better claim to be the legitimate descendants of the Axumite civilization."[2]

The Colonial Period

Eritreans do not, however, base their claims to independence on the political geography of ancient Africa. The borders of all current African states have been inherited from the European colonial period. "During this period," from the sixteenth to the nineteenth centuries, "Eritrea is identified as politically distinct from Ethiopia" by a number of European explorers and travelers.[3] While control of the Eritrean highlands shifted among different invading Ethiopian and Somali kingdoms, Portuguese military expeditions, the Ottoman Empire, and local peoples, the ports of Eritrea continuously "looked eastward" to the Red Sea world

> rather than inland to the African continent. While the Ethiopians were effectively cut off from the outside world for over three centuries, the Eritreans enjoyed continuous contact with the Middle East, a contact which resulted in a distinctive economic and political development.[4]

The Ottoman Turks ruled the port of Massawa and its coastal plains from 1517 to 1848, when they were displaced by Egypt.[5] With the opening of the Suez canal in 1869, the Red Sea coast gained strategic and commercial importance.[6] In that year the Italian government, "something of a late starter" in "the European scramble for African colonies" purchased the port of Assab from the local sultan.[7] The Italians occupied Massawa in 1885. In 1889, in the Treaty of Wichale, or Uccialli, King Menelik of Shoa "'traded' Eritrea and its inhabitants" to the Italians in return for a military alliance "to ensure his title and crown" against his Tigrayan rivals.[8] Still, Italian war preparations in Eritrea "worried the new emperor," and "worry turned to stupefaction when [Menelik] learned that the Italian prime minister had notified the Powers of Europe . . . that Ethiopia was an Italian protectorate."[9] In 1895, Italian legions crossed the Mareb River into Tigray, and fighting began.[10] Menelik's troops fought well, although the poorly provisioned army would probably not have held together for a long war. However, the Italian generals, seeking a decisive victory, blundered fatally at Adwa on March 1, 1896, losing 43 per cent of their 10,000 Italian and 7,000 Eritrean troops in six hours.[11] "For the white world . . . Adwa was an immense surprise, if not a bewildering shock," earning Ethiopian sovereignty the grudging respect of the European Powers.[12] In the Treaty of Addis Ababa, signed on October 26, 1896, Italy renounced claims to Ethiopia, while Menelik affirmed Italian control of Eritrea[13]—not without, however, asserting a cunning "perpetual Ethiopian claim to Eritrea: 'In the case where the Government of Italy should wish to abandon, by its own decision, a portion of territory in its possession, it will return to Ethiopia.'"[14]

Through this treaty, Ethiopia became the only African country protected from European colonization. Menelik used his access to European weapons to consolidate, over the next forty years, an empire in which the Shoan, or Amhara, ethnic minority dominated larger ethnic populations, principally the Tigrayan and Oromo peoples. Amharic rule and policies favoring the Amharas have since been the principal source of conflict in Ethiopia. Successive regimes, the Haile Selassie monarchy and the avowedly Marxist military government of Mengistu Haile Mariam, continued the Amhara domination of Ethiopia's and Eritrea's diverse populations, in land policies, military conscription, and access to government, education, and famine relief.[15]

Development Under the Italians

Whatever the basis of Ethiopian claims to "traditional historical rights" in segments of the pre-colonial territory, the Italian occupation established the basis of a different historical and political claim for Eritrean independence and set in motion the socio-economic forces which were to underpin an Eritrean national identity.[16]

Armed resistance kept the Italians from consolidating their rule until 1897, when the first civilian governor was appointed.[17] The Italians ruled Eritrea for the next 45 years until their defeat by the British in 1941. Eritrea's boundaries, therefore, and the unified political identity fostered by direct colonial control within those boundaries, date from the same era in which most of today's independent African states were undergoing similar developments.[18] There was, however, "a readiness to invest more in Eritrea than was often the norm for European colonial powers in Africa," due in part to Italy's design for "making Eritrea a base for its wider geographical aspirations."[19]

Nevertheless, the economic power of local and regional chiefs and nobles, based on taxation and land rental, was squeezed and diminished by Italian seizure of land on the one hand and by increased economic opportunities available to serfs on the other, for example as soldiers. However, "even as the nobility was destroyed economically, the Italians worked hard to preserve its political influence because they wanted to rule the peasantry through this caste."[20] As an adjunct to colonial rule, the Italians

> encouraged the emergence of tribal and village leaders and the consolidation and legitimation of their community position through their power to settle "collective disputes," that is disputes involving the tribe or the village which came neither under the Italian penal nor civilian codes.[21]

This "emphasis on social stability," Edward Paice concludes, "served largely to freeze social relationships. Eritreans were never treated as equals and there was no emergence of a petty bourgeoisie, although it was not until the fascist era that active discrimination was practiced."[22]

After Mussolini's rise to power, the Italian Fascist regime gradually increased the settler population from around 5,000 to 60,000.[23] The vast majority of settlers lived in towns and were shopkeepers, small craftsmen, and professionals, but there were a significant number of medium and large scale farmers and factory owners. As the Italian population grew, "stringent racial laws were implemented establishing segregation and wage differentials based on color."[24] Benefiting from low wages and extensive use of child

A graffitist's tribute to Mussolini, presumably from the 1930s, near Decamhare.

labor, the Italians built diverse manufacturing concerns, increasing the drift to the towns, with the result that Eritrea was rapidly urbanized. "By the end of Italian colonial rule, about 20% of the population were living in urban centers, albeit restricted by racial legislation to 'native quarters.'"[25] Similar trends transformed Eritrean agriculture and rural life. The commercialization of agriculture, introduction of new crops such as cotton and coffee, introduction of veterinary medicine to improve the health and productivity of livestock, the importation of agricultural machinery and tools, and the consolidation of vast parcels of land cultivated under Italian ownership "hastened the disintegration of the traditional . . . socioeconomic structure in the lowlands and the feudal social structure in the highlands."[26] At the same time, the Italians constructed roads, railways, ports, military installations, and towns for the settler population, making Eritrea "increasingly a unified economic and social unit" as well as "facilitat[ing] potential external intercourse."[27] The Eritrean road system, the best in Africa,[28] was a part of Italy's plan for eventual occupation of Ethiopia, which the Italians invaded in 1935. In the invasion and throughout the occupation, there were mass desertions of the Italian colonial army's Eritrean troops.[29] Eritreans played key roles at all levels of the Ethiopian resistance—as advisors to Haile Selassie's government in exile, in pitched battles against the invaders, and in assassination plots against Italian colonial officials.[30]

In the late 1930s the colonial government sought to control the growth of Eritrean political power, for example the "influence of Eritreans of mixed race . . . [who], unlike Eritreans, were given an education," and of foreign missionaries. In 1937 the Italians tightened racial laws, prohibiting mixed marriages, assigning the mother's nationality to any child, and expelled all foreign missionaries, "angering many Eritreans."[31]

By 1940 Asmara's population had grown to over 100,000, with modern services. Massawa, with over 10,000 inhabitants, was a fully equipped port and naval base. Other ports and inland cities were rapidly expanding. But Italian colonialism was an early casualty of World War II. British forces entered Eritrea in January 1941, and by April all of Eritrea was under British occupation.[32]

British Administration

Eritrea was controlled by a British Military Administration from 1941 to 1949, and then administered by the British Foreign Office until 1952. During the war, the United States also began using Eritrean ports, establishing a naval base, an aircraft assembly plant, and supply depots.[33] Britain built up Eritrean industry—and employed the skilled working class of the Italian period—to meet the needs of a war economy, but after the war Eritrea suffered an industrial slump. "The British removed or sold an estimated £86 million worth of industrial plant [sic] and equipment, including port facilities at Massawa and Assab." In 1948, the worst year of the post-war depression, 637 businesses closed and 10,000 Eritreans became jobless.[34] Combined with increased local taxation, the large scale unemployment contributed to the growth of political consciousness among Eritrea's urban working class. Further contributing to Eritrean political participation, the British gradually removed the color bar, and began an "Eritreanization" of lower administrative positions. The British "promoted the formation of . . . political parties and trade unions," and a new public health service with some hospitals and clinics provided services to Eritreans in cities and towns.[35]

Federation and Annexation

The peace treaty with Italy provided that the future of its former colonies, Libya, Somalia, and Eritrea, would be decided by the Allied powers. Libya and Somalia became independent, but the four powers failed to agree on the status of Eritrea, whence a United Nations Commission was sent to Eritrea for two months in early 1950 to consider

> the wishes and welfare of the inhabitants of Eritrea ... the capacity of the people for self-government ... the interests of peace and security in East Africa ... [and] the rights and claims of Ethiopia, including in particular Ethiopia's legitimate need for adequate access to the sea.[36]

Following an investigation which commentators have labeled "perfunctory," "indifferent," "casual," and "superficial,"[37] the UN Commission "produced two separate reports and no less than three sets of proposals."[38] The Commission's findings were further compromised by an Ethiopian-sponsored campaign of bombings and assassinations of independence supporters, eighteen of whom were murdered,[39] and religious pressure from the Ethiopian Orthodox Church, which declared that "those supporting independence would not be baptized, married, buried, or receive communion."[40] Haile Selassie's promise to return church lands taken by the Italians, Jordan Gebre-Medhin asserts, "made the Coptic Church the center of Ethiopian ambitions." However,

> Unionism attracted the ex-ruling classes of Eritrea regardless of their religion. They had lost or were in the process of losing their privileged status with the "development of underdevelopment" during the Italian era. The Church hierarchy and the nobility of the highlands and lowlands—basically those who exploited and appropriated the peasant surplus—congealed themselves as a force and began to support the return of feudalism

which was being attempted by the feudal rulers of Ethiopia.[41]

After lengthy debate, the UN General Assembly voted to federate Eritrea with Ethiopia. The position of the United States in the matter was stated by Secretary of State John Foster Dulles before the UN Security Council:

> From the point of view of justice, the opinions of the Eritrean people must receive consideration. Nevertheless the strategic interest of the United States in the Red Sea basin and considerations of security and world peace make it necessary that the country has to be linked with our ally, Ethiopia.[42]

A payoff for the United States was the Kagnew military station in Asmara, the largest communications base of its time, which, before the advent of satellites, was the base for "eavesdropping" on the Middle East, Africa, and the Soviet Union.[43]

Eritrea was to be an "autonomous unit 'with its own legislative executive and judicial powers in the field of domestic affairs,' but federated with Ethiopia under the sovereignty of the Ethiopian crown."[44] The contradictions of federation were immediately apparent. Ethiopia's feudal economy and imperial political system clashed with the capitalist development of Eritrea and the democratic constitution approved by the elected Eritrean Assembly in 1952.[45] Haile Selassie outlawed Eritrean political parties and trade unions. In 1956, the Eritrean native languages were banned and replaced by Amharic in schools and public life. Strikes and demonstrations were attacked by police. Newspapers were censored. When the Eritrean flag was banned, police fired on protesters, killing many. Entire factories were dismantled and transferred to Addis Ababa. Meanwhile, repeated Eritrean missions to the UN were ignored.[46] Finally,

> the end of federated Eritrea came with a "vote" in the Eritrean Assembly in 1962, in favor of annexation by Ethiopia. Prior to the vote, Ethiopia increased its campaign of bribery and intimidation. Eritrean police surrounded the assembly; the police were surrounded by men of the Ethiopian Second Division under the

command of General Abbiye Abebe, who controlled all urban areas and most of the countryside. On November 13, a motion to dissolve the federation was defeated four times. No vote was taken on the next day, Asfaha Wolde Micael merely read a statement prepared for the emperor several weeks in advance by his adviser, John Spencer, requesting the assembly to dissolve the federation and unite with "our motherland, Ethiopia." Asfaha read the statement in Amharic, a language understood by only a handful of the Eritrean representatives. . . .

On the following day, the emperor, without consulting the United Nations, proclaimed Order No. 27, terminating Eritrea's federal status.[47]

The Eritrean Liberation Front

In 1961, the Eritrean Liberation Front, or ELF, was formed, its members "arguing that the only remaining path to Eritrean independence was through armed resistance."[48] After annexation, the ELF's guerrilla activities increased, bringing harsh reprisals. By 1963, an estimated 3,000 Eritrean civilians were in prison on suspicion of sympathizing with the ELF. Villages were burned and their inhabitants massacred. In 1970, after an ELF ambush in which an Ethiopian general was killed, 600 civilians were shot in nearby villages, and the town of Keren was bombed with a reported 500 civilian casualties. Thousands fled from the area. Arrests, detention, and torture became common.[49] Saleh Meki, an Eritrean exile at the time he was interviewed by Susan Kalish in her film, *Eritrea*, spoke of this period:

> Haile Selassie really represents the ultimate suffering that has been inflicted on our people. Still his picture outside has been deliberately presented as a peaceful man, a father of Africa. To us, he brought death and destruction, and we remember him that way.[50]

The ELF and the EPLF, which split off from the ELF in 1970, attracted many recruits from those who escaped from the towns. The ELF maintained an Arab and Muslim orientation and conservative social policies. The ELF lacked democratic structure and condoned corruption.[51] The dissident EPLF represented a Christian-Muslim coalition; its first "manifesto placed strong emphasis on overcoming ethnic and religious differences and on launching revolutionary struggle *during* the independence war."[52] Between 1972 and 1974, however, the two fronts fought each other. Although casualties were low, the civil war sapped the morale of the Eritrean populace, especially in the countryside.[53] Finally, in November 1974, between 20,000 and 30,000 Eritrean civilians converged on two villages, fifteen miles from Asmara, where the fronts were holding peace talks.[54] "The irate and impatient population prevailed upon them to call a formal truce,"[55] an important example not only of mass political action but of the Eritrean people's willingness to assume collective responsibility for their liberation struggle by taking the movement to task.

Not only, before this civil war ended, had "the EPLF generally inherited some of the ELF's strength, as the ELF tended to grow weaker and lose some of its military superiority,"[56] but the EPLF's "program of social transformation and their secular nationalism proved attractive to the younger generation of Christian students at high schools, colleges and university, who, after 1973, joined the EPLF in large numbers."[57] After 1978, Soviet-backed Ethiopian invasions devastated the ELF. By the early 1980s, the ELF had ceased military operations inside Eritrea.[58]

The Dergue

Corruption and incompetence in the Haile Selassie regime, and the drain on the Ethiopian economy of the war against Eritrea, led to the overthrow of Selassie in 1974.[59] No one faction of the popular movement which toppled Selassie was strong enough to form a new government, which "led to a creeping transfer of power to the military."[60] Infighting and murder marked the Dergue—the military government—until Mengistu Haile Mariam, his major rivals eliminated, emerged as chairman.[61] At this time, superpower alliances in the Horn of Africa shifted; the United States, adopting a cautious stance in the wake of the Vietnam war, denied Mengistu's requests for increased arms, and the Dergue turned to the Soviet Union.[62] "In an unprecedented show of skill and coordination, the Soviets were able to send, by air and sea, more than 2 billion dollars' worth

of arms ... in a very short time."[63] In July 1978, five separate
Ethiopian forces, totaling 100,000 troops, pushed into Eritrea to
crush the independence movement.[64] In the next five months, the
EPLF evacuated its liberated towns and cities and withdrew into the
northern mountains. Although the liberation army survived what
came to be known as the "first offensive"[65] with its hardware
intact,

> [w]ith the retreat into the mountains, the EPLF could
> no longer command an audience for its appeals to jus-
> tice and democratic process. Over the next few years,
> the movement entered a phase of extreme isolation, as
> the Soviet-led political embargo took effect, and the
> West simply walked away. This lasted until regional
> famine pushed Eritrea back into the news in the mid-
> 1980s.[66]

Meanwhile, the Dergue became

> steadily more Marxist and pro-Soviet in its pronounce-
> ments. A host of delegations from the socialist camp vis-
> ited Ethiopia and began to send aid. On December 11,
> 1977, the Cuban head of state, Fidel Castro, declared
> that while the Eritrean liberation movement had once
> been progressive it was now controlled by reactionary
> states such as Sudan and Saudi Arabia; this was why the
> Eritreans continued to fight against a socialist regime.[67]

In 1984, Mengistu formed the Workers Party of Ethiopia. Elections
were held in 1987, and a civilian socialist government was proclaimed.[68] However, Mengistu remained

> the head of state and the commander-in-chief of the
> armed forces. He appoint[ed] all ministers, judges and
> top officials of government. Moreover, President
> Mengistu [wa]s also Secretary-General of the Party.
> Given all these powers, Mengistu may have emerged as
> the most powerful "communist" leader in the world.[69]

The Workers Party of Ethiopia joined the "bloated bureaucratic
machine ... of state control and repression"[70] comprising the
Revolutionary Ethiopian Youth Association, Revolutionary

Ethiopian Women's Association, the All-Ethiopia Trade Union, Worker's Control Committees, the Urban Dweller's Association, called the *kebeles*, and other organizations. The membership and attendance at the *kebeles* were compulsory, and members could not change their residence without obtaining permission. The *kebeles* acted as a security service for the Dergue, keeping dossiers on residents and interrogating less-enthusiastic members. Infractions were punished with detention or imprisonment. In Asmara, *kebeles* included non-Eritrean and Soviet members, owing to the presence in Eritrea of Ethiopian government employees and nearly 9,000 Soviet troops and advisors.[71] The atmosphere of fear, suspicion, and harassment was the milder end of the spectrum of terror Eritrean civilians endured under Ethiopian military occupation in the Dergue years. Villages were subject to random air attack and ground massacres.[72] Arbitrary arrest, imprisonment in "overcrowded ... small, airless and often stinking cells," torture, and summary execution were "a persistent fact of life in Eritrea."[73]

Eritrea in World Politics

Along with repression and terrorism against Eritrean civilians, the Soviet-supplied Dergue mounted massive military campaigns against the EPLF. In five campaigns between 1978 and 1981, huge armies of peasant conscripts swept into Eritrea. Each of these assaults failed.[74] In 1982, in a sixth offensive of over 100,000 peasant troops, "the Ethiopian army ... received a severe setback with estimates of their killed and wounded varying between 37,000 and 43,000."[75] Over the next nine years, the EPLF slowly surrounded Ethiopian garrisons.

> The decisive battle of the thirty-year war took place in Afabet on March 17, 1988. Breaking with the conventions of people's war, the EPLF hit the Ethiopians at their strongest point, taking advantage of their enemy's demoralization to shatter the ten-year stalemate. In forty-eight hours, Eritrean forces wiped out three crack Ethiopian divisions and overran the largest ammunition and supply depot in Eritrea, capturing enough heavy weapons, ammunition and equipment to supply (and

substantially expand) their army over the next year. British historian and author Basil Davidson described it on the BBC as "one of the biggest [victories] ever scored by any liberation movement anywhere since Dien Bien Phu in 1954."[76]

The stunning Eritrean military victories of the mid-1980s fueled western speculation of secret ties and arms deals between the Eritreans and revolutionary and extremist states of various political persuasions. Although journalists in Eritrea during the 1980s set EPLF troop strength at between 40,000 and 50,000 men and women, and vouched that arms, tanks, and heavy artillery in large numbers were captured from the Ethiopians,[77] this seemed so unbelievable that numerous attempts were made to identify backers and suppliers of the EPLF, primarily in the Arab world.

In fact, the EPLF had little choice but to be self-supplying. Self-reliance was a result not only of tradition but also of Cold War *realpolitik* in which, Kwame Anthony Appiah states, the United States and the Soviet Union "play[ed] out their mutual antagonisms with African lives."[78] The EPLF waged a self-sufficient war out of necessity. Ethiopia is huge, populous, and strategically located, a desirable African ally for contending superpowers. Even while Ethiopia was armed by the Soviet Union, the United States continued massive humanitarian aid to the Dergue—much of it diverted to military use, for example famine aid used to feed Ethiopia's swollen military.[79] U.S. policy hinged on confidence that Ethiopia's alliance with the Soviets would eventually sour.[80]

> While the State Department acknowledged that the U.S. wanted to destabilize the Mengistu government, the only instrument in sight potentially strong enough for the job, the EPLF, was both leftist and set on independence, not to mention uninterested in any alliance with Washington. The United States has maintained a steady opposition to the EPLF although the front moved in recent years from Marxism-Leninism to a broad progressive stand that does not preclude a free market. As recently as March [1991], Undersecretary of State Herman Cohen said . . . that the United States would oppose any Eritrean breakaway from Ethiopia.[81]

However, when the insurgents' victory was imminent in May 1991, the United States arranged Mengistu's departure and "assuming the dubious mantle of 'honest broker' . . . chaired talks in London between the EPLF and the new Addis regime."[82] Thus, until the EPLF's final victory, both superpowers had rebuffed the Eritrean struggle. Then the United States accepted the Eritrean *fait accompli*. Speaking in Oakland, California, on May 20, 1992, Herman Cohen, Assistant Secretary of State for African Affairs, outlined the U.S. position on Eritrea: support for the right of Eritreans to self-determination, acceptance of the expected landslide vote for independence, and the hope (or wish) that Eritreans would opt for political alliance with Ethiopia. When the landslide came, the United States immediately extended recognition to Eritrea. It was less forthcoming with aid.[83]

Support for the Eritreans by Arab nations has had a complicated history. What backing there was for the Eritrean struggle was mainly for the predominantly Muslim ELF, "which was supported by many Arab governments which regarded the country as an extension of the Arab world. Israeli assistance to Haile Selassie was an additional incentive for Arab support."[84] The ELF, however, fielded no army for the last decade of the war. In surveys by James Firebrace and Stuart Holland in 1985 (prepared for the British Labour Party)[85] and Roy Pateman in 1990, no significant or consistent support for the EPLF was found, with the exception of Sudanese toleration of EPLF supply lines and refugee camps. Pateman concluded:

> An EPLF commander stated that from 1980, no country gave the EPLF military aid; before that, Iraq, Kuwait and certain Palestinian organizations provided it with limited aid, especially shells and ammunition. A judicious view would seem to be that Arab military support has been relatively modest; while financial assistance, although significant in early years, is by no means the primary reason for the success of the Eritrean struggle.[86]

"More important" than external financial support (and "an important indication of popular support") "have been revenues derived from small scale taxation in some private sectors of the economy (mainly distribution), and above all, the financial contributions systematically made" by Eritrean refugees, exiles, and expatriates.[87] Wolde Mesghinna, an engineer living in Berkeley, explained:

> Most of us who live abroad and those people who live inside Eritrea give a portion of their income to the EPLF and using that revenue, the EPLF buys its needs. I am constantly working to help the struggle. And this is a way of life to us. It gives us satisfaction. It gives us hope. We are not like other people who are refugees and never think back about their country. We live in *hope.*[88]

Eritreans in the Middle East, Europe, and North America (about 50,000 reside in the United States) joined EPLF organizations by the thousands, and contributed up to 20 percent of their salaries annually. Some of the organizations, such as the Eritrean Relief Association, the Eritrean Medical Association, and the Research and Information Center on Eritrea "have generated appreciable (given the lack of more substantial support) humanitarian and political support for Eritrea. Drawing on this kind of minimal, yet meaningful support the EPLF has been able to successfully implement its policy of self-reliance."[89]

Self-Reliance in War

> The EPLF tries to be as self-sufficient as possible. . . . A very effective communication network has been developed. Their workshops are unique in Africa. They handle the repair of trucks, metal work, carpentry and joinery, textiles and radio repairs. Skilled manual labor is the basis of all these operations. . . . [T]heir military achievements are unique in Africa.[90]

An important factor in the EPLF's military effectiveness was that the infrastructure of the EPLF, and all of the fighters, have always been inside the country, in the northern, mountainous regions which provided natural defenses against both land and air attacks. The morale of EPLF fighters, Pateman reported in 1990, "is extraordinarily high. The fighters are all volunteers and there is no shortage of applicants."[91] Recruits were drawn from all nine Eritrean nationalities. About thirty-five percent of the fighters were women.

Each recruit, male or female, is given a minimum of six months' training combining political and military education. In the early years, the EPLF political training stressed Marxism; now the emphasis is very much on national and democratic issues. Female fighters are trained separately for the first six months in order to overcome the timidity of many recruits and to accustom them to strenuous physical exercise. They then join units on the same terms as male recruits.[92]

By 1975, the Eritreans were able to switch from guerrilla to positional war. They repeatedly devastated huge Ethiopian assault and occupation forces, capturing Soviet-made arms and heavy equipment. In 1985, Firebrace and Holland reported,

[t]he EPLF has captured and can now mobilize some 150 tanks and armored vehicles, as well as heavy and light artillery, rocket launchers and anti-aircraft guns. The [Eritrean People's Liberation Army] is now a larger and better equipped army than those of most African states.[93]

By 1990, the Eritrean People's Liberation Army fielded

twelve infantry brigades, each with three battalions having 450 fighters at full strength. There are a number of semi-regular regional armies and some 20,000 fighters in militia units. There are a heavy weapons brigade, artillery units and an engineering corps. The EPLA can mobilize over 200 tanks and armored vehicles, all captured from the Ethiopians; there are two tank battalions. Naval operations are carried out by a fleet of fast attack speedboats. The EPLA ranks eleventh in size among African armies. . . . It is better equipped than any other African conventional army except those of Angola, Egypt, Ethiopia, Mozambique, Nigeria and South Africa.[94]

Most important to the military self-reliance of the Eritreans, however, was their ability to repair and maintain captured arms and equipment, and to manufacture practical necessities from captured material. EPLF factories and workshops employed captured trucks, generators, metal and woodworking machines, sewing machines, and x-ray units.

The most remarkable aspect of this captured material is the EPLF's efficiency in using it. . . . Not only are spare parts, cooking utensils, teaching materials, aids for the disabled, and hospital equipment put together from the captured debris of war, but the EPLF is also constructing many of the machines necessary for producing these items. . . . The process is almost literally from shells to ploughshares.[95]

When machines needed to be replaced or their output increased, EPLF technicians "simply copied the principle from an imported model and built [another] one themselves."[96] The EPLF was equally thoughtful in matching work to workers.

The watches of EPLF fighters are fixed in an underground watch repair shop. Broken watches are collected from the EPLF units, including those operating behind the Ethiopian lines. They are registered and marked, so that they can eventually be returned to the same individual, and sent to this workshop which is run by 28 staff, most of whom have been disabled in the fighting. A few staff had watch-repairing skills before they joined the EPLF and are now teaching their skills to others.[97]

EPLF doctors, this woman said, came to her village, Nefasit, and performed the surgery that cured her blindness.

The EPLF developed the capacity to do brain surgery, dental surgery, open heart surgery, eye surgery, and microsurgery to repair wounds. Surgery was performed in shipping containers converted to sterile operating theaters.[98] Among other innovations, the Eritrean Health Service produced a simple plastic microscope, well-suited to rural health work, manufactured for $70, compared to $500 for a standard microscope.[99]

If the minute skills of watch repair and surgery are located at one end of a scale of EPLF capability, perhaps the other end is the more than 1,000 kilometers of road through rugged mountainous terrain which the EPLF constructed during the war, including the

> "Challenge Road" cut in 1982 into the precipitous east-ern slopes of the Sahel mountains . . . [which] twists and winds its way from valley floor to mountain ridge with 37 hairpins built over fortress-like supporting walls in a stretch 12 kilometers long. Swiss engineers, in peace-time, without air attack, would be proud of it.[100]

Other public works projects in liberated areas included building dams and irrigation systems.[101]

From War to Peace

In February, 1990, the Eritrean People's Liberation Army, "using a flotilla of speedboats to mount a surprise attack," captured the port city of Massawa, cutting Ethiopian-occupied Asmara, Eritrea's cap-ital, off from supplies.[102] During the 1980s the EPLF had built strategic alliances with the Oromo and Tigrayan rebels fighting inside Ethiopia to topple Mengistu. In May 1991, the EPLF marched into Asmara and the panicking remnants of 150,000 Ethiopian troops, their officers taking off in tanks and jeeps, fled inland toward the Ethiopian and Sudanese borders. A few days later, Addis Ababa fell to the Ethiopian Peoples Revolutionary Democratic Front.

The Provisional Government of Eritrea

The new government in Addis Ababa immediately recognized Eritrea's right to self-determination and confirmed an agreement with the EPLF to allow a popular referendum to decide Eritrea's political future. The Provisional Government of Eritrea was formed "within days of liberation," stating its priorities as the reconstruction and restoration of normal economic life, repatriation of refugees, and preparation for the referendum on independence.[103] The referendum was scheduled for 1993, to give the new Ethiopian regime two years to "stabilize its position" among the traditionally dominant Amharic ethnic minority who opposed the "loss" of Eritrea.[104]

The new government faced a country whose "antiquated physical infrastructure was in ruins," Dan Connell reported.[105] "Only 44 factories existed when the EPLF took over—and none of them were operating. The . . . key port of Massawa was crippled from the heavy fighting. Roads, bridges and railroads had all been damaged in the war."[106] Agriculture, too, had been devastated by the war and years of drought. "An estimated eighty percent of the country's 3.5 million people, many of whom were displaced by the fighting, were surviving on international relief."[107]

Access to aid, however, was stymied by the country's odd political status, no longer a part of Ethiopia and not independent either. The government "plunged ahead" in its customary self-reliant mode: the entire EPLF army volunteered to work without pay for

Retaliating for the EPLF's capture of Massawa, Eritrea's largest port, the Ethiopians bombed the city for 10 consecutive days. This was Haile Selassie's Red Sea palace.

two years to rebuild the country's infrastructure: roads, power, water, communications. A major project was clearing land mines from agricultural areas. In addition, all citizens eighteen to forty years old were required to register for twelve to eighteen months of compulsory national service. Universal primary education and expanded health care were seen as essential services. Schools opened with new curricula in four languages in October 1991, five months after the government was installed. The process of consolidating local and regional self-government was continued in the previously liberated areas, and was begun, under the guidance of EPLF organizers, in the newly liberated villages and towns. Attempting to "jump-start" the economy by attracting small-scale investment by Eritrean expatriates, the government adopted a business code favorable to foreign investment.[108]

Attracting educated and skilled Eritrean exiles back to the country was foreseeably difficult, as Eritrean salaries and the standard of living could not compete with conditions in the West and the Middle East. Large-scale repatriation of refugees (estimated at half a million) was also stalled for lack of jobs, housing, and other needs, although refugees were free to return on their own.[109] Nevertheless, Eritreans world-wide have tended to maintain relations with their homeland, and continued to respond to the EPLF's fundraising.

Eritrea also emerged from diplomatic isolation, and seemed especially determined to foster regional stability:

> In 1992, the Eritreans were already trying to play a stabilizing role in the Horn of Africa. EPLF leaders engaged in mediation efforts among warring Somalis and among contending Ethiopian groups; they held talks with rival Djibouti factions; and they initiated diplomatic contacts with states throughout the region, even Israel and Saudi Arabia, despite the long-standing hostility of both states toward the Eritrean revolution.[110]

This, then, is a brief account of the economic, human resources, and development outlook of Eritrea at the time I arrived there to conduct my research. Even before I stepped off the Ethiopian Airlines jet in Asmara, I was immersed in the celebratory mood of preparations for the referendum on independence. As the plane touched the tarmac in Asmara, the women aboard erupted in ululations. In Asmara, where I spent most of my time teaching and interviewing, the population was busy repairing, painting, building, planting, and beautifying their stately Italianate city. Driving out to nearby towns and villages, more than once I ran into pro-independence parades culminating in street parties.

Two days before the vote, the party started in Asmara—non-stop street dancing, parades, lights, music piped into the streets, traditional costumes and headdresses, even saber dancing.

On April 23, in predawn darkness, crowds began lining the streets around the polling places. Beginning at seven a.m., a million and a half Eritreans would tear their ballots in half, separating the blue side (yes) from the red side (no) and dropping one or the other into the ballot box. Everyone knew—the outcome was certain—when the boxes were dumped, blue ballots would overwhelm red ones. Elsewhere in the Horn of Africa, nothing was certain. Somalia, and especially Mogadishu, had devolved into armed compounds, the streets patrolled by beleaguered U.S. and UN troops. In Ethiopia, Oromos and Amharas still contested the legitimacy of the new government in Addis Ababa. Civil war seethed in the Sudan. But in Asmara civilians had no weapons and fighters displayed none. Enthusiasm for the referendum cut across religious and ethnic lines and political allegiances. Some ELF leaders, their organization long inactive, had flown into Asmara, stating support for the vote and respect for their rival's, the EPLF's, Provisional Government.

Outside, even in the back streets, there was a rush of excitement. White-swathed women and men (many men, today, had eschewed their western suits or work clothes for crisp white tunics and head wrappings) walked purposefully to the schools and offices designated as polling places. Women and men glowed with happiness in the brittle morning sunlight. Some had begun to line up at four a.m. Dignitaries—government officials, leading clergy—were scheduled to vote first, with cameras clicking, when the polls opened at seven a.m. I was told, though, of one old woman who had spent the night camped outside the school, determined to cast the first blue ballot. The Muslim cleric deferred the honor.

Eritreans were clearly making a statement to the world. Walking into polling places with just a snapshot camera and no press or observer ID, I was welcomed into the courtyards, the registration areas, the balloting rooms. I went everywhere but into the white-curtained booths where voters tore their secret ballots into two pieces. But the voters had no secret to keep. They held up their blue ballots to the cameras, prayed over them or over the ballot box. Some shouted "Awet Ne Hafash" (Victory to the Masses, an EPLF slogan) and raised their fists, as they dropped the blue slip in the box. Through unstoppable tears, I tried to focus my camera and get their faces on film.

Outside a kindergarten, women filled the street, four and six abreast, drumming, chanting, strutting in a high-stepping, swaying dance, entertaining a block-long line of voters leaning into the shade. A woman offering *embaba*, popcorn, from a tublike basket worked her way along the line and through knots of chatting, fanning bystanders. A video team from Boston aimed their equipment at an Eritrean man, one of the first to emerge from the polling place. "How do you feel today?" Nervous before the camera, he chose his words carefully. He wanted to make his feelings perfectly clear: "This is the most beautiful day for me. It is my birthday."

On Tuesday, April 27, people were saying that election results might be announced that afternoon. In the morning I drove out to Nefasit and Ghinda. I wanted to talk to people and take pictures of the celebrations I had heard were going on in all the villages. Nefasit was dreary, literally falling off the bare, muddy hills its stone houses hug—people were digging their huts out of the mudslides that a heavy rain had brought the night before. But Ghinda was all smiles and celebration. I was ushered into a courtyard where women were cooking for the festivities, producing huge stacks of *injera* from a steamer trunk full of batter and a single *mogogo*, the round charcoal-fired baking griddle, and cutting and cooking meat and vegetables. A party atmosphere prevailed, with enormous enameled cups of *sewa*, homemade beer, close at hand. I was treated to the resulting delicious stew, and tiny cups of sweet black coffee. At the same time, down the road, contingents of men and women were drumming, clapping, singing, and chanting. When I joined them, about 200 Tigre women, in bright yellows, purples, and pastels, were crowding and dancing into the road under strings of EPLF and Eritrean flags.

Back in Asmara, about 3 p.m., Dr. Amare Tecle, the head of the Referendum Commission, in a hastily called press conference at the

Selam Hotel, announced that 1,516,280 Eritreans had voted and 99.805 percent of them had voted yes—99.8 percent!

Much of what followed I heard in snatches, from the summary translations of Eritreans clustered around radios in the street, in hotels, in a few offices where people gathered to share the news. Italy immediately extended recognition, followed by the United States, Ethiopia, and the Sudan. The first speech broadcast came from the Ethiopian representative and was an important symbol of Meles Zenawi's government's unequivocal endorsement of Eritrean independence.

As dusk fell, crowds surged into the streets. The music and drumming started up again. For me that night was bittersweet, as I ran into friend after friend to hug, congratulate, and bid farewell—in a few days I would be leaving Eritrea and the rare company of people who face a daunting future with brave and joyous hearts. So my joy was mixed with sadness. But after a while I didn't care. I was dancing.

Notes

1 Ethiopia, Ministry of Foreign Affairs, *Eritrea Then and Now* (Addis Ababa: Press and Information Department, 1976; reprint, New York: Committee to Defend the Ethiopian Revolution, 1978), 4.

2 Roy Pateman, *Eritrea: Even the Stones Are Burning* (Trenton, NJ: Red Sea Press, 1990), 30. See also Jordan Gebre-Medhin, *Peasants and Nationalism in Eritrea: A Critique of Ethiopian Studies* (Trenton, NJ: Red Sea Press, 1989), 9.

3 Richard Sherman, *Eritrea: The Unfinished Revolution* (New York: Praeger, 1980), 9.

4 Pateman, *Eritrea: Even the Stones Are Burning*, 30.

5 Pateman, *Eritrea: Even the Stones Are Burning*, 35.

6 Pateman, *Eritrea: Even the Stones Are Burning*, 48; Yemane Mesghenna, *Italian Colonialism: A Case Study of Eritrea, 1869-1934—Motive, Praxis, and Result* (Lund, Sweden, 1988; reprint, Maryland: International Graphics, 1989), 242.

7 David Pool, *Eritrea: Africa's Longest War*, Anti-Slavery Society Human Rights Series Report No. 3 (London: Anti-Slavery Society, 1979), 17.

8 Sherman, *Eritrea: The Unfinished Revolution*, 11.

9 David Levering Lewis, *The Race to Fashoda: European Colonialism and African Resistance in the Scramble for Africa* (New York: Weidenfeld and Nicolson, 1987), 109.

10 Lewis, *The Race to Fashoda*, 112.

11 Lewis, *The Race to Fashoda*, 116-120.

12 Lewis, *The Race to Fashoda*, 120-121.

13 Bahru Zewde, *A History of Modern Ethiopia, 1855-1974* (London: James Currey Ltd., 1991), 83-84.

14 Lewis, *The Race to Fashoda*, 122.

15 Bereket Habte Selassie, "From British Rule to Federation and Annexation," in *Behind the War in Eritrea*, ed. Basil Davidson, Lionel Cliffe, and Bereket Habte Selassie (Nottingham, England: Spokesman, 1980), 32-47; James Firebrace and Stuart Holland, *Never Kneel Down: Drought, Development, and Liberation in Eritrea*, 2nd printing (Trenton, NJ: Red Sea Press, 1986); Pateman, *Eritrea: Even the Stones Are Burning*.

16 Pool, *Eritrea: Africa's Longest War*, 17.

17 Pateman, *Eritrea: Even the Stones Are Burning*, 52.

18 John Sorenson, "Discourses in Eritrean Nationalism and Identity," *Journal of Modern African Studies* 29 (1991): 302.

19 Edward Paice, *Guide to Eritrea* (Chalfont St Peter, Bucks, England: Bradt Publications, 1994), 23.

20 Gebre-Medhin, *Peasants and Nationalism*, 65.

21 Pool, *Eritrea: Africa's Longest War*, 17.

22 Paice, *Guide to Eritrea*, 23.

23 Pool, *Eritrea: Africa's Longest War*, 17.

24 Pool, *Eritrea: Africa's Longest War*, 18.

25 Pool, *Eritrea: Africa's Longest War*, 18.

26 Gebre-Medhin, *Peasants and Nationalism*, 59.

27 Gebre-Medhin, *Peasants and Nationalism*, 61.

28 Pool, *Eritrea: Africa's Longest War*, 17.

29 Bahru Zewde, *A History of Modern Ethiopia*, 158, 169; Pateman, *Eritrea: Even the Stones Are Burning*, 56.

30 Pateman, *Eritrea: Even the Stones Are Burning*, 56-58.

31 Pateman, *Eritrea: Even the Stones Are Burning*, 57.

32 Sherman, *Eritrea: The Unfinished Revolution*, 16.

33 Sherman, *Eritrea: The Unfinished Revolution*, 16.

34 Paice, *Guide To Eritrea*, 26.

35 Firebrace and Holland, *Never Kneel Down*, 18; Sherman, *Eritrea: The Unfinished Revolution*, 17.

36 Quoted in Firebrace and Holland, *Never Kneel Down*, 19.

37 Firebrace and Holland, *Never Kneel Down*, 19; Pateman, *Eritrea: Even the Stones Are Burning*, 70; Sherman, *Eritrea: The Unfinished Revolution*, 22-23.

38 Sherman, *Eritrea: The Unfinished Revolution*, 22.

39 Pool, *Eritrea: Africa's Longest War*, 29.

40 Firebrace and Holland, *Never Kneel Down*, 20; Pool, *Eritrea: Africa's Longest War*, 29.

41 Gebre-Medhin, *Peasants and Nationalism*, 90-91.

42 Quoted in Bereket Habte Selassie, "From British Rule," 58.

43 Sherman, *Eritrea: The Unfinished Revolution*, 141, 143; Bereket Habte Selassie, "From British Rule," 38.

44 Firebrace and Holland, *Never Kneel Down*, 20.

45 Gebre-Medhin, *Peasants and Nationalism*, 38, 180; Pool, *Eritrea: Africa's Longest War*, 36-37.

46 Firebrace and Holland, *Never Kneel Down*, 20-21.

47 Pateman, *Eritrea: Even the Stones Are Burning*, 73.

48 Firebrace and Holland, *Never Kneel Down*, 21.

49 Firebrace and Holland, *Never Kneel Down*, 21.

50 Susan Kalish, *Eritrea*, prod. Susan Kalish, dir. Susan Kalish, Yasha Aginsky, and John Knoop (Cinema Guild, Inc., 1697 Broadway, Suite 506, New York, NY 10019-5904), 1990, film.

51 Dan Connell, *Against All Odds: A Chronicle of the Eritrean Revolution* (Trenton, NJ: Red Sea Press, 1993).

52 Connell, *Against All Odds*, 83, emphasis in original.

53 Sherman, *Eritrea: The Unfinished Revolution*, 82.

54 Connell, *Against All Odds*, 83; Sherman, *Eritrea: The Unfinished Revolution*, 82.

55 Connell, *Against All Odds*, 83.

56 Sherman, *Eritrea: The Unfinished Revolution*, 81.

57 Firebrace and Holland, *Never Kneel Down*, 30.

58 Connell, *Against All Odds*, 165; Firebrace and Holland, *Never Kneel Down*, 30; Pateman, *Eritrea: Even the Stones Are Burning*, 106.

59 Pateman, "Eritrea Is Free, While Ethiopia Scrambles for Unity," *Guardian*, 26 June 1991, 14

60 Pateman, *Eritrea: Even the Stones Are Burning*, 78.

61 Bereket Habte Selassie, *Conflict and Intervention in the Horn of Africa* (New York: Monthly Review Press, 1980).

62 Firebrace and Holland, *Never Kneel Down*; Pateman, *Eritrea: Even the Stones Are Burning*; Sherman, *Eritrea: The Unfinished Revolution*.

63 Araya Tseggai, "The History of the Eritrean Struggle," in *The Long Struggle of Eritrea for Independence and Constructive Peace*, ed. Lionel Cliffe and Basic Davidson (Trenton, NJ: Red Sea Press, 1988), 80.

64 Connell, *Against All Odds*, 160.

65 Connell, *Against All Odds*, 165.

66 Connell, *Against All Odds*, 177.

67 Pateman, *Eritrea: Even the Stones Are Burning*, 81.

68 Pateman, *Eritrea: Even the Stones Are Burning*, 78, 226.

69 Kola Olufemi, "Stalinism in Ethiopia," *Journal of Eritrean Studies* III, no. 2 (1989), 4.

70 Olufemi, "Stalinism in Ethiopia," 7.

71 Mary Dines, "Ethiopian Violation of Human Rights in Eritrea," in *The Long Struggle of Eritrea for Independence and Constructive Peace*, ed. Lionel Cliffe and Basic Davidson Trenton, NJ: Red Sea Press, 1988), 139-141; Pateman, *Eritrea: Even the Stones Are Burning*, 83.

72 Dines, "Ethiopian Violation," 148; Robert Papstein, *Eritrea: Revolution at Dusk* (Trenton, NJ: Red Sea Press, 1991), 97; Sherman, *Eritrea: The Unfinished Revolution*, 84-86.

73 Dines, "Ethiopian Violation," 149. See also Abeba Tesfagiorgis, *A Painful Season and a Stubborn Hope: The Odyssey of an Eritrean Mother* (Trenton, NJ: Red Sea Press, 1992).

74 Tseggai, "The History of the Eritrean Struggle"; Firebrace and Holland, *Never Kneel Down*; Pateman, *Eritrea: Even the Stones Are Burning*.

75 Firebrace and Holland, *Never Kneel Down*, 55.

76 Connell, *Against All Odds*, 228, brackets in original.

77 Firebrace and Holland, *Never Kneel Down*, 51.

78 Kwame Anthony Appiah, *In My Father's House: Africa in the Philosophy of Culture* (New York: Oxford University Press, 1992), 167.

79 Pateman, *Eritrea: Even the Stones Are Burning*; Jane Perlez, "Peace Is Bursting Out; Will Crops Do As Well?" *New York Times*, 16 July 1991, A6.

80 Firebrace and Holland, *Never Kneel Down*, 47.

81 Pateman, "Eritrea Is Free."

82 Pateman, "Eritrea Is Free."

83 Stephen Hubbell, "The Next Fight for Independence," *The Nation*, 31 May 1993, 732-735; Connell, *Against All Odds*, 250.

84 Liberation Support Movement, "Hurricane In the Horn," *LSM News*, 15 (1978): 13.

85 Firebrace and Holland, *Never Kneel Down*, 49-50.

86 Pateman, *Eritrea: Even the Stones Are Burning*, 102.

87 Richard Leonard, "Popular Participation in Liberation and Revolution," in *The Long Struggle of Eritrea for Independence and Constructive Peace*, ed. Lionel Cliffe and Basil Davidson (Trenton, NJ: Red Sea Press, 1988), 111.

88 Kalish, *Eritrea*.

89 Leonard, "Popular Participation," 111.

90 Gerard Chaliand, "The Guerrilla Struggle," in *Behind the War in Eritrea*, ed. Basil Davidson, Lionel Cliffe, and Bereket Habte Selassie (Nottingham, England: Spokesman, 1980), 51-52.

91 Pateman, *Eritrea: Even the Stones Are Burning*, 125.

92 Pateman, *Eritrea: Even the Stones Are Burning*, 125.

93 Firebrace and Holland, *Never Kneel Down*, 51.

94 Pateman, *Eritrea: Even the Stones Are Burning*, 120-121.

95 Firebrace and Holland, *Never Kneel Down*, 74.

96 Firebrace and Holland, *Never Kneel Down*, 78.

97 Firebrace and Holland, *Never Kneel Down*, 78.

98 Connell, *Against All Odds*, 230; John Kifner, "Rebels Working to Modernize Eritrea," *New York Times*, 21 August 1988, 1, 14; Papstein, *Eritrea: Revolution at Dusk*, 62; Provisional Government of Eritrea (EPLF), Mission to the USA and Canada, "In Memoriam: Fred Hollows," *Eritrea Update*, February 1993, 7; Amrit Wilson, *The Challenge Road: Women and the Eritrean Revolution* (Trenton, NJ: Red Sea Press, 1991), 142.

99 Michael G Hiwet, "Field Evaluation of the EPHP Plastic Microscope," in *Proceedings of the First International Conference On Health In Eritrea: Milan, November 1st And 2nd 1986*, ed. John Black and Yohannes Fassil, 33; Papstein, *Eritrea: Revolution at Dusk*, 152, 161.

100 Firebrace and Holland, *Never Kneel Down*, 75.

101 Dan Connell, "A New Country Emerges," *Links, Health and Development Report* (National Central America Health Rights Network), Spring 1992, 10.

102 Connell, *Against All Odds*, 234.

103 Provisional Government of Eritrea (EPLF), Mission to the USA and Canada, "Editorial: Eritrea Is Free!" *Eritrea Update*, January 1992, 1.

104 Connell, *Against All Odds*, 248.

105 Connell, *Against All Odds*, 248.

106 Cameron McWhirter and Gur Melamede, "Breaking Away," *Africa Report*, November-December 1992, 60.

107 Connell, *Against All Odds*, 248.

108 Connell, *Against All Odds*, 247-253.

109 As of April, 1993, 80,000 refugees had returned to Eritrea from the Sudan. Provisional Government of Eritrea, Commission of Eritrean Refugees, "Problems of Eritrean Refugees," in *Eritrea: The Long Trek to Self Determination*, information package (Asmara, April 1993), 2.

110 Connell, *Against All Odds*, 265.

III

EDUCATION, PRECOLONIAL TO POSTLIBERATION

The following account of the major periods in the history of education in Eritrea is based, in its outline and for much information, on published sources; however, it includes information from documents I collected in Eritrea and the conversations I held there.

In Eritrea, educational *policy* has been an instrument of colonial control and an instrument of liberation. Educational *experience*, however, has tended to be seen (with the exception of Asmara's youth educated under the Dergue, 1980 to 1991) as liberating and possibility-opening. Even so, education cannot be understood apart from its traditions; and possibility, while infinite, is always historically effected.

> [H]istorically effected consciousness . . . is an element in the act of understanding itself and . . . is already effectual in *finding the right questions to ask.*
>
> Consciousness of being affected by history . . . is primarily consciousness of the hermeneutical *situation.* To acquire an awareness of a situation is, however,

> always a task of peculiar difficulty. The very idea of a situation means that we are not standing outside it and hence are unable to have any objective knowledge of it. We always find ourselves within a situation, and throwing light on it is a task that is never entirely finished. This is also true of the hermeneutic situation—i.e., the situation in which we find ourselves with regard to the tradition that we are trying to understand.1

I sought a view of educational history from within education's post-liberation horizon, and to understand the current situation in the light of history. Because it reflects Eritrean educators' current thinking on the legacy they have inherited, I have especially relied on a history of education which is part of the document *Science and Technology Education in Eritrea*, prepared in April 1993 by the Science Panel of the Curriculum Development Institute in the Department of Education.[2] It is also useful for its data from Italian sources. This document reveals, at least in part, the historical consciousness of Eritrean educators, and inasmuch as I, working with Eritrean educators, shared their "situation," this document formed a historical horizon for my own understanding of the nature of the educational work I was doing.

It is, says Greg Sarris, a "necessity for collaborators in any cross-cultural project to see themselves as present, as persons working in a given place at a given time, if they are to begin to understand the nature and consequences of their work."[3]

The Tradition of Exemplary Practice

Information on precolonial education in Eritrea is sparse. An EPLF account (published in 1984) of formal education before the arrival of the Italians reads:

> Pre-colonial education in Eritrea was essentially religious and totally dominated by the Orthodox Christian Churches and the Islamic Mosques. These churches and mosques took in children who professed their respective faiths and produced advocates who dogmatically tried to divide the people on religious and tribal lines. Superstition became so dominant that even the rudi-

ments of scientific outlook were lacking. This greatly hampered the people's ability to be equipped with even the elementary know-how that could be useful in an improvement of their living conditions. Furthermore, a fatalistic attitude towards their conditions of oppression, which they were constantly told was pre-ordained by the supernatural, was a great obstacle to any organised struggle that they could have waged against the bonds of ignorance and oppression.[4]

Given these effects—or rather, the polemicized understanding of them (which, I would venture, has changed since the early 1980s)—one might conclude that it is fortunate that formal education in the pre-Italian, "precapitalist and basically feudal"[5] period was limited, it may be assumed, to a small percentage of the population. In the highlands, the Coptic Church "was the carrier of high culture"[6]—literacy, historical documentation and interpretation, legitimation of feudal class distinctions. Muslim societies, of course, have strong traditions of learning,[7] and the coastal lowlands of Eritrea, as I pointed out in chapter 2, were a crossroads of African and Middle Eastern traffic and trade, including, of course, cultural exchange. "The complexities of war and trade, dominance, and clientage, migration and diplomacy, in much of pre-colonial Africa," Kwame Anthony Appiah reminds us, "are simply not consistent with the image of peoples unaware that there is a world elsewhere."[8] One legacy of this, as well as of colonialism, is the multilingual ability of many, especially older, Eritreans living today, who might be found to speak—besides their mother tongue, other Eritrean languages, and Ethiopia's Amharic language—Arabic, Italian, and English.

Education as an informal practice is present in every society: training in productive skills, home construction, traditional medicine, music-making, storytelling, decorative arts, and so on. In Eritrea, I believe, can be detected the traces of ancient modes of instruction in the force of authority, especially generational authority, and the function of exemplary behavior, demonstration, and imitation. "In African society, lifelong learning has always been the norm, with children beginning to learn the history of the clan in lullabies. In the educational continuum, the elders have the continuing responsibility to teach the younger elders" in religious, family, and practical matters.[9] Ethiopia, Birgit Negussie points out, "has a rich oral culture, and much knowledge is transmitted from generation to generation," including health, medical, dietary, and pharmacological knowledge; agricultural and ecological knowledge; housekeeping, child-bearing, and childrearing techniques; multiple languages; genealogy, and socio-cultural values.[10] But the traditional "curriculum" is not inalterable. Innovations which clearly demonstrate material improvements and advantages form a touchstone for development in education in literate and non-literate societies.

> In precolonial African societies th[e] purpose [of education] was clear: Functionalism was the main guiding principle. . . . African societies regarded education as a means to an end, not as an end in itself. Their education emphasized social responsibility, job orientation, political participation, and spiritual and moral values; it was an integrated experience which combined physical training with character building and manual activity with intellectual training.[11]

Many examples of *example* appeared in my conversations with Eritrean educators: the adoption of sanitation methods among rural Eritreans (see pages 197–199); a woman merchant coerced into literacy classes by the EPLF under threat of punishment, who later was found teaching her own children to read (page 213); EPLF gardening techniques imitated by villagers who saw higher yields; changes among a semi-pastoralist group over five or six years, due to the example of school children wearing clean clothes, washing themselves, learning useful skills such as health care, and earning salaries (pages 198–199). Many other examples abound. Wolde Mesghinna told me he was the first child in his village to attend school—a disgrace in a community which measured success by the size of a family's herd and the attention it required.

> They were telling my parents, "How can you send your kid to school? People who go to school are those poor people who have no herds to look after, who have no cows, no goats," or something like that. You know? And there was no school in my village.

However:

> After I went to high school, I sort of became a role model for the village, and the village built its own school by itself. It was a three-room school and they asked the government, "Okay, now we've built a school here, and we will build also his house, for the teacher, and we want you to bring us a teacher." So the government brought them a teacher. And, you know, it starts to flourish, and then they have more rooms, and more rooms, and the village, now they have a lot of educated people right now.

Wolde's account, and other examples, suggest, however, that generational influence, in traditional societies, is bi-directional. Certainly the key concept, the test of an idea's spread and endurance, is its fittingness or social efficacy: "The aim of traditional African education has always been for the good of the community as whole."[12] Change comes from within by example and from without through "fusion of horizons," which chapter 5 discusses at length. Or, as Arnold Krupat finds compelling, like "Bakhtin's claim that language in society is always and inevitably a plural concept . . . it may be useful to see culture . . . as never absolute and exclusive unto itself."[13] For Bakhtin, "at any given moment of its historical existence, language"—and for Krupat, culture—

> is heteroglot from top to bottom: it represents the coexistence of socio-ideological contradictions between the present and past, between differing epochs of the past, between different socio-ideological groups in the present, between tendencies, schools, circles and so forth, all given a bodily form. These "languages" of heteroglossia intersect each other in a variety of ways, forming new socially typifying "languages."[14]

Such theories help explain the potency of small doses of example, and why rapid cultural shape-shifting is not confined to metropolitan areas of the world; a young teacher, Solomon Woldmichel, described this process in the relatively remote western lowlands of Eritrea:

> For example, in Maria Tselam, in 1981 when I went to
> that region, the people that were at that time and the peo-
> ple that are found now are quite different. For example,
> the way of marriage at that time was obligation. The
> woman and the boy—even the boy—had no chance to
> prefer his woman. At this time, even the girl has a right to
> prefer her husband and to refuse the man who gave her
> father. And there is no girl of sixteen years to be married
> to man older than her by twenty years or thirty years, at
> this time. One of the changes is this in the social field. This
> comes from the education because most of the girls that
> are now at the marriage age are students, and they know
> what is the benefit of marriage with one who loves you
> and what is the benefit of the previous way of marriage.
> And they got a chance to communicate with other soci-
> eties, to see other societies how they marry, even in Eritrea
> or outside Eritrea. For example, people like you came
> from outside, and they saw them in video cassettes, and
> you teach them, for example in history, in geography, and
> sometimes they came from, for example, from Senhit and
> went to Semhar—in this exchange of cultures.

Of course, throughout the world it is not uncommon for love of
learning to be handed down within a family. Mohammedin Jassir,
of the largely illiterate Saho nationality, came from an atypical, educated family, and was motivated toward schooling, the university,
and now a teaching career. Salome Iyob listed the educational
accomplishments of her nine brothers and sisters. What, I asked her,
had inspired them?

> Ah, yes, my father was a doctor in jurisprudence. But he
> studied by correspondence. He became a doctor by corre-
> spondence. Well, my father was an intellectual. He liked
> people to study, and I think we took from him: we liked to
> read books. I do, because he used to read a lot to me. When
> he came back from work, he just laid down and read a lot.

Generational influences from outside the family can be efficacious,
too. Professor Kiflemariam Zerom, of the University of Asmara,
told me that as a child he wanted to be a jet pilot, following the

example of an uncle who was an Ethiopian Airlines pilot, but later he was influenced by the example of Peace Corps volunteers who were his teachers in the town of Adi Teclesan. Ambitious, public-spirited, or successful individuals are likely to be looked up to and imitated, even in highly distressed populations, such as the predominantly female refugee communities (at least in communities large enough for women's work to be significantly differentiated) that Elsa Gebreyesus and Sherry Phillips surveyed in western Eritrea:

LES GOTTESMAN: Were there some women who really set an example for other women, who other women would say, "This is an example of what I can do, independently, on my own"?

SHERRY PHILLIPS: Yes.

LG: "And I see this person who has this ability, so that shapes my own aspirations"?

ELSA GEBREYESUS: Yes.

LG: Do you think that's very instrumental in the process that women go through?

EG: Yes.

SP: Very much so! I think that was much more visible, though, in the urban centers where women's activities were more diverse, where you had professional or semi-professional women in business or in commerce, as opposed to the smaller communities where, pretty well, I can safely generalize to say that most of the women were involved in the same activity, whether making handicrafts out of palm leaves or having teashops or whatever. But in the larger communities, in Barentu and Tessenei and Agordat, there were more examples of women who had managed to have more education, who had more skills, and therefore had more choices.

LG: And this formed an example then for other women?

SP: Yes. I found that, for instance, in Barentu among the Kunama women, there were a few women that I met.

One woman for instance who works in the economics department, Ministry of Agriculture, is very skilled, is very collaborative with other Kunama women. On a number of occasions in different interviews with Kunama women they referred to her as an example. She speaks good English, and some women would say to me, "I really want to learn English." And when I would ask why, they'd say, "Well, Lucia has managed to do so well. In comparison to other Kunama households, female-headed households, hers is much more stable and secure," and so on and so forth. And among the Kunama, it seemed to me that there was a tighter or very strong network of communication between households, so I would venture to guess that most women in Barentu know Lucia.

Many openings for innovative social practice were provided by the emergencies and dislocations of war, with the EPLF playing an influential role in education and social change. The tradition of exemplary practice continues today, though not without problems. For example, Paul Highfield explained,

one of the problems is that a lot of these role models have been EPLF members, and the EPLF is not really integrated fully back into the communities. The demobilization has only just started, and the vast majority of the EPLF is outside of Asmara; some are living in army barracks, not with their families, and they haven't got civilian jobs—whereas they might be doing something different or developing themselves in a different way from what's happening in the community, or having different attitudes which would have an influence. So to some extent that situation has the potential of happening in the future, but it's not happening as much as it could be because of that gap that exists between the separate lives of the EPLF and the civilians.

Demobilization could introduce powerful progressive elements into Eritrean communities and families, Highfield agreed,

if the resources were there to provide training centers for

the fighters who are being demobilized. But to a large extent the resources are not there because the vast majority of the EPLF fighters are illiterate or semi-literate ex-peasants who joined from the mid-1980s onwards. The highly educated, politically conscious members, most of those were killed during the war. And because political education almost stopped from the late 1980s onwards, they're not particularly highly conscious. They've been through a different experience in the war, physically fighting the enemy, and to some extent living in a collective way, but for quite a short period of time, and it's certainly not long enough for them to have changed their attitudes—the men, anyway. So unless they have skill training courses, take courses that give them skills in auto mechanics, in how to build simple pumps for water, handicrafts, that sort of thing, then there's going to be widespread unemployment amongst the EPLF and, the members when they go back, they're not going to be role models. Resources are really the key.

This is one threatening scenario that postliberation Eritrea must struggle against, in which the tradition of exemplary practice—in, for example, community-based technical innovation, expanded social roles for women, improved hygiene and health, local democracy—is jeopardized, forestalled, even atrophied, by the lack of jobs, job-training, and other resources for reintegrating the EPLF fighters, the people's heroes, into Eritrean society.

Education in Italian Eritrea

Education in Italian Eritrea prior to fascism was almost entirely in the hands of Protestant and Roman Catholic missionaries. The former included two Swedish missionary societies which established schools in eight centers, serving over 1,100 students in the late 1920s, while Catholic missionaries were encouraged to run the government schools which came into existence.[15] In 1909, the first colonial educational policy was declared, based on separate schools for Italians and Eritreans. Schooling was compulsory for Italians aged seven to sixteen, and the curriculum followed the curriculum of the schools in Italy. Education for Eritreans, however,

> was to be under full control of the governor. He was responsible for laying down the rules . . . for natives in terms of attendance requirements and programs. The school program was to include the Italian language, arts and crafts, hygiene, agriculture, geography and arithmetic.[16]

Prior to 1938, "half-castes" who were recognized by their Italian fathers were admitted to Italian schools, but with the tightening of racial laws by the Fascist regime they too were denied admission.[17]

In 1932, the first central office for primary education was established in Eritrea, "the purpose of which as defined by its director, Andrea Festa, was to exercise technical and disciplinary supervision to ensure that education accorded with the principles of the Italian regime."[18] A 1938 confidential directive from Festa to headmasters makes these principles explicit:

> By the end of his fourth year the Eritrean student should be able to speak our language moderately well; he should know the four arithmetical operations within normal limits . . . and of history he should know only the names of those who have made Italy great.[19]

To the third Colonial Congress in 1937, Festa explained:

> It is desirable above everything that the child knows and feels the need to wash himself. These are the best results that a teacher can obtain in the colonies. The rest, reading and writing will certainly be seen later; but it is necessary to waste time with soap.[20]

The emphasis on hygiene was, in part at least, meant to reduce the dangers of contamination to the Italian population.

Berhane Teklehaimanot finds ample evidence in Italian sources that education of Eritrean males was explicitly designed to train them for military functions, to be soldiers, telegraph operators, clerks, typists.[21] In textbooks, "[m]ilitary service was lauded. Boys were encouraged to become 'little soldiers of the Duce', the Fascist salute was compulsory, and at the morning hoisting of the flag,

Italian songs were sung."[22] According to Festa,

> the program of studies had the following aims: to make
> the child a "conscious propagandist" of Italian civiliza-
> tion and so to proselytize the parents; to inform the
> native child of Italy's ancient and present glory and
> greatness, so the child might become a "conscious mili-
> tia man" under the protection of the Italian flag; and to
> give him a knowledge of hygiene, geography, and histo-
> ry.... [S]chools designed with these programs had
> already established "future soldiers for Italy."[23]

Additionally, boys were trained in agriculture, girls for domestic
roles. Starting in 1921, educational policy required every school "to
establish training in gardening or in one of the local industries."
The Fascist Government specified agriculture as one of the subjects
of instruction. Festa advocated the establishment of agricultural
schools, "to the exclusion of arts and crafts schools, whenever
favorable agricultural conditions prevailed."[24]

Instruction in the government schools was in Italian. Education
was never widely available to Eritreans. Essentially, fourth grade was
the highest level an Eritrean was allowed to reach.[25] Starting in 1927,
two-year secondary school courses were available, in the Vittorio
Emanuel III School in Asmara, "for the children of some selected
Eritrean notables" who had completed four years of elementary
school. Enrollment in the secondary program topped at 38 students
in 1934; by 1940, only ten students were in attendance.[26] Country-
wide, "there were 20 elementary schools ... in 1938–39 for the
native Eritreans. Two of the elementary schools had trade schools
attached to them. The number of students in 1938–39 is reported to
have been 4,177." This shockingly small number of Eritrean students
had further declined by 1941. Then, "there were only 16 schools in
operation. ... [T]here were 152 teachers in these schools including
33 Italian elementary school teachers, 86 nuns and 27 Eritrean assis-
tants." Moreover, "only one out of five students remained in these
schools until the end of the school year."[27] The "unexplained diffi-
culty which the Italians ... had in persuading native children to come
to school"[28] could have been due to the educational policies and
goals: instruction in Italian, political indoctrination, preparation for
military service, and discouragement from "acquiring professional or

political aspiration[s] out of harmony with the fascist ethos."[29] For their part, Italian officials complained of the "diversity in the degree of civilization" of Eritreans, and their racial, religious, language, and "prejudicial" divisions that made "the problem of education in the colony of Eritrea very complex and difficult to solve."[30]

"In general," the Science Panel history concludes, "the Italians neglected the development of education for the native Eritreans. The educational facilities were limited; there were few and unqualified teachers. The schools served for the propaganda dissemination of the colonialists."[31]

Educational Development in the British Decade

"The Italian neglect of education in Eritrea left the British with a huge task."[32] It was also a new task: Britain's educational goal in Eritrea, as Berhane Teklehaimanot describes it,

> was to train interpreters, clerks, and paraprofessionals who would act as vanguards in the "civilizing" mission. Thus, when the British Military [A]dministration was installed in 1941, the authorities saw the need for an educational process that would also force the Eritreans into a money economy and help break down tribal solidarity.[33]

At the beginning of British rule, "[t]here were no native trained teachers."[34] The Department of Education, created by the administration in August 1942,

> looked for old records and ha[d] a talk also with Eritreans to see if there were individuals interested in teaching and who had sufficient knowledge and skill of the three R's and that could also be trained for the work.
>
> By the end of the year, 1942, the Department of Education came up with nineteen "potential" teachers. . . . One of the candidates was Isahac Teweldemedhin[,] who had attended the Swedish Mission School. He had studied for two years at the American University in Beirut and after that he taught for a number of years until the Italians closed the Mission. He was an able man, and with good will and initiative for the promotion of edu-

cation in Eritrea. He was appointed as native assistant to
the British education officer in January of 1943. . . .

The Department of Education organized two weeks
of intensive instruction for the potential teachers. The
crash programme was largely a matter of refreshing and
increasing their knowledge of the basic subjects of reading, writing, arithmetic, geography and a little history.
Several periods were also devoted to the subject of conducting a school, how one should go about teaching children, and the preparation of instructional materials. Such
was the limited preparation of the first group of teachers
as they departed for their schools in the villages.[35]

Over the next 10 years, the British "quadrupled the number of primary schools, from twenty-four to 100, and also introduced fourteen
middle schools with 1,200 students and two secondary schools with
167 pupils."[36] The curriculum introduced in 1943 covered agriculture, woodwork, clay-modeling, carpet-making, shoe-making, reading, writing, and hygiene for boys, and reading, writing, hygiene,
weaving, sewing, basket work, and domestic science for girls.[37]
Textbooks in Tigrinya (the principal Eritrean language) were locally
printed, and books in Arabic and English were provided.[38] "English
became more important than before as entrance to the middle
schools"—introduced in 1947—"required students to be able to
read and write English."[39] In 1946 a trilingual manual for Eritrean
teachers was issued, and a teacher training college was established
with an initial enrollment of fifteen student teachers.[40] By 1950,
fifty-three men and seven women were in training to be teachers.[41]

Through school committees organized in the villages, Eritreans
were "active . . . in the expansion of education. They funded the
school building and paid the salaries of the teachers. The school
committees were also responsible for the smooth running of the
schools and the welfare of the teachers."[42] But the demand for education far exceeded "the limits of the budget," a 1950 British government report admitted (a situation the government of independent Eritrea would face in the 1990s, the next period when communities would be allowed to exercise initiative and control over an
expanding educational system). "Many children were rejected
owing to lack of buildings, equipment and staff."[43]

The Science Panel history of education credits the British for utilizing and training Eritrean educators; producing textbooks in Tigrinya and Arabic, the instructional languages at the primary level; and "appointing dedicated local education inspectors . . . who, in one way or another, played a significant part in selling modern education to the Eritrean people." Overall, the Science Panel concludes, "the British educational system . . . enhanced the educational awareness and the political consciousness of the Eritrean people."[44]

Education in the Federal Period, 1952–1962

Eritrea passed from the British Military Administration to the federal arrangement with better educational facilities than Ethiopia. "The enthusiasm and thirst for education that was aroused during the British Administration also continued during the Federation. Teachers were recruited locally, student enrollment [increased, and] schools were built,"[45] but the government was unable "to meet the popular demand for primary and secondary education."[46] The 1952 Eritrean constitution guaranteed residents the right to education; it also declared Tigrinya and Arabic the official languages, and these were used for primary education up to grade four, with English thereafter. The Department of Education was founded in 1953 with a British director. A Publications Committee developed its own Tigrinya textbooks and imported Arabic textbooks from Egypt.[47] Education was extended for the first time to rural areas and to girls in significant numbers.[48] The system included primary and middle schools inherited from the British administration, two new secondary schools which were established during the federation, and three "professional schools" in vocational trades, teacher training, and nursing, "which had somewhat equivalent grades to the academic secondary schools."[49]

During the federal period, Haile Selassie began to undermine Eritrean education, along with other institutions.[50] In 1956, Amharic "was proclaimed as the only language for public offices, schools, law courts and business documents."[51] Ethiopian teachers brought in to teach Amharic "received 30 percent higher pay than their Eritrean counterparts, as a 'hardship allowance.'"[52] The first of many student strikes occurred in 1957 at the Haile Selassie

Secondary School in Asmara (now the Red Sea Secondary School), the first school at which Amharic was made compulsory; in response, 300 students were jailed for a month. "No sooner was this strike settled than discontent spread to the Prince Mekkonen Secondary School; frequent strikes occurred for a decade."[53]

Imperial Education

Following annexation in 1962, all education decisions were made in Addis Ababa.[54] The policies of "Ethiopianization" and "Amharization" intensified, the latter becoming one of the factors which awakened national consciousness and united diverse ethnic groups against the imperial regime. In 1963 the Publications Committee was abolished and Arabic and Tigrinya textbooks were burned.[55]

> One of the important accomplishments of annexing Eritrea to Ethiopia, from the latter's point of view[,] was halting Eritrea's progress in order to bring it down to the level of the other provinces. This covert and overt policy of undermining the Eritrean[s'] confidence in their democratic practices and procedures and of making them more dependent (economically and educationally) on Ethiopia proper was vigorously pursued.[56]

Thus, enrollment in Eritrean schools was frozen, despite "the public outcry for more schools," while other areas of Ethiopia received expansion funds.[57]

In 1962, following the abrogation of the Federation, the Santa Familia University, founded in Asmara by the Comboni Sisters in 1958, obtained recognition from the Ethiopian government, changing its name to the University of Asmara.[58] The obstacles which beset the development of the university reveal something of the intrigues which fractured the court of Haile Selassie, who was personally supportive of the university and intervened repeatedly when the Ethiopian Ministry of Education objected to its status as a degree-granting university.[59] The Italian community in Asmara, historically hostile to Eritreans obtaining an education, conspired with the Ministry of Education to prevent the university's campus being built, until the university's lawsuit won on appeal and the building was completed.[60]

> Perhaps the most successful measure by the Haile
> Selassie government to deny higher education to
> Eritreans was the . . . calibration of examination scores
> according to the province of origin. Students from
> provinces with poor educational endowment . . . had to
> achieve lower marks to gain entrance to university com-
> pared to those with better schools—such as Eritrea.
> What made this otherwise acceptable scheme into a
> form of discrimination was that the threshold score for
> Eritrea was set higher than for other Ethiopian
> provinces, such as Sh[o]a, which were given better edu-
> cational resources.[61]

Meanwhile the university, which offered instruction in Italian, had
been recognized by the Superior Council of the Institute of Italian
Universities in 1960, and began offering instruction in English as
well as Italian in 1964.[62]

In 1963, elementary and secondary teachers went on strike,
ostensibly over the pay differential between Eritrean and
Ethiopian teachers. Underlying reasons for the strike, however,
were "unhappiness at the Ethiopian government's policies and
sympathies for the Eritrean Liberation Front" which had begun
the guerrilla war. Teachers were active in clandestine nationalist
organizations, and many were arrested, jailed without trial, or
transferred to Ethiopia.[63] However, starting in 1967 when large-
scale military confrontations broke out between the Ethiopian
army and the ELF, young nationalists began joining the guerrillas
outright,

> and—especially after the declaration of a State of Emer-
> gency in 1970—any sign of dissent in the schools was
> immediately identified with subversion and dealt with
> accordingly. The new governor, Ras Asrate Kassa, also
> took a more conciliatory line to teachers and students
> who showed no overt dissent. Teachers and students
> thus became more cautious, and the beginning of a long
> period of 24 years of enforced self-censorship began. In
> contrast to Addis Ababa, students in Eritrea played lit-
> tle part in the events of the revolution of 1974 [the
> overthrow of Haile Selassie].[64]

Education Under the Dergue

Educated Eritreans were a particular target of Dergue "harassment and violence. . . . Thousands were detained," and many met horrible deaths, including dozens of young Eritrean students who were strangled with piano wire by Ethiopian security services in the late 1970s. Amharic remained compulsory, and the number of Ethiopian teachers increased—up to 2,000 by 1980. "Little additional pressure was needed to ensure that the educational system remained in quiescent conformity with the government's aims." Nevertheless, "[s]urveillance was constant in the educational system. All teachers were obliged to attend weekly classes in Marxism-Leninism, in which their adherence to the official philosophy could be scrutinized and assessed."[65] Professor Kiflemariam Zerom of the University of Asmara described the frustrations of those years:

> Since we were under the Ethiopian regime, up to the time of liberation, 1991, our teaching—or my teaching—has been affected very much. I think it has been affected very much. Of course, I believe that I was doing my best in my teaching, but I believe that I'd have done more, I'd have been motivated more, had the situation been more favorable. But there was frustration. There was dissatisfaction. I shouldn't have waited. We have been waiting for a scholarship in order to go and finish the rest of our education that we have to finish, and come back to the university and do justice to our students, to our university. Because of these problems, frustrations, and dissatisfactions, I believe that my teaching has been affected. I believe that I would have been more motivated, I would have done more, my teaching would have been more effective if these expectations had been met or fulfilled. But with the passage of time, with all this experience, I believe the level of my teaching, the level of my performance has been fairly increasing, has been progressing or growing. But *more* could have been done, more could have been achieved under favorable situations. I repeat, I emphasize: scholarship, promotion, salary—in all these matters or respects, we were

frustrated. If we take scholarships, for example, the Ethiopian regime gave priority to its nationals in Addis Ababa University, in other colleges. One time, two of my colleagues and myself, we were promised we would be going to Cairo to do our master's degree. We waited for one year, we waited and waited, and nothing materialized. Very frustrating! And then after we did our master's degree in Addis Ababa University, we have been waiting, but nothing, nothing. The opportunities that came here were very nominal. They were given here just for political titles.

Highfield described the effect of this atmosphere on students in Asmara:

The students had no hope at all, because what were they going to do when they leave school? The standards were terrible. The teachers were totally demoralized and demotivated. They weren't paid enough. Some of them—there were more members of the security forces among the students than among teachers, and students were there to spy on their teachers. And so the teachers couldn't discipline the students; they couldn't give them homework. If they tried to give them homework, you know, there'd be a riot. So gradually the standards got lower and lower, and the students became less and less enthusiastic about schooling. And no matter what marks they got at the end of the year, they were promoted to the next grade because the Dergue was afraid if they didn't do that then students would run away and join the EPLF. So they encouraged them—they set up these Kinet clubs, sort of these youth associations and encouraged them to drink, take drugs, have sex. And encouraged them to spy on their parents as well, these members, the ones they recruited to the security forces: they paid them to spy on their parents—and so break up family unity that way.

In 1990 the Dergue disbanded the University of Asmara, taking its staff and movable property to Ethiopia. Following the liberation of

Asmara in 1991, the university was reestablished by the Provisional Government as an autonomous university.[66] Kiflemariam Zerom, and other educators who had remained in Ethiopian-administered Asmara expressed deep bitterness over the destruction of education. Sister Mary Thomas Johnston, Chair of the English Department of the university, who was in her twenty-ninth year of teaching in Asmara, told me:

> You can't get thinking, intelligent, educated people out *en masse* just because they're going to get a couple of bottles of beer at the stadium to shout down was so and so out with something else. . . . And this is what these regimes wanted. And that's oversimplification, I know, but that's it.

Nevertheless, Eritreans' tradition of reverence for learning became the basis, ultimately, for a tentative optimism by the end of the following few minutes of my conversation with Sister Thomas:

> SISTER THOMAS: A few months ago—he's dead now; he died a few months ago—it must have been about just after liberation, or just before it—it was 'round about that time—where a man called Memher Ghebrehiwet—he was a teacher, he was a playwright and a poet in Tigrinya—he knew Tigrinya extremely well —and he loved to help Father Agostino with his youngsters in the house, have them all 'round about him, like teachers of old, you know—really a lovely setting—and this man a few months or weeks before the liberation said, "Things

Sister Mary Thomas Johnston has taught at the University of Asmara since 1964.

are so destroyed." He said, "There's no school. Now—nowadays," he said, "everything has been destroyed and taken away. We used to have education everywhere. The parents, mother and father, were the first educators. The schoolhouse, the teacher, was well respected, and they learned. The church, the priest taught, and their fellows in the school—and the street. When they were in the street playing, they learned. If you did something wrong, you were scolded by *any* grownup around. And they didn't take it bad." He said, "Now, none of these things exist. This regime has destroyed the family hold because they can go and tell on their family to the [Ethiopian authorities]. And all these things have been broke." But, you know, they had had the traditional sense of the teacher, the learning, the education, they had it here, and they've lost it. And I think it will be quite quick, really, before they regain it—come back—no? It won't be a *very* long process.

LES GOTTESMAN: I think the potential is really there. This is a very interesting, very amazing country.

ST: 'Tis, isn't it? [Laughs.]

EPLF Education Programs

During the war the EPLF served civilian as well as military needs. A "revolutionary"[67] example of this was the manufacture of sanitary napkins,

> a product which previously had been used only by a tiny elite of educated urban women. The bulk of the population had to make do with much less hygienic methods. Tigre women in the lowlands, following traditional taboos, sit inside a tent sited over absorbent sand when menstruating. They would prepare food for the family in this tent and pass the prepared meal under the flap of the tent to the men outside.... The mass production and distribution of sanitary towels ... is transforming both the self-image and the role of Eritrean women.[68]

With the end of the war, the production and services of the EPLF's camouflaged and underground workshops and hospitals were directed to civilian needs,[69] but transformation of people's lives can occur only if the material changes, such as the availability of sanitary napkins, are preceded and accompanied by educational work among adults. In this regard the EPLF has proceeded persistently but carefully, recognizing and honoring the traditions of the Eritrean nationalities while seeking to improve the lives and fortunes of all the groups. The following sections of this chapter provide a brief overview, based on conversations and documents, of the history, policies, and practices of EPLF education programs.

Development of Country-wide Schooling

> SALEH MAHMUD: Even though the slogan "Illiteracy is our main enemy" was among the first slogans of the EPLF, until 1976 it was not possible to implement the educational policy in a systematic way, because of the civil war that was going between the EPLF and ELF.

"The only thing that the EPLF could do at that time was to run literacy campaigns for its fighters," Beraki Ghebreselassie, head of the Department of Education, explained. This first educational goal—to make each fighter literate—was achieved by 1972.[70] In 1985, EPLF practice, James Firebrace and Stuart Holland observed, had

> [a]ll new recruits with less than seven years [of] schooling complet[ing] their education within the EPLF. . . . [W]e often saw fighters sitting in the shade of trees studying. In this respect the [Eritrean People's Liberation Army] differs from almost every other Third World army. For the EPLF, high levels of literacy and education among the fighters ensure a more effective fighting force, because fighters are highly motivated combatants, not just passive recipients of orders. We were surprised by how well-informed and interested many fighters were about world affairs.[71]

Alula Mesfun, a 16-year old combatant in 1977, spoke of "many doctors," university students, and "many intellectual people" who functioned as teachers at that time. Study was required of all, men and women, with formal classes for approximately six hours a day, followed by political "discussion group." Many rural villagers and farmers, he said, encountered education for the first time in the front.

LES GOTTESMAN: Was it hard for them?

ALULA MESFUN: Yeah, of course. But they are motivated, you know. When you go to fight, and to die, you are another person. You will be serious, and you will accept everything.

Frits Eisenloeffel, a Dutch journalist, reported (and Alula Mesfun confirmed) that "even during the smaller battles . . . classes continue, with fighters taking turns in fighting and studying."[72] Difficulties, Alula Mesfun said, included the small number of teachers qualified to teach higher level students (he had attended school in Asmara) and the transition from learning in Amharic, the Ethiopian language imposed on Eritrean schools, to learning in Tigrinya, the predominant Eritrean mother tongue.

At the end of 1974, with the cessation of the civil war, liberated areas began to expand, raising the demand for educational programs and services. In essaying the beginnings of a national school system, the EPLF began the Zero School in Sahel Province—"it started with nothing, or with zero, or we might say, less than zero," Saleh Mahmud, who had been a student there, told me—a boarding school for orphans, refugees, children of fighters, and those who had run away to join the front but were too young to fight. The Zero School, Saleh Mahmud said,

> started with about 150 students and not more than ten teachers. The situation was very difficult; imagine what you can do with ten or less than ten teachers, and inexpert teachers. There was no curriculum, there were no school supplies, there was no school experience. But they did a miracle. They sketched the elementary curriculum and started the education, or the teaching process, for the first time in Eritrean languages, Tigre and Tigrinya, since the federation administration.

The Zero School "was designed as a teaching laboratory"[73] and "came to be the workshop for the . . . expanding national education system. The lessons of Zero were learned and relearned."[74] The Zero School eventually offered five years of elementary education and two years of middle school, adding grades as students continued.[75] By 1983, the school had over 3,000 students. Subjects taught were the geography and history of Eritrea, Africa, and the world; science; arithmetic; Tigrinya, Tigre, Arabic, and English; arts, music, sports; and handicrafts at the elementary level and technical education at the middle level. Zero graduates have "played a vital role in opening up schools in other parts of the country and in teaching peasants to read and write,"[76] most significantly in the national literacy campaign of 1983 to 1987.

"The Education Department sees its history in terms of two distinct periods—before and after the withdrawal of the independence forces from the towns and cities" in 1978.[77] "Prior to the strategic withdrawal . . . there were some 30,000 students attending 150 schools," predominantly in the countryside, including schools to serve the pastoralist and semi-pastoralist populations at four locations.

> One notable outcome of opening such schools was the unveiling and full participation of the women who had traditionally had no opportunity to go out of their huts. There is no doubt that these schools marked a historical point in the effort to emancipate women.[78]

Country-wide schooling, however, was aborted in 1978, and education briefly contracted again to the Zero School. But "[t]he early 1980s saw the successive flourishing of schools, first in the towns and in refugee camps in the Sudan," where thousands of Eritrean civilians had fled the Ethiopian invasion, "then in Barka and Sahel"[79] as the EPLF pushed Ethiopian military forces from these provinces.[80]

The National Literacy Campaign

In 1983 the national adult literacy campaign was begun with the dispatch of 451 Zero School students to serve as teachers[81] "behind enemy lines" (Ayn Alem Marcos).

> The rationale behind this dispatch was to give the students firsthand experience of being integrated in the

community as the few nomads in the surrounding area were not a typical representative sample of the people; and also for them to conduct a pilot study in the eradication of illiteracy from society. In their first year in the community, the students gained much knowledge and experience as well as contributing in terms of their sociopolitical and economic impact and their improvement of the people's reading and writing abilities. These positive results encouraged the continuation of the campaign and students stayed longer, receiving correspondence courses. In the meantime, attempts were also made to enlist people who could take part in the teaching campaign from within the communities themselves.[82]

The literacy campaign reached 56,000 adults, 60 percent of them women, Kaleab Haile, director of the Adult Division of the Department of Education, told me. The campaigners taught reading, writing, numeration, hygiene, sanitation, and health,[83] and participated in agriculture in the rural communities. The literacy campaign is discussed at length in chapter 6.

Drought and Ethiopian military offensives after 1985 disrupted the literacy campaign, and the EPLF abandoned the campaign form altogether when it began its own offensives in 1988, continuing adult education only for civilian health, agricultural, and political workers brought in groups to protected areas for one and two months at a time. By 1990, with the war intensifying to its climax, adult education was available only to combatants.

Nevertheless, in the vast areas of liberated countryside, primary schools continued. Textbooks, published by the EPLF, were in short supply, and many classroom materials nonexistent—including in some areas classrooms themselves: students sat on stones in the shade of trees. Schools had to be camouflaged against air attack and students prepared to take cover.[84] In the 1985-1986 school year, the EPLF reported 24,000 students enrolled in 154 schools inside Eritrea.[85] In (probably) 1990, a year before liberation, Robert Papstein reported 165 schools, 1,782 teachers, and about 27,000 students.[86]

Educational Objectives

In 1989, Girmai Abraham cited "two broad objectives" in the EPLF's educational system:

> (1) the transmission of skills that can be used to solve practical problems, and (2) the creation of a well-informed, literate populace such that democracy and freedom are not threatened by the emergence of an authoritarian or even tyrannical governments [*sic*].[87]

In regard to the first objective, Abraham credited the success of Eritrean self-reliance to the existence of a "'critical minimum' of skilled people in many key areas . . . and the crash training programs by which the Front has multiplied that critical minimum."[88] This was done formally in vocational schools offering two-year courses in auto mechanics, electrical engineering, metal work, carpentry, civil engineering, and other skills, and informally in workshops and on farms.[89] Besides the Department of Education, the departments of Health, Communication, Transportation, Construction, and other departments trained people in their own programs, Beraki Ghebreselassie explained. However, in fostering technical expertise, the EPLF cautioned against technocracy:

> The prime objective of education, as we view it, is not limited purely to the attainment of material values. . . . The limitations of the integration of theory with practice in education only to scientific experiments, to the exclusion of the student's participation in the struggle for social justice may result in the production of an intelligentsia that applies its knowledge and skills without regard to its [*sic*] social consequences. . . . The natural sciences must be presented to [the student] in such a matter [*sic*] that he must be able to use them both in his everyday life and in his future role as a scientist, engineer, doctor, geologist and so on.[90]

In regard to education's second objective, fostering mass participation in democratic processes, Australian novelist Thomas Keneally, who spent three and a half months in Eritrea, observed:

> The whole of Eritrea goes to school. . . . 15 meters from
> the front trenches, as in far villages, you can see classes
> in progress. The Eritrean axiom is that a tyrant cannot
> arise if there is a universally literate and aware popula-
> tion. The day seems consumed by education. In big cen-
> tres such as Jani regional school, the children might have
> desks. In desperate little towns flayed by war and
> famine—Endalal, Nacfa, Erota, Adashi, Hishkub—they
> sit on stones in brush shelters or mud brick bunkers. In
> the afternoons, the adults are taught. . . . Even the
> Ethiopian prisoners of war . . . have to attend four class-
> es a day, five days a week.[91]

Both objectives were served by the participation of the populace in setting educational policy through People's Assemblies, parents' committees, and mass organizations.[92] Roy Pateman reported that "all of the
mass organizations, i.e., those involving workers, peasants, women
and youth" took an active part in deciding the curriculum and organization of the Zero School.[93] The EPLF explained this policy:

> Through them the school comes to grips with the socio-
> economic problems that have to be tackled. . . . In the
> long run, these mass organizations will, through the
> expertise they provide to schools, enable students to
> obtain some of the basic skills they will need as future
> producers. Furthermore, the various mass organizations
> will have to participate both in the running of the
> schools and, [w]henever the need arises, in the prepara-
> tion or modification of the curriculum.[94]

"Education is also part of our strategy of integrated development,"
Andebrhan Woldegiorgis, deputy director of the Department of
Education, told Papstein: local communities "define priorities, and
then ask the civilian departments of the EPLF to help in developing
projects to meet their needs."[95]

In 1993, parent committees and elected village assemblies continued to be involved in the daily running of schools. The EPLF's
strategy reflects the strong Basic Needs Approach to development,
and the education for self-reliance model, described and advocated
by Ben Wisner:[96]

> Education for self-reliance bases all educational activities (literacy, primary and vocational) on the daily realities and needs of the local people. . . . It reflects as far as possible the local culture, and minimizes the distinctions between school and community and between study and production. . . .
>
> While education for self-reliance is linked in practical ways to production and to daily life, its implications go further. Participation here begins with the study of the local social and physical environment—the first step in an ongoing process of people defining their own needs.[97]

Wisner's statements accurately characterize the EPLF's educational practice, especially in health education and support for agriculture. A few examples must suffice here, highlighting program, policy, and pedagogy respectively.

1. The first example is the EPLF's program for retraining traditional village birth attendants. "The status, function and networks of these highly respected women have been preserved but their role has been transformed by training and equipping them" with modern, hygienic methods, saving many mothers' and babies' lives.[98] Richard Leonard reported that birth attendants and paramedics were elected at the local level for training.[99]

2. In an example of policy which encourages self-reliance, Highfield described the government's view of health education:

> PAUL HIGHFIELD: From a ministry or national point of view, we already want to incorporate health care and preventative health measures into the curriculum. Well, that's an obvious thing. What the people are demanding is better health care. But most of the people are demanding it from the government or from their representatives. They don't realize that they can do a lot themselves to minimize some things that will harm their health, and so if that sort of knowledge is incorporated into the curriculum, how to do things that reduce the number of flies, the correct handling of water, toilet areas, that sort of basic stuff, if that's incorporated into curriculum that's going to go some ways toward meeting the demands of the people. But

now those demands are directed at an outside body, not to themselves.

LES GOTTESMAN: Not specifically to education.

PH: Right. And I think also that raises the point that one of the most important things of education, of the curriculum, is that it needs to teach—I don't know if teach is the right word—the people that a lot of the problems need to be solved by their own collective efforts, not by putting demands on an outside body, which to some extent you can do for certain things like overall defense and security, main roads, or that sort of thing, but a lot of things have to come from within the community itself, so the skills have to be created from within the community itself.

3. In a final example, Solomon Woldmichel told me how he "taught" agriculture to adult peasants during the mid-1980s literacy campaign:

> For example, terracing. Terracing is a scientific way, terracing is the important thing to keep our soil. Traditionally our people used such methods. And when I'm teaching them agriculture, for example, instead of teaching them myself, first I participate in the terracing activity with the peasants. I go to the terracing activities with them. When I came to class also, instead of teaching, terracing is this, this, and this, teaching them on the blackboard, I prepare certain questions, to invite them to discuss or to open a sort of discussion among the peasants. And I give some well-skilled people in the society, known for their agricultural activity, give them the chance to come and teach the people what they are doing. I use their own teachers, and I sit down. I also myself learn from the teachers. That is the way we teach the peasants. And we don't really—I myself for example, I don't know anything; I learned from books, theoretically, but practically they are very advanced from me—I know that. And I let them learn and I learn myself from them. I only create a sort of discussion.

Education After Liberation

> BERAKI GHEBRESELASSIE: Immediately after the liberation
> of the whole country, in fact a very conducive situation
> was created, because, you see, during the liberation war
> it was really very difficult to run schools very easily
> because there were aerial bombardments. So we in fact
> were forced to run schools at night—in caves.

The post-liberation challenge of education can be simply stated:
extending education to every community, including pastoralist
groups, in a physically devastated country. This task fell to an
impoverished government. Major problems cited by the Department
of Education[100] included:

- Unequal distribution of educational opportunities

- A big shortage of schools, and a large number of
  schools badly damaged

- [S]evere shortage of school materials and equipment[,]
  etc[.]

- Shortage of teachers both quantity and quality wise

- A very low academic level among students, and also
  among many teachers

- An ac[ut]e shortage of technicians, technical students
  and technical know-how

- An illiteracy rate of over 80%

- A depressed state of Eritrean culture and language
  among the nine groups, due to the imposition of
  Amharic language and culture inside and outside
  schools.

Each of the these problems was defined by the Department of Education as a task.[101] The Department immediately took over the
urban schools previously administered by the Ethiopian government, and began opening new schools and rehabilitating those damaged or destroyed in the war. The Department saw its first priority
as opening schools in the most underserved areas, primarily the
lowland provinces, Beraki Ghebreselassie said. Communities were

enlisted in repairing and refurbishing schools, according to Semere Solomon, director of the Planning and Programming Division of the Department of Education; many of the school buildings had been dismantled or stripped by Ethiopian soldiers for construction materials, used by them as barracks, or bombed.[102] In Seraye Province, for example, Solomon Ghebremariam, an administrator there, told me, 20 new schools had been opened since liberation, and enrollment had jumped from 12,000 to 40,000.

> Schooling is mandatory up to Grade 7 for all children, [but] at present large numbers of school-aged children are not attending school due to the shortage of schools and teachers. Existing schools are overcrowded, and many operate a 2 shift (morning and afternoon) system. By early 1991, 30,000 students were being taught in [the] EPLF's schools. Today, throughout Eritrea, the figure is 251,698.[103]

Communities were encouraged to set up their own schools, which they did "in quite large numbers," according to Paul Highfield; however, responsibility for staffing the schools and providing supplies fell on the Department of Education. In a 1992 consultancy report to the department, Berhane Woldemichael concluded that

Classroom at Sembel Elementary School, in a poor neighborhood of Asmara, 1993.

not only were resources limited, but plans for redressing regional imbalances might have to be compromised; in any case, either purchasing or manufacturing enough school furniture, blackboards, teaching aids, and other materials would depend on international aid.[104] I saw relatively privileged classrooms in Asmara and Arreza with broken windows, "blackboards" merely a square of black paint on the wall, and students crowded three to each planklike, dilapidated desk. Solomon Woldmichel, a former literacy campaign teacher who was, until he entered the University of Asmara, the supervisor of schools in Tessenei, gave me a "verbal tour" of the school and the town in his account of the educational issues that western Eritrea was grappling with:

> SOLOMON WOLDMICHEL: I was there from 1988 up to 1991. And most of the town is totally destroyed. No building is available there, because of the continuous air raiding of the Ethiopian air force. We have a very small building, but most of the classes are just simple huts— something, a hut which is made of grasses and materials which are available in that area. The area is very hot; climatically, it is very tough to live there without any ventilator, you know, and without any materials, a fridge or something else to keep the house cold. And to learn in such grass-made rooms is very hard for the students. And it's a windy area—a lot of dust. Sometimes maybe you are teaching the students, totally the whole class is covered with dust. The students are burning with sunstrokes. And really it's very hard.

> LES GOTTESMAN: How do the students feel about coming to school? Do they want to come to school?

> SW: Yes, they are very interested, even four or five year old children came to school, and they wait to learn, and most of the time they came to school and just play around the area. They ask every now and then to be admitted in the class, but since they are very small, we don't accept them, and we just give them something, a ball or something to play with. And they just play in that area. Or sometimes we put them in some area,

some shade of a tree, and just every free teacher teaches them some songs and other things, just to play with them, and takes them to their homes, because they are very interested.

LG: What about the adults? Do they want education too, even if it's not available now?

SW: Yes. Sometimes they ask, but when you look, really the situation is very hard because people are at this time struggling for survival, as you know, in Eritrea. Most came from refugee centers; they don't have anything.

LG: Were there any schools in the refugee centers?

SW: Yes, there were schools, but when they migrate to this area, they have to have a shelter, they have to have something to build their living here now, and they are struggling for such things, and it is hard for them to ask to learn at this time because first of all in order to learn you have to survive, and it is a question of survival for them at this moment, especially for the Eritreans who came from the refugee centers. And we don't ask them. That's not the only problem: we don't have enough teachers to teach them. Not just the adults—we couldn't teach the younger generations at this time, because there is a shortage of teachers also, trained teachers, devoted teachers. It's one type of problem at this time.

LG: Do the adults want education for their children, or do they want to have their children help them survive, or how do they feel about education for their children?

SW: No. They want their children to learn only.

LG: They want their children to go to school, even though it's difficult?

SW: Yes. After the school is finished, most of the children are participating in trading activities, some helping their fathers or mothers in buying, making some trading activities, small business, making things to sell, small breads, which are made in the home by the mothers, and they take it from their mothers to the market, and they sell. Or chewing gum, cigarettes, anything they can find they sell. And this also has a great effect on their learning because they don't study when they go home, because they are working. And this also, a trading activity, with their small age, makes them participating in some unnecessary behavior, to develop unnecessary behavior because they are interrelating with money, cheating, and so on. It's a social problem.

LG: But they always come to school?

SW: Yes, because the school is running from eight in the morning up to twelve and a half. They have their own time for business.

LG: But it has an effect on their studying.

SW: Yes. If you give them homework, or if you want them to study, they don't study, because they have to participate in that activity.

LG: But still there's a lot of interest and enthusiasm for education everywhere in this country.

SW: Oh, yes.

Even in urban areas, the schools lacked duplicating machines and typewriters. At the Provincial Office of Education in Keren, Eritrea's second largest city, Woldemichael Ghebretensae, the director there, told me administrators must walk down the street and pay the commercial rate for photocopies. At the Curriculum Development Institute in Asmara, where I worked, the first drafts of textbooks, reports, and funding proposals were being written out in longhand. Printing facilities in Eritrea are limited, and paper must be imported; nevertheless, the government has continued to develop and mass-produce elementary textbooks.

As well as materials, qualified teachers were in short supply. Only one Teacher Training Institute was in existence, in Asmara. There were plans to build a second institute "either in Senhit or in Barka," Highfield said, "but again we're running to keep up with the situation. We're having enough problems trying to upgrade the level of the teacher trainers first." Another priority, Beraki Ghebreselassie said,

> is to open or to establish various vocational training centers. In fact, these vocational training centers are also meant for the fighters of the EPLF, because the fighters have to be integrated into the civilian society. In fact, the majority of the fighters will be demobilized. If they get some skills, they'll be really an asset to the country; in fact, their contribution to the construction of the country will be really very productive.

An additional need was for vocational training for 15,000 undereducated graduates of Ethiopian-administered high schools, who have remained unskilled, unemployed, and "idle" for "the last five to seven years," according to Beraki. The country also lacked mid-level technicians; Beraki explained:

> The era of reconstruction needs skilled manpower at this middle level. Vocational schools have to be established. We do have so far two technical schools; one is at Nacfa, and the other one is in Asmara. The technical school in Asmara is a school founded in the early '50s. It needs total rehabilitation. So these two technical schools are not enough. So new technical schools or new vocational centers have to be opened or have to be established so as to meet the rising demands for the new era that we are starting.

Beraki Ghebreselassie, head of the Department of Education, Provisional Government of Eritrea, joined the EPLF in 1972.

It was clear that Eritrea's 80 percent illiteracy rate could only be lowered significantly with the relaunch of a national literacy campaign for adults. Following liberation, however, only former combatants were being provided with large-scale literacy and primary education (through fifth grade), although smaller programs for civilian adults were available in a few cities, according to Kaleab Haile, the director of adult education. Although an earlier generation of fighters had been relatively well-educated in the front, "the vast majority of the EPLF fighters are illiterate or semi-literate ex-peasants who joined from the mid-1980s onwards. The highly educated, politically conscious members, most of those were killed during the war," according to Highfield. Indeed, Solomon Woldmichel told me,

> most of our teachers are sacrificed. They lost their lives in the field. They were killed by the enemy. Sometimes we were participating in the front lines to defend the serious problems of the war, and most of the teachers have lost their lives. Only remaining are very few, and it's quite difficult to spread what we know.

The final task is curriculum revision. An important principle of revision is making the curriculum relevant to local culture and needs.

> BERAKI GHEBRESELASSIE: The people in the lowlands, particularly the nomads, what they gave priority is their livelihood. Generally speaking, the people's attitude towards education, for sending their children to school, is really very positive. But still a lot of efforts have to be done to make people realize that education is beneficial to improve their livelihood. And to do that, you can't convince people by talking. Action speaks. So the main effort of the Department of Education is to make educational services be relevant to their livelihood.

Highfield illustrated the curricular deficiencies with the example of the Afar, merchants and fishers of the southern Red Sea coast:

> At the moment we're not offering them anything relevant in their own terms. I mean our curriculum is totally irrelevant from the point of view of their daily lives. It teaches nothing about the seas, the oceans, wind patterns, how to build a boat, how to engage in trade, that sort of thing.

Highfield described the Department of Education's four-year research and development plan to revise the curriculum, which began in 1994 with department members traveling throughout the country to consult with community groups. We discussed the process by which the community's curriculum needs will be ascertained. An excerpt indicates the scope of the problem, the tricky heuristics of the dialogue proposed, and the high stakes, especially for rural people, of the outcome:

> PAUL HIGHFIELD: It's not going to be a question of when we go around in this big research study, this discussion, that we're going to just say to people, "What do you need from a national curriculum?" But we'll be raising questions as well which will make them think about what a curriculum is and what they themselves think they need and how to articulate that.

> LES GOTTESMAN: For example, what would be a kind of line of questioning that would elicit that?

> PH: Some people in rural areas, in settled rural areas, might for instance say, "Look, we've had drought here for so long. We've got no future left there, in this area. We can't even grow enough to feed ourselves. Therefore, it's best if we move to the nearest town," wherever that is. And you don't want to create a situation where that's encouraged. Rather than say, "Okay, the situation's bad," you want to say, "Look, what can be done in this area to improve it?"—so that it is worthwhile for people to stay where they are, and they can get a worthwhile, fulfilling life by doing certain things, like building dams. Even if not enough water falls during the year, if you've got water management and irrigation, then you can do something. That sort of thing.

> LG: So what you're saying is that by engaging in this discussion, this dialogue, new ideas and new approaches will emerge out of the people's needs and whatever level of expertise can be brought to the discussion.

> PH: That's what I hope would happen.

Both Beraki and Highfield envisioned a national core curriculum—to continue building the unity and national identity which emerged during the independence struggle and which is seen as essential to national reconstruction—with local variations aimed at the individual communities' prosperity and development.

> PAUL HIGHFIELD: What I accept, what a lot of people accept is the majority of people are going to finish education at the elementary level. They're not going to go on beyond that. So they've got a different set of needs. So you've got to have a curriculum which provides skills for those people who're going to leave elementary level, skills that are necessary within the community to improve the whole community economically, and also create social change, at the same time as providing a different set of needs for people who are going to go on higher in the system. And that's a pretty complicated thing to do.

The main resource in educational development, educator after educator told me, is the Eritrean people, their energy, self-reliance, and determination. Shortly after liberation, Karen A. Hauser observed:

> The tremendous intellectual and spiritual strength of its people is perhaps Eritrea's greatest asset right now. There is a large number of highly educated and highly skilled Eritreans. Among all Eritreans there is a tenacity and a wisdom that have helped them survive, and community-based self-identity that encourages individuals to act for the common good. . . . Civilians who stayed in Eritrea, either in Ethiopian-controlled or EPLF-controlled areas, had the supreme wit and skill to survive and to keep their society functioning through the war. Many Eritreans who live abroad are professionals, academics, and successful entrepreneurs whose experiences and insights (and capital!) will be invaluable now in integrating Eritrea into the world community.[105]

I spoke with Semere Solomon, Director of the Department of Education's Planning and Programming Division. His strong, personal convictions about parent involvement emerge, I think, from his recitation of the department's policy:

SEMERE SOLOMON: Now we are trying to reactivate the whole educational activities all over Eritrea. And what I believe is, we have to be able to involve the whole population in the management or betterment of education. We have already established an inbuilt mechanism whereby in every school the parents could be involved in the running, management, and cultivation of their children in the most proper way. In every school, for example, we have this school committee, which is composed of the representatives of the parents' association— in every village, in every zone, for example in Asmara—and democratically elected teachers, and a school director.

LG: They're elected locally?

SS: Locally, yes. For example, we have a village; in the village is the parents' association, and the parents' association democratically elects some members of its association to be their representatives in the school committee. For example, if the number is ten, five of them are members of the parents' association, four are teachers, and one is the school director. And in secondary schools, we even involve the students in the school committee. So having built such a mechanism, established such a mechanism, we are trying to involve the parents, first and foremost, in bringing up their children according to our educational objectives and philosophy. The child has to be taught the same thing in the school and in his house. Both of them have to take care of the children, not only the school staff but also the parents. They have to approach them the same way, and so if a student is given some assignments in the classroom, the parent or the family has to be able to follow it up at home. This is, of course, how we try to bring up the children. The second one is that of managing the school—the parent has to be involved in the management of the school, the running of the school. The government doesn't have to be involved in every aspect of every school, in the management of every school. One has to be able to shift it to the population and carry it out themselves. So, for example, parents contribute in labor, money, material, and also moral support. And also they participate in the actual management of the school, by having to discuss things related to discipline, things related to maintenance of different classrooms, the introduction of teaching aid materials, the introduction of books, and so forth and so forth, so that jointly they produce something. What the population in different parts of Eritrea is demanding is— of course, the first priority is food, the second is education, and the third one is health care—they want to have a school *in their village*, or in the vicinity of their village, so that their children could have access to educational services. They are even committing themselves, in certain parts of Eritrea, to providing teachers' salaries, maintaining the damaged schools, whitewashing, and fencing the school courtyard.

It was, in fact, a fenced courtyard that neighborhood volunteers had built that I was shown at Sembel Elementary School, two ramshackle buildings serving the children of a poor district of Asmara. In the absence of material resources, parents and community members were in and around the schools, constructing, repairing, planting, improving, and talking to the teachers and administrators. The obvious, acute needs in every school and the imperatives of the government's strategy of community involvement had combined to gather, focus, and release community energy.

Notes

1   Hans-Georg Gadamer, *Truth and Method*, trans. Joel Weinsheimer and Donald G. Marshall, 2nd rev. ed. (New York: Crossroad, 1989), 301-302, emphasis in original.

2   Provisional Government of Eritrea, Department of Education, Institute of Curriculum Development, Science Panel, *Science and Technology Education in Eritrea*, 1993. I have a photocopy of the hand-written, unedited manuscript of this document and have been unable to obtain a final or published version.

3   Greg Sarris, *Keeping Slug-Woman Alive: A Holistic Approach to American Indian Texts* (Berkeley: University of California Press, 1993), 110.

4   Eritrean People's Liberation Front, "Social Transformation in Eritrea I: Education Prior to the Liberation Struggle," *Adulis* I, no. 8 (1984): 6.

5   Jordan Gebre-Medhin, *Peasants and Nationalism in Eritrea: A Critique of*

Ethiopian Studies (Trenton, NJ: Red Sea Press, 1989), 38.

6   Gebre-Medhin, *Peasants and Nationalism*, 48.

7   Cheikh Anta Diop, *Precolonial Black Africa: A Comparative Study of Political and Social Systems of Europe and Black Africa, From Antiquity to the Formation of Modern States*, trans. Harold J. Salenson (Chicago: Lawrence Hill Books, 1987), 176-186.

8   Kwame Anthony Appiah, *In My Father's House: Africa in the Philosophy of Culture* (New York: Oxford University Press, 1992), 125.

9   Beverly B. Cassara and George N. Reche, "Traditional Adult Education in Kenya: Some Thoughts for Today's World," *Adult Learning* 1, no. 8 (1990): 15.

10 Birgit Negussie, "Oral Skills and Knowledge of Language: A Resource in Development" (paper presented at the 10th annual meeting of the International Conference of Ethiopian Studies, Paris, August, 1988), 2-8.

11 Josiah Tlou and Hubert Dyasi, "Part I, Education for Rural Development: Introduction," *Rural Africana* 28-29 (Spring-Fall 1987): 1.

12 Cassara and Reche, "Traditional Adult Education in Kenya," 14.

13 Arnold Krupat, *Ethnocriticism: Ethnography, History, Literature* (Berkeley: University of California Press, 1992), 18.

14 M. M. Bakhtin, *The Dialogic Imagination*, ed. Michael Holquist, trans. Caryl Emerson and Michael Holquist (Austin, TX: University of Texas Press, 1981), 291.

15 Provisional Government, *Science and Technology Education*, 11.

16 Provisional Government, *Science and Technology Education*, 10.

17 Berhane Teklehaimanot, "Education in Eritrea During the European Colonial Period," *Eritrean Studies Review* 1, no. 1 (1996), 6.

18 Provisional Government, *Science and Technology Education*, 11-12.

19 Quoted in David Pool, *Eritrea: Africa's Longest War*, Anti-Slavery Society Human Rights Series Report No. 3 (London: Anti-Slavery Society, 1979), 18.

20 Quoted in Provisional Government, *Science and Technology Education*, 13.

21 Teklehaimanot, "Education in Eritrea," 4.

22 Teklehaimanot, "Education in Eritrea," 5.

23 Teklehaimanot, "Education in Eritrea," 4-5.

24 Teklehaimanot, "Education in Eritrea," 5, 8.

25 Roy Pateman, *Eritrea: Even the Stones Are Burning*, (Trenton, NJ: Red Sea Press, 1990) 218.

26 Provisional Government, *Science and Technology Education*, 14.

27 Teklehaimanot, "Education in Eritrea," 7.

28 Four Power Commission, quoted in Teklehaimanot, "Education in Eritrea," 7; also suggested in Provisional Government, *Science and Technology Education*, 14.

29 Provisional Government, *Science and Technology Education*, 13.

30 Teklehaimanot, "Education in Eritrea," 6.

31 Provisional Government, *Science and Technology Education,* 15.

32 Teklehaimanot, "Education in Eritrea," 11.

33 Teklehaimanot, "Education in Eritrea," 11.

34 Provisional Government, *Science and Technology Education,* 20.

35 Provisional Government, *Science and Technology Education,* 20-21.

36 Pateman, *Eritrea: Even the Stones Are Burning,* 218.

37 Teklehaimanot, "Education in Eritrea," 11.

38 Provisional Government, *Science and Technology Education,* 19.

39 Teklehaimanot, "Education in Eritrea," 14.

40 Provisional Government, *Science and Technology Education,* 19, 21.

41 Teklehaimanot, "Education in Eritrea," 17.

42 Provisional Government, *Science and Technology Education,* 22.

43 Teklehaimanot, "Education in Eritrea," 13

44 Provisional Government, *Science and Technology Education,* 24.

45 Provisional Government, *Science and Technology Education,* 27.

46 Provisional Government, *Science and Technology Education,* 34.

47 "Eritrea—Freedom of Expression and Ethnic Discrimination in the Educational System: Past and Future, *Africa Watch* V,. no. 1 (1993), 2; Provisional Government, *Science and Technology Education,* 25-26.

48 Pateman, *Eritrea: Even the Stones Are Burning,* 218.

49 Provisional Government, *Science and Technology Education,* 27

50 "Eritrea—Freedom of Expression," 2.

51 Pool, *Eritrea: Africa's Longest War,* 37.

52 "Eritrea—Freedom of Expression," 2.

53 "Eritrea—Freedom of Expression," 2.

54 "Eritrea—Freedom of Expression," 2.

55 "Eritrea—Freedom of Expression," 2; Provisional Government, *Science and Technology Education,* 38.

56 Provisional Government, *Science and Technology Education,* 38.

57 Provisional Government, *Science and Technology Education,* 38.

58 "Eritrea—Freedom of Expression," 5; Asmara University, *Fact Sheet,* 1.

59 "Eritrea—Freedom of Expression," 5.

60 "Eritrea—Freedom of Expression," 5-6.

61 "Eritrea—Freedom of Expression," 6.

62 Asmara University, *Fact Sheet.*

63 "Eritrea—Freedom of Expression," 2-3.

64 "Eritrea—Freedom of Expression," 3.

65 "Eritrea—Freedom of Expression," 1, 3, 4.

66   Asmara University, *Fact Sheet*, 1.

67   James Firebrace and Stuart Holland, *Never Kneel Down: Drought, Development, and Liberation in Eritrea*, 2nd printing (Trenton, NJ: Red Sea Press, 1986), 81.

68   Firebrace and Holland, *Never Kneel Down*, 81.

69   Provisional Government of Eritrea, Department of Industry, "Rehabilitating the Industrial Sector," in *Eritrea: The Long Trek to Self Determination*, information package (Asmara, April 1993).

70   Firebrace and Holland, *Never Kneel Down*, 118.

71   Firebrace and Holland, *Never Kneel Down*, 118.

72   Quoted in Girmai Abraham, "Political Will, Self-Reliance, and Economic Development," *Journal of Eritrean Studies*, III, no. 2 (1989), 35.

73   Pateman, *Eritrea: Even the Stones Are Burning*, 219

74   Eritrean Relief Association, *Developing a National Education System for Eritrea: The Beginnings* (Khartoum, 1986), 1.

75   Eritrean Relief Association, *Developing a National Education System*.

76   Pateman, *Eritrea: Even the Stones Are Burning*, 219.

77   Eritrean Relief Association, *Developing a National Education System*, 2.

78   Eritrean Relief Association, *Developing a National Education System*, 16.

79   Eritrean Relief Association, *Developing a National Education System*, 3.

80   Pateman, *Eritrea: Even the Stones Are Burning*, 219.

81   Eritrean Relief Association, *Developing a National Education System*, 12.

82   Eritrean Relief Association, *Developing a National Education System*, 12-13.

83   Eritrean Relief Association, *Developing a National Education System*, 23-28.

84   Firebrace and Holland, *Never Kneel Down*, 119; Thomas Keneally, "Let Eritrea Live," *Adulis* IV, no 3 (1987): 14-15, first published in the *Sydney Morning Herald*, 20 June 1987; Robert Papstein, *Eritrea: Revolution at Dusk* (Trenton, NJ: Red Sea Press, 1991), 138-140.

85   Eritrean People's Liberation Front, "Recent Progress in Education," *Adulis* IV, no 3 (1987): 6.

86   Papstein, *Eritrea: Revolution at Dusk*, 138.

87   Abraham, "Political Will," 34.

88   Abraham, "Political Will," 35.

89   Pateman, *Eritrea: Even the Stones Are Burning*, 219.

90   Eritrean People's Liberation Front, "Social Transformation in Eritrea V: Education as a Part of the Liberation Struggle—III," *Adulis*, I, no. 8 (1985): 12.

91   Keneally, "Let Eritrea Live," 14-15.

92   Eritrean People's Liberation Front, "Social Transformation in Eritrea VI: Education as a Part of the Liberation Struggle—IV," *Adulis*, I, no. 9 (1985): 10.

93   Pateman, *Eritrea: Even the Stones Are Burning*, 219.

94 Eritrean People's Liberation Front, "Social Transformation in Eritrea VI," 10.

95 Papstein, *Eritrea: Revolution at Dusk*, 138, 140.

96 Ben Wisner, *Power and Need in Africa* (Trenton, NJ: Africa World Press, 1989); and see chapter 4.

97 Wisner, *Power and Need in Africa*, 44.

98 Amrit Wilson, *The Challenge Road: Women and the Eritrean Revolution* (Trenton, NJ: Red Sea Press, 1991), 147-149; see also Eritrean Relief Committee, *Project to Retrain Traditional Birth Attendants in Eritrea*, 1990.

99 Richard Leonard, "Popular Participation in Liberation and Revolution," in *The Long Struggle of Eritrea for Independence and Constructive Peace*, ed. Lionel Cliffe and Basil Davidson (Trenton, NJ: Red Sea Press, 1988), 139.

100 Provisional Government of Eritrea, Department of Education, *Basic Information on Education in Eritrea*, January 1993, 1.

101 Provisional Government of Eritrea, *Basic Information on Education*, 3.

102 Berhane Woldemichael, *Primary Education In Eritrea: Issues, Challenges and Prospects* (consultancy report, 1992).

103 Provisional Government of Eritrea, *Basic Information on Education*, 3.

104 Woldemichael, *Primary Education*, 60.

105 Karen A. Hauser, *Eritrea After the War: Findings of a Trip There in Early July-Early August 1991* (New York: Eritrean Relief Committee, 1991), 11.

IV

EDUCATION AND DEVELOPMENT: TWO MODELS

The history of literacy efforts is the history of varying and contending ideas about how literacy can and should serve the goal of meeting the basic needs."[1] In this debate, literacy and adult education policies and pedagogy are often posed as adhering to one of two general development models, either a "narrowly economic" emphasis on "basic human needs" or one which emphasizes "empowerment" of communities.[2] In his discussion, *Power and Need in Africa* (1989), Ben Wisner reformulates the two models as "the weak" and "the strong" Basic Needs Approach (BNA) to development:

> The strong BNA *begins* when the poor themselves reflect collectively on their own needs. "To need" is a verb, an experience of deprivation that has been created socially. The strong BNA encourages poor people to understand the social origins of their poverty and to struggle to change them. . . . Most commonly, the weak BNA involves the delivery of a bundle of goods and services (e.g. school lunches, clean water, housing sites, health care) thought to correspond to needs. . . . [T]he essence

of the weak BNA is that the poor are recipients, not activists.[3]

Wisner contrasts the assumptions and intentions of education in each of these paradigms:

> The weak BNA accepts the existing arrangements of productive and power relationships. Education, in this perspective, is "education for employment"—as opposed to "education for self-reliance." . . . Thus many of the non-formal as well as formal "delivery systems" for education discussed approvingly by the World Bank . . . have tended to teach skills that are applicable only in the formal labour market. . . . Education for self-reliance bases all educational activities (literacy, primary and vocational) on the daily realities and needs of the local people. . . . It reflects as far as possible the local culture, and minimizes the distinctions between school and community and between study and production.[4]

The Weak Basic Needs Approach

Wisner asserts that a "weakened view of participatory development [has] prevailed." The "'weak' interpretation of participatory development" sees "participation as a limited, formalized process, stripped of the political volatility of direct popular involvement."[5]

"In its weakened, technocratic form, the BNA could appear to be—and indeed was—a product of planning and of detached or neutral science."[6] César Picón Espinoza[7] locates this approach in the "idea of literacy as a principal cause of underdevelopment. . . . Thus interpreted, illiteracy may be seen as an illness or 'social blindness.' Consequently, 'illiterates are ignorant people to whom "the light of knowledge" must be given.'" In this account, "Literacy work should be selective[,] concentrating on those sectors of the population which will most enhance economic development." This reasoning, Raja Roy-Singh asserts,

> gave rise to methods of teaching literacy in which adult illiterates are seen as passive objects to be salvaged by the literary process, in which they need not intervene

until they have mastered the salvationary words in the right way and at the right time. This "salvationary" literacy practice is almost exclusively based on technical drills of reading and writing and often uses the same methods and texts which are used for children in their early grades at school.[8]

The weak BNA paradigm is the newest generation of the "planned social change" theories of the 1960s. Walter Leirman's account of this earlier model is interesting for the world-view it exposes:

> Adult education became part of the world-wide social change enterprise, where "change agents" would guide their "clients" through a process that started with a diagnosis and the establishment of a change relationship, moved toward the setting of goals and the construction and execution of a program, and ended in evaluation, generalization and the termination of the change relationship.[9]

Leirman's language here aims to reveal how such theories served Western political and economic interests in the pre-Vietnam war era. That is, western interests can be inferred not only in the history of neo-colonial manipulation and displacement of traditional cultures of the period but also in the entrepreneurial, instrumental, and transactional vocabulary of development theory. Education was an "enterprise." The enterprise was elaborated in purely instrumental terms. The change agent-client paradigm had at its center "the man of knowledge," the "change agent," the expert clearly external to the changing community, since the relationship had to be "established" and was later "terminated." Change was "evaluated" and "generalized" so that a better product (tool for change) could be supplied to the next client. This and other paradigms of the post-World War II era, extending into the 1960s, were based on an assumption of unlimited growth, and on the idea that growth was always positive and desirable.

> The assumption has been that the cultural context is largely irrelevant to the dictates of rationality and that the introduction of new ideas and techniques automatically represents a progressive development. The view of society as something to be engineered has further conditioned us

to ignore questions about the cultural consequences of new technologies and abstractly formulated ideas. But . . . the rapid rate of technological and ideological change, along with the nihilistic orientation which is fostered by the liberal view of a context-free form of rationality, puts the culture on an uncharted trajectory.[10]

This paradigm called on the global village metaphor which rationalized, for the West, technical assistance (or virtually any intervention) as being "all in the family": "The 'Global Village' was believed to be in a firm orbit of continuous growth and expansion, and science, technology and the UN would solve the undeniable but curable problems of the world."[11] Such optimism was based on a world of prospective clients for technology and expertise, in a market system dominated by the West—the "owners" of science, technology, and, in another sense, of the UN. Now, 25 years later, UNESCO finds,

> *contrary to all logic and expectations*, during the last years of the [1980s], the net capital flow has been from the poor countries to the rich ones, from the "have-nots" to the "haves" of the world. Education has been especially hard hit. Many countries have seen the goal of universal primary education, a prerequisite for creating a literate society, slip further from their grasp.[12]

Rather than a global village, a metaphor suggesting almost familial participation in a process of slow-moving, non-disruptive growth, the world system has evolved in a stark division of labor—with assets accruing in fewer and fewer hands:

> The concentration of economic power far outweighs the puny national sovereignty of Third World countries. 80% of all foreign investment is accounted for by the top 500 companies. One-third of all world trade is accounted for by the top 100.[13]

From 1960 to 1987, the Gross Domestic Product (GDP) per capita of African countries (South Africa excluded) fell from 6.9 to 3.5 percent of the GDP of developed countries.[14] African exports as a portion of world exports of manufactured goods fell from 2.4 percent in

1966 to 0.7 percent 20 years later.[15] Individual income, Walden Bello points out, declined with GDP.

> Total debt for sub-Saharan Africa now amounts to 110 percent of GNP, compared to 35 per cent for all developing countries. Cut off from significant capital flows except aid, battered by plunging commodity prices, wracked by famine and civil war, and squeezed by structural adjustment programs, Africa's per capita income declined by 2.2 per cent per annum in the 1980s. By the end of the decade it had plunged to its level at the time of independence in the early 1960s.[16]

While Bello sees the last 20 years as a reversal, other commentators point to a longer, consistent process:

> Most Afrikans [*sic*] lived better in 1600 than they do now in 1992. Hunger and certainly famine were not common. When the first white explorers and settlers came to Zimbabwe in the 1890s they were shocked—*the Afrikans were living better than most people did back in Europe.*[17]

But all the versions of history and blame converge in one prognosis:

> Some 200 million of the region's 690 million people are now classified as poor, and even the least pessimistic projection of the World Bank sees the number of poor rising by 50 per cent to reach 300 million by the year 2000. If current trends continue, the United Nations Development Program estimates that the continent's share of the world's poor, now 30 per cent, will rise to 40 per cent by the year 2000.[18]

Workers follow money. Fueled by the international mobility of capital, "vast movements in the world population of workers are afoot . . . Whatever happens to work and unemployment in any particular country, the market in jobs is now global."[19]

The curriculum and the rhetoric have changed to meet this restructuring of global labor patterns, but the general terms of the educational contract remain the same. The World Bank states: "Educational spending must be treated as investment in human

capital—complementing investment in physical capital and technological innovation."[20]

> The education and training of men and—although often
> neglected—of women contributes directly to economic
> growth through its effects on productivity, earnings, job
> mobility, entrepreneurial skills, and technological inno-
> vation. In addition, education has indirect effects, stem-
> ming mainly from the education of girls, as female par-
> ticipation in schooling slows population growth and
> spreads better health and nutrition practices.[21]

UNESCO advances an identical argument using the same terms:
"Illiteracy can only be vanquished if its global nature is recognized
and policies are adopted to enrich the *human capital* of African
countries. Decision-makers must realize that investment in education and public health brings a high economic return."[22] But the
question remains: to whom?

World Bank lending for education has shifted from a 1970s
focus on "basic education programs—adult literacy, nonformal
training, and primary education.... Most recently, support for
broad-based programs of sectoral reform and adjustment has
become a high priority, especially in Sub-Saharan Africa." World
Bank lending policy emphasizes "sound management to flexibly
adapt programs and create the capacity to monitor and evaluate program cost and effectiveness."[23] Wisner's explication of these formu-
lae echoes Leirman's analysis (see page 113) of the transactional
change paradigm of the 1960s:

> The World Bank stresses that a better educated popula-
> tion—in particular, a literate and numerate one—is
> capable of responding to opportunities for improving
> the techniques of production. It further notes the statis-
> tical correlation between mothers' level of education and
> the health of their children, suggesting that the more
> women are educated, the greater the social benefits. ...
> The response, according to this view, should be to
> increase the "inputs" (measured as literacy teachers per
> thousand of the population and classrooms), encourage
> "participation" (defined as attendance at and exam
> scores in literacy and other programmes) and evaluate

the "results" (measured as the percentage of adult literacy, female literacy and female children in school).[24]

Empowerment, or The Strong BNA

In contrast to the "myth," in the weak Basic Needs Approach, that illiteracy causes underdevelopment,[25] is the "view that illiteracy is one consequence of underdevelopment. Therefore *all* illiterates should be given preferential treatment." In this (empowerment) paradigm, literacy "is both a basic human right and a major contributor to meeting basic human needs."[26]

"There can be no confusing the value-orientation of the strong BNA. It is not a 'scientific,' externally imposed plan but is, instead . . . a dynamic, participatory struggle for development."[27] Education builds the "skills," in addition to literacy, that are "necessary" for "effective political participation" in "the struggle for bread and health": critical understanding of social change, knowledge of organizing strategies, self-esteem and self-confidence. "Most importantly, new locally-based knowledge becomes the foundation of self-reliance."[28]

Pronouncements on development and education in 1980s EPLF publications echo these principles, albeit within the framework of a Maoist structuralism. The "strategy and tactics of the struggle," according to a 1983 document entitled "Creating a Popular Economic, Political and Military Base,"[29] must be based on an "all-sided analysis of the different basic and secondary classes and social groups," must "start from above and below simultaneously," and "should encourage the constructive activities, self-improvement, creativity and initiative of the masses." The EPLF realized, says Lionel Cliffe, "that different patterns of mobilisation are required in different regions" to meet the "changing network of social relationships in which the peasantry of different regions and nationalities are embedded."[30] "A key part" of this mobilization, says Richard Leonard, "involved raising the political consciousness of the Eritrean peasants."[31] Doris Burgess notes that "[b]eing able to read and write is seen as a prerequisite for political literacy,"[32] but, Leonard makes clear, political education was not deferred.

Political education, in the case of Eritrea, must include literacy if it is go beyond very elementary stages and if it is to have lasting effects. . . . Literacy classes . . . are carried out around specific topics . . . such as elementary class analysis of Eritrean society, agrarian reform, status and role of women, cooperatives in rural society, organs of people power and people's militia.[33]

In 1986, the Maoist phraseology had faded:

The aim of the [literacy] program is to serve the entire adult population, heightening people's awareness of their living conditions and enabling them to strive for improvement. It therefore covers political education, language, arithmetic, general science (including health and agriculture), skilled trades and social studies. In addition, the program includes training in technical skills relevant to rural economic development plans.[34]

And, by 1987, Bruna Sironi's report from the EPLF's base area places development of pedagogy within, not prior to, the processes of material development and social transformation.

Curricula are set up, didactics and methodology studied in detail and an analysis made of the pedagogic questions that arise in a society that is being constructed and which intends to rely on its own resources, particularly as regards the economic development of one of the poorest countries in the world . . . as well as the challenges created by a multi-ethnic people, whose various languages and culture are to be respected.[35]

Self Reliance: Trial and Trend

Roy Pateman argues that

the experiences of Nigeria, Zimbabwe and a number of more economically developed Latin American countries show that a period of involuntary self-reliance—perhaps brought about through civil war or prolonged depression—can be a spur to developing an industrial economy; Eritrea has also passed through this period of trial.[36]

I would add that perhaps the major reward of these trials is not the level of industrial development achieved, but—certainly in the case of Eritrea—the creative energies released and the innovative solutions applied to the problems of survival or minimal growth. In the case, such as Eritrea's, of extreme political isolation necessitating extreme self-reliance, a dividend lies in the challenge of enlisting the people's creative energies and cooperation which cannot, especially in the long run, be achieved without the legitimation of the leaders and their policies, which, in its turn, cannot be achieved without policies which specifically ascertain, respect, and address the people's history and traditions, as well as their current wants and needs—policies that the EPLF has considered the benchmark of authentic political leadership:

> [A] liberation struggle must also be, indeed is above all, a process in which there is a specific political design which promotes participation and the development of awareness among the population, at the same time as satisfying their basic needs. This requirement is always neglected by regimes that are not authentically democratic and people-oriented.[37]

The period of self-reliance in Eritrea, and the process of development it catalyzed, corresponded to diverse and unfolding practices of education for community empowerment, participatory development, liberatory social transformation, and political mobilization throughout the Third World. In education

> [t]he exponents of these new approaches do not use the same terminology and emphasize different aspects of the literacy process but they have certain points in common. Firstly, they recognize that adult learners have a central role in the process and should be active in defining their learning needs and the goals which they serve. Secondly, they regard learning as a continuous, integral and deepening process of critical awareness of the self within and the world without. Thirdly, they see diversity and not uniformity or homogeneity as the true characteristic of literacy action. Fourthly, this "dynamic literacy process" finds its full expression in engaging and participating in authentic social change and developments.[38]

The political and social upheavals of the 1960s in Europe and America gave birth to the alternative education movement, based on a variety of sources including critical theorists of the Frankfurt School, the Brazilian educator Paulo Freire, and western psychologists.[39] At the same time in the anti-colonial movements of developing countries, "[t]he concept of lifelong education . . . [found] new definitions and practices related to 'struggle' situations."[40]

> [S]tarting from the early 1970s an indigenous and . . . radically democratic conception of liberation took root in various African liberation struggles. This perspective . . . commenced by critically differentiating itself from the kind of "independence" established in the late 1950s and early 1960s. . . . In concrete and practical terms, this critique was grounded on the contrast between the miserable situation of post-colonial Africa and the purely formal and empty status of political "independence." It was grounded on the lived and stark contrast between unfulfilled *ideals* and harsh unforgiving political *realities*. This immanent and critical orientation was thus directed internally toward its own lived historical situatedness. In countering itself to the despotic politics of post-colonial "independent" Africa, this trend established the practice of participatory popular democracy as the cornerstone and gauge of its own political existence.[41]

In this climate, "[c]ountries and populations [began] to 'reappropriate' their educational and cultural histories, and cultural creativity [became] a major source of strength in the struggle against the national and international social hierarchies that the division of labor creates."[42]

Leirman argues that the new trend of adult education paired with, and as a form of, political action aimed at social change and democracy finds an "objective basis" in the environmental "limits to growth" recognized in the 1970s. In the understanding of the tasks entailed in saving the planet, "the HOPEFUL statements in [global studies] nearly always include an appeal to education (both school and adult education) as a saving tool of change."[43]

Facing a situation of growing scarcity and ecological constraints, the modern state has developed two alternative strategies: either the *growth-regenerating* strategy of stimulating investment and technological innovation, or the strategy *of adapting to ecological constraints*, either in a limited sense of redistribution of the cost of scarcity over different social groups, or in the sense of a comprehensive strategy of "deliberate scarcities" and social control.[44]

Wolde Mesghinna spoke of the EPLF's choice of adapting investment policy to ecological considerations:

The EPLF is very conscious of the environment. In fact, I'm sure there are many people, especially Eritreans, who want to start various kinds of businesses, small factories, and so on, but the EPLF has very—even with all the problems that they have, that they have revenue problems and so on—they are very strict in terms of the environment. They have very strict guidelines, if you want to develop certain things.

Paul Ricoeur, speaking at the University of Chicago in 1975, formulated the problem in broader terms. For developing countries, Ricoeur said,

their arduous task is to find their own identity in a world already marked by the crisis of industrial societies. Not only have the advanced industrial societies accumulated and confiscated most of the means and the tools for development; they have engendered a crisis of advanced society which is now a public and world phenomenon. Societies are entering into the process of industrialization at the same time as nations at the top of this development are raising questions about the process. Countries have to incorporate technology at the same time that the critique and trial of technology has begun. For intellectuals in these countries, the task is an especially difficult one, because they live in two ages at the same time. They live at the beginning of the industrial period, let us say the eighteenth century, but they are also part of the twentieth century, because they are raised in a culture which has already entered into the crisis of the relation between its goals and the critique of technology. . . . . People in developing countries are educated at the same time with the intellectual tools of their own culture and the tools of the crisis of the developed countries.[45]

These examples—Ricoeur's 18th-20th century time-warp, and Leirman's dilemma of strategies, and Wolde's concern over the clash of business ambitions and environmental policy—all point to vexing social, economic, and political contradictions. In the potential conflict within the EPLF's own goals and among the Eritrean people's most pressing needs, I think Wolde discerned (judging not only from his words but also from a tone of concern, even consternation, as he spoke) the type of situation which could lead to legitimation questions and crisis in Eritrea. While the new paradigm of adult education, stressing "the involvement of the widest possible representation of the people in the management of educational systems with open access to all the necessary information in order to perform the function effectively,"[46] seeks to involve all relevant social groups in averting a social or political crisis, it does not alter the social forces from which conflict arises. In fact, a crisis may surface earlier due to the fact that the participation of social forces is sought and encouraged, rather than ignored, suppressed, worn down by the co-optation of leaders, or overwhelmed by material incentives and consumerist values as in the instrumentalist change-agent paradigm.

Notes

1   Manzoor Ahmed, quoted in Paul Fordham, ed., *One Billion Illiterates, One Billion Reasons for Action: Report and Extracts of an International Seminar On: Co-operating for Literacy, Berlin (West), October 1983* (Toronto: International Council for Adult Education/Conseil International d'Education des Adultes, 1983), 26.

2   Fordham, *One Billion Illiterates*, 31.

3   Ben Wisner, *Power and Need in Africa* (Trenton, NJ: Africa World Press, 1989), 27, emphasis in original.

4   Wisner, *Power and Need*, 44, emphasis in original.

5   Wisner, *Power and Need*, 14.

6   Wisner, *Power and Need*, 20.

7   Summarized and quoted in Fordham, *One Billion Illiterates*, 32.

8   Raja Roy-Singh, "The Mind Transformed," *Unesco Courier*, July 1990, 21.

9   Walter Leirman, "Adult Education: Movement and Discipline Between the Golden Sixties and the Iron Eighties," in *Adult Education and the Challenges of the 1990s*, ed. Walter Leirman and Jindra Kulich (London: Croom Helm, 1987), 2.

10 C. A. Bowers, *Elements of a Post-Liberal Theory of Education* (New York: Teachers College Press, 1987), 27.

11 Leirman, "Adult Education," 6.

12 John Ryan, "From Rhetoric to Reality," *Unesco Courier*, July 1990, 11, emphasis added.

13 Colin Griffin, "Ettore Gelpi," in *Twentieth Century Thinkers in Adult Education*, ed. Peter Jarvis (London: Routledge, 1987), 281.

14 Harry Magdoff, *Globalization: To What End?* Monthly Review Pamphlet (New York: Monthly Review Press, 1992), 26.

15 Magdoff, *Globalization*, 34.

16 Walden Bello, *Dark Victory: The United States, Structural Adjustment and Global Poverty* (London: Pluto Press/Food First/Transnational Institute, 1994), 54.

17 Butch Lee and Red Rover, *Night Vision: Illuminating War and Class on the Neo-Colonial Terrain* (New York: Vagabond Press, 1993), 140, emphasis in original.

18 Bello, *Dark Victory*, 54.

19 Griffin, "Ettore Gelpi," 282. See also Lee and Rover, *Night Vision*.

20 Adriaan Verspoor, "Educational Development: Priorities for the Nineties," *Finance and Development*, March 1990, 22.

21 Verspoor, "Educational Development," 20-21.

22 Baba Haidara, "Africa: Disturbing Trends," *Unesco Courier*, July 1990, 15, emphasis in original.

23 Verspoor, "Educational Development," 23.

24 Wisner, *Power and Need*, 43-44.

25 Roy-Singh, "The Mind Transformed," 21.

26 Espinoza, summarized in Fordham, *One Billion Illiterates*, 32.

27 Wisner, *Power and Need*, 20-21.

28 Wisner, *Power and Need*, 45.

29 Quoted in Lionel Cliffe, "The Eritrean Liberation Struggle in Comparative Perspective," in *The Long Struggle of Eritrea for Independence and Constructive Peace*, ed. Lionel Cliffe and Basil Davidson (Trenton, NJ: Red Sea Press, 1988), 99, 102.

30 Cliffe, "The Eritrean Liberation Struggle in Comparative Perspective," 100.

31 Richard Leonard, "Popular Participation in Liberation and Revolution," in *The Long Struggle of Eritrea for Independence and Constructive Peace*, ed. Lionel Cliffe and Basil Davidson (Trenton, NJ: Red Sea Press, 1988), 128.

32 Doris Burgess, "Light Out of Darkness: The EPLF and Education. *Adulis*, III, no. 4 (1986): 10.

33 Leonard, "Popular Participation," 128-129.

34 Eritrean Relief Association, *Developing a National Education System for Eritrea: The Beginnings* (Khartoum, 1986), 38.

35 Research and Information Centre on Eritrea (RICE), "The Educational System in Liberated Eritrea," *Eritrea Information*, 9, no. 8 (1987), 10.

36 Roy Pateman, *Eritrea: Even the Stones Are Burning* (Trenton, NJ: Red Sea Press, 1990), 217.

37 Research and Information Centre on Eritrea (RICE), "The Educational System in Liberated Eritrea," 10.

38 Roy-Singh, "The Mind Transformed," 22.

39 Leirman, "Adult Education."

40 Ettore Gelpi, *Lifelong Education and International Relations* (London: Croom Helm, 1985), 7.

41 Tsenay Serequeberhan, *The Hermeneutics of African Philosophy: Horizon and Discourse* (New York: Routledge, 1994), 89-90.

42 Griffin, "Ettore Gelpi," 291-292.

43 Leirman, "Adult Education," 8, 9, 11, emphasis in original.

44 Leirman, "Adult Education," 13, emphasis in original.

45 Paul Ricoeur, *Lectures on Ideology and Utopia*, ed. George H. Taylor (New York: Columbia University Press, 1986), 262-263.

46 Griffin, "Ettore Gelpi," 290.

V

HERMENEUTIC AND
CRITICAL PROBLEMS

> Rebellion presupposes a viable set of critical categories
> which enables people to discredit the legitimacy of the
> present order, legitimate resistance and opposition to
> this order, and anticipate future, alternative arrange-
> ments. Such critical categories develop from the interac-
> tion of tradition (or the remembered past) and play.[1]

Involvement," "representation," "participation" by a wide range
of social forces, as called for in chapter 4, are necessary but not
sufficient to guarantee innovation, creativity, change, or—Frank
Hearn's concern in the statement above—rebellion against oppressive social relations. "[I]ntellectuals," whom Paul Ricoeur addresses,
"who are looking for ways they can honestly exercise effective action
as political educators,"[2] must be hermeneuticists prepared to inter-
vene[3] in the "breaches in intersubjectivity . . . all those situations in
which we encounter meanings that are not immediately understandable but require interpretive effort,"[4] for it is clear from Hearn's formulation that political action supposes acts of interpretation—such
are the "interactions" between the "imaginative reconstruction of

the past" on the one hand and the "freedom from everyday forms of reality" of play on the other. In interpretation, the meaningful thrust of "the remembered past," its "moral imperatives and structural necessity," meet the possibilities of freedom discovered in play.[5] Play may be occasioned but is not defined by or confined to leisure; in fact, hermeneutics finds adults at play in situations that are far from unserious. For Hans-Georg Gadamer, just as players lose themselves in play,[6] so in adults' conversations the conversants are "conducted by the subject matter":[7]

> the form of operation of every dialogue can be described in terms of the concept of the game. It is certainly necessary that we free ourselves from the customary mode of thinking that considers the nature of the game from the point of view of the consciousness of the player. . . . Rather, the very fascination of the game for the playing consciousness roots precisely in its being taken up into a movement that has [its own] dynamic. . . . Now I contend that the basic constitution of the game, to be filled with its spirit, the spirit of buoyancy, freedom and the joy of success—and to fulfill him who is playing, is structurally related to the constitution of the dialogue in which language is a reality. When one enters into dialogue with another person and then is carried along further by the dialogue, it is no longer the will of the individual person, holding itself back or exposing itself, which is determinative. Rather, the law of the subject matter is at issue in the dialogue and elicits statement and counterstatement and in the end plays them into each other.[8]

For Ricoeur, play—and self-understanding—characterizes a reader's encounter with a text: "as a reader, I find myself only by losing myself."[9]

The meeting of meaning and possibility suggests what individuals and collectives can be and do.

> Everyday reality is abolished and yet everyone becomes himself. Thus the child who disguises himself as another expresses his profoundest truth. The player is metamorphosed "in the true"; in playful representation, "what is

emerges." But "what is" is no longer what we call everyday reality; or rather, reality truly becomes reality, that
is, something which comprises a future horizon of unde-
cided possibilities, something to fear or to hope for,
something unsettled.[10]

"Players" are not mere dreamers, but act and communicate. As educators, they acknowledge a part in shaping consciousness; as moral
agents, they face Ricoeur's question, "What kind of man are we making?" For Ricoeur, "The educator ... ought ... to prepare men for
th[e] responsibility of collective decision" by "mak[ing] apparent all
the moral implications of a collective choice."[11] Educators, then, as
storytellers, conversationalists, analysts, and critics, presenting the past
and conducting the play of students encountering it, are, finally,
responsible, to return to Hearn's formula, for the form of the critical
categories that result. Educators are hermeneuticists, interpreters, and,
Ricoeur demands, must be critics of ideology,[12] unmasking "meaning[s] for which the subject lacks the key," for "[i]n principle an ideology is not aware of itself as an ideology."[13] "Ideologies succeed,"
Kwame Anthony Appiah points out, "to the extent that they are invisible, in the moment that their fretwork of assumptions passes beneath
consciousness; genuine victories are won without a shot being
fired."[14] Yet, as a site of victories, obviously ideology, invisible or not,
is not without inner tension and contention. Ideology itself is a "space
of play, where opposing normative claims confront one another;
between these claims practical reason operates as an arbiter and judge,
ending debate by decisions that can be likened to judgments in a court
of law."[15] Archaeologist, archivist, storyteller, detective, lawyer, and
judge—Ricoeur's political educator is asked to perform many difficult
roles. Problems of interpretation and critique, with specific attention
to the Eritrean situation, are addressed in the several parts of the following discussion.

Legitimation

"If governmental crisis management fails ... the penalty for this
failure is withdrawal of legitimation."[16] Jürgen Habermas delin-
eates tendencies toward legitimation crisis in three types of society: traditional, liberal capitalist, and advanced capitalist. Eritrea

will not fit easily into these categories. Eritrea is not an advanced capitalist country—yet will soon enough be a target of capital penetration. Significant portions of the country are inhabited primarily by traditional societies—nomads and small subsistence-farming communities—yet the capital city, Asmara, is a metropolitan center of half a million people, and 20 percent of Eritreans are in the working class. It is perhaps closest to the model of liberal capitalism, yet is poor, war-ravaged, and drought- and famine-wracked. Habermas's analysis of legitimation based on stages of structural development of societies[17] will not neatly accommodate the conditions of Eritrea. However, many of Habermas's specific ideas about legitimation do apply to government in general and to Eritrea at a time when a new government must respond aggressively to new political and economic conditions. It is *generally* true that

> expanded activity of the state produces an increase in the need for legitimation, for justification of government intervention into new areas of life. At the same time, the very process of subjecting sectors of social life to administrative planning produces the unintended side-effect of undermining traditional legitimations. "Rationalization" destroys the unquestionable character of validity claims that were previously taken for granted; it stirs up matters that were previously settled by the cultural tradition in an unproblematic way; and thus it furthers the politicization of areas of life previously assigned to the private sphere. For example, educational (especially curriculum) planning, the planning of the health system, and family planning have the effect of publicizing and thematizing matters that were once culturally taken for granted.[18]

Habermas's critique of capitalism's need to legitimate its inability to distribute wealth equitably is both moral and empirical.[19] While, in applying certain of Habermas's empirical propositions to Eritrea and ignoring others, I recognize that any conclusions must be tentative, I feel more assured in stating that the moral outlook of Habermas's study of advanced capitalism can be retained and ought to be applied, for "in most Third World countries, the productive system itself is defenceless in the face of the global movement of investment, technology and workers as a result of the operations of multinational corporations," as Colin Griffin rawly puts it.[20]

I think there are three social forces that, in conflict in any combination, pose the threat of crisis in Eritrea: *(a)* the traditional ways of life of smaller, rural-based ethnic groups, those Wolde Mesghinna described as "backward in their thinking" ("of course, you can't generalize it—but in many cases they don't know education, they don't know public health, they don't know doctors, and so on"[21]); *(b)* the EPLF and its adherents who have established a style of leadership which encourages participation, discussion, and a carefully thought-through process of change and growth; *(c)* entrepreneurial Eritreans, residing inside or outside of Eritrea, influenced or not by non-Eritrean investors, who see the potential for investment, technological development, and rapid growth. In addition, the EPLF now administers a population which, divided by war, has had two fundamentally different experiences: those who have lived in the liberated zones and those who have suffered under the Ethiopian occupation.[22] Aspects of the social gulf which divides the newly-liberated country are clear in Wolde's account of the corruption of teachers under Ethiopian rule:

> What the Ethiopians introduced in Eritrea is tremendous corruption. In school, for example, if the child is to pass from one grade to another grade, he gives some kind of money or some favor to his teacher. That's the only way things were working there. So the country was completely corrupt. So the EPLF has to retrain the teachers that were there; they need them, the Eritrean teachers. Everything that was being conducted there by a teacher was *corrupt*—everything starts from corruption. And everybody was corrupt. The girls, instead of going to school, they go to villas, or to some places, you know— they were using them, the government was using them for all kinds of stuff. It's just horrible.

To this account of social groupings, I will add, as a known variable with unpredictable effects, the Eritrean tradition, virtually a character feature of Eritreans, of self-reliance, which during the war was raised to the status of national precept, analogous perhaps to the ideology in the United States of "American individualism."

These social forces and factors are facing the needs, opportunities, and inevitabilities of a new era in Eritrea, calling for a level of cooperation, leadership, legitimation, coordination, and social transformation which are comparable, perhaps, only to the changes in Eritrean society, indeed to the formation of the Eritrean nation itself, in the period of Italian colonialism. At the same time, Eritrea has the opportunity to avoid a legitimation crisis, to take advantage of the leadership's very lengthy apprenticeship in the process of war and social transformation which it has stewarded in the most difficult situations. The postwar era poses specific challenges and dangers. During the war, the choices which confronted the Eritrean population were stark. Now, opportunities are beginning to open up that are highly attractive to spontaneous and individual initiative which government policy (environmental law, business regulation) may stymie. On the other hand, governmental policies, such as the emphasis on English in the high schools, reveal the state's awareness of Eritrea's future in a global economy.

Ricoeur's "Political Educator"

The EPLF, and the teachers and administrators developed by the EPLF, are in the position of mediating these forces: the entrepreneurial world, internal and external to the country; the urban worker; and the traditional Eritrean whose material conditions have changed little since the eighteenth century. The Eritrean leaders, literally and figuratively, stand in the position of "the political educator" whom Ricoeur describes: "The major task of the educator is to integrate the universal technical civilization with the cultural personality . . . with the historical singularity of each human group."[23]

Ricoeur identifies three omnipresent social realities: industry, institutions, and values.[24] Industry refers to the means by which any society creates goods, and corresponds to Habermas's "technical interest in prediction and control of objectified processes."[25] In the realm of industry,

> [w]e are doubtless the first historical epoch to include as a dominant fact the consciousness of belonging to a single global civilization, to experience ourselves as a single humanity which enlarges its capital, its instruments and

means of working, living and thinking. This single humanity, which is developing a single global civilization, experiences itself as a single historical subject which adds to [its] knowledge and power.[26]

At the level of institutions, however, societies are historically and experientially plural. It is through its own institutions that each society "appropriates its own technical and economic reality."[27]

What do we mean here by institutions? Two things, it seems to me. First, the forms of social existence in which the relations between men are regulated in normative fashion. . . . If we now consider institutions from the angle of social dynamics, the institution is no longer represented by rights but what we could call, in the broader sense of the word, politics—that is to say, the exercise of decision-making and force at the level of the community.[28]

The third social dimension, that of values, "the practical mores" of "the life of the people" discloses "traditions, which are like the living memory of a civilization."[29]

Each historical group in this sense has an *ethos,* an ethical singularity which is a power of creation linked to a tradition, to a memory, to an archaic rooting. It is doubtless here that we reach the concrete heart of civilization, whereas the available industry only represents the collection of abstract mediations of the group's existence. It is only by the collection of concrete attitudes, shaped by the valorizing imagination, that the human phenomenon historically realizes itself.[30]

Although tools and production are common and identical across civilizations, there is no universal ethos. The ethical—that is, the social—dimension of life depends on language. "Whereas on the technical level men can become identical with one another, on the deeper level of historical creation, diverse civilizations can only communicate with each other according to the model of the translation of one language into another."[31]

The political educator, says Ricoeur, acts on all three levels.

It would be a clumsy error to believe that the action of
the political educator remains confined to the third level,
that of values. . . . There is on each of the three levels a
specific type of intervention which can be reduced neither
to that of the technocrat on the first level, to that of the
professional politician on the second level, nor to that of
the writer, professor or the cleric on the third level.[32]

The rational economic plan at the level of industry "represents a conquest of decision over chance and fate."[33] People determine themselves collectively as active agents of their destiny.[34] The educator
must prepare the people for the "responsibility of collective decision"
by making apparent the moral implications of decisions.[35] Short of
this, "in the present African situation" that Kwame Anthony Appiah
writes about, the future will be "decided by the fact of the technological superiority of the already hegemonic cultures of the metropolitan world."[36] Ettore Gelpi is worth recalling here. Technology, Gelpi
sees,[37] is globally ubiquitous but "hardly . . . neutral"; education
which merely "adapt[s] people to change" (i.e. workers to technology and jobs) is "deeply implicated in the exploitation of the poor
countries of the world by the rich." Educational policy, such as a curriculum of adaptive job training, emerges at the institutional level of
society. What is central at this level "is the role of the political decision and the exercise of force by the public power."[38] Because "institutional dynamics are tied to power structures," the exercise of collective choice is therefore possible at the institutional level only
through participation in democratic processes.[39]

The task of the educator, then, appears twofold: first
he should make apparent the ethical significance of
every choice appearing to be purely economic.
Secondly, he ought to struggle for the erection of a
democratic society.[40]

There are indications that the EPLF recognizes elements of the necessary tasks of the political educator. While "the EPLF is vitally
involved in all aspects of Eritrean life and nowhere more so than in
education,"[41] its goals are democratic rather than authoritarian. In
1989, Girmai Abraham summarized the objectives of the EPLF's
educational system as

> (1) the transmission of skills that can be used to solve
> practical problems, and (2) the creation of a well-
> informed, literate populace such that democracy and
> freedom are not threatened by the emergence of an
> authoritarian or even tyrannical governments [*sic*].[42]

Solving practical problems, the EPLF makes clear, is a praxis, the
exercise of ethical, rather than technical, "know-how":

> The prime objective of education, as we view it, is not
> limited purely to the attainment of material values. . . .
> T]he limitations of the integration of theory with prac-
> tice in education only to scientific experiments, to the
> exclusion of the student's participation in the struggle
> for social justice may result in the production of an intel-
> ligentsia that applies its knowledge and skills without
> regard to its [*sic*] social consequences. . . . The natural
> sciences must be presented to [the student] in such a
> matter [*sic*] that he must be able to use them both in his
> every day life and in his future role as a scientist, engi-
> neer, doctor, geologist and so on.[43]

Here the EPLF distinguishes, as Richard J. Bernstein does, the "different conceptual relation between means and ends" in *techne*, or
technical know-how, and *phronesis*, "the form of reasoning appropriate to *praxis*":

> [W]hile technical activity does not require that the
> means that allow it to arrive at an end be weighed anew
> on each occasion, this is precisely what is required in
> ethical know-how. In ethical know-how there can be no
> prior knowledge of the right means by which we realize
> the end in a particular situation. For the end itself is only
> concretely specified in deliberating about the means
> appropriate to a particular situation.[44]

Most important in reaching the objective of solving practical problems is the participation of the populace in setting educational policy. The "possibly most consequential emphasis in Aristotle's definition of praxis," Calvin O. Schrag concludes,

> falls in its directedness toward the achievement and

> maintenance of the virtuous life among the citizens who
> constitute the *polis*. There is an indissoluble linkage
> between praxis and the *polis* in the thought of Aristotle.
> The *polis*, as the interwoven fabric of . . . ethical and
> political existence, is displayed by Aristotle as the dis-
> tinctive *topos* or locality for the exercise of practical wis-
> dom. It is the institutionalized context provided by the
> *polis* that regulates and vitalizes the interaction of
> human beings in the ongoing life of society.[45]

During the war, Roy Pateman reported, "all of the mass organizations, i.e., those involving workers, peasants, women and youth,
[took] an active part" in decisions affecting the curriculum and
organization" of Eritrean schools.[46] The EPLF explained this policy:

> In the long run, these mass organizations will, through
> the expertise they provide to schools, enable students to
> obtain some of the basic skills they will need as future
> producers. Furthermore, the various mass organizations
> will have to participate both in the running of the
> schools and, [w]henever the need arises, in the prepara-
> tion or modification of the curriculum.[47]

The EPLF seems to recognize, along with Ricoeur, "that the development of a rational economy represents a conquest of decision
over chance and fate."

> It is a question each time of giving consumption, leisure,
> exhibitions of prestige and power, and culture their
> respective place and relative urgency. What do we final-
> ly want? An economy of consumerism? Or power? Or
> prestige? Or is it necessary to sacrifice the consumption
> and enjoyment of one or two generations to some later
> virtue? What do we want through this choice? What
> kind of man are we making? That is the question. More
> and more it will be the task of the political educator of
> modern times to initiate the citizen continually to the
> exercise of collective choice.[48]

The Eritrean people will have to make difficult choices: "all the values of the past cannot survive," says Ricoeur; "only those can

which are susceptible to what I have come to call reinterpretation." However,

> [o]nly a return to the past and a living reinterpretation of tradition can permit modern societies to resist the leveling to which the consumer society submits. We are touching here on the work of culture, more precisely, on the work of language, which our criticism of the idea of civilization entrusts to the hermeneutic problem.[49]

Fusion of Horizons

Paul-Henry Chombart de Lauwe proposes:

> Every culture, in every country, and in every social group ... thanks to its cultural heritage which is constantly being renewed as a result of contact with other cultures and transfers of industrial technology and know-how, contributes something original to the construction of a new world. Culture asserts itself as a movement that starts within groups and which leads them to define their own identities and to formulate intentions.[50]

Knowledge exchange can also be intentional and guided, as it is by educators, researchers, or development workers. Eritrean educators and development workers can be key mediators among the discourses of tradition and modernization. In outlining Eritrea's development challenges in agriculture and forestry, for example, Scott Jones writes, "Western ideas about research and development need to be coordinated with local environmental knowledge to obtain the best of both approaches. A sensitivity toward and close cooperation with local people surely is a fundamental tenet of development work."[51] In May 1992, I telephoned Jones at Oregon State University and asked him what he had meant. A lengthy excerpt from our conversation is worth reprinting here:

> LES GOTTESMAN: I was interested in something you wrote about local environmental knowledge. I was wondering if you could give me some examples of local knowledge being useful in more Western-oriented environmental research.

SCOTT JONES: The sort of thing I think I had in mind when I was writing that was, there are certain things that would be investigated by a one-time or a two-time visitor to a research site. Those would include temperature, rainfall, vegetation cover, that sort of thing, whereas I might really want to focus on the soil question, and the local knowledge would be less inclusive of those concepts and think more about where the wind comes from at a particular time of year, and that's something that I would not know unless I asked some questions about what was important to them agriculturally.

LG: That's not even a question that you would come up with.

SJ: I wouldn't know to formulate a question—"Can you tell me where the wind comes from in the summer and how that influences your crops?"— because that would not be the frame of references that I go out with. I'd simply have to go out with a different approach, and start saying, "Well, what's important to you when you're growing crops? Why do you grow crops here and not there?"—even obvious things—and then wait for information to come and explore, as local people start to give their own perceptions or their own ideas about things, then pick up on that and go with that rather than my own particular bent. A classic one that I got involved with was, I was determined to ask questions about soil, but when I asked a question, "Is the soil here fertile?" they would say "the land"; they would respond with the word "land." As it turns out, land is a much more inclusive concept than soil, and you can learn a lot more by taking their concept of land because then they'll include a whole bunch of other things that you're not even thinking about.

LG: For example, what would be included in the concept of land?

SJ: Soil fertility is not so important as slope, aspect, whether there is grass in the vicinity or whether there was tree cover upslope, the level of stoniness of the soil, and then also within those things soil color, things like that. But by using the word land you can have a much broader discussion about agriculture than you can just using the word soil. Whereas in Kansas we tend to ask questions about soil. Since farmers here can manipulate soil circumstances very nicely, with chemicals and other things, and farmers in Eritrea cannot, there is a greater focus on soil here. Also we have soil science departments, and soil comes up as a concept much more here.

LG: So then again it ties in with what kinds of customary practices are already in existence.

SJ: So in your field, adult education, there's a language component to the local culture which should guide, hopefully, adult education. The idea of teaching or thinking about soil and all the other things that agriculturalists, foresters think about, would be limiting to most farmers there, whereas if you went into the education thing with a much broader concept of land, then you might have more success with your adult education. I've asked some farmers why trees are important and they give one set of answers and in a different area you get a different set of answers. If a farmer really wants trees because they afford good shade, well then there's no point in gearing your education about trees or how to propagate trees and get them growing in order to produce soil erosion control, because it's not that high up on his list of priorities. Or if the farmer is really interested in soil erosion control or woodfuel, there's not a lot of point in saying, "Hey, let's look into this from the point of view of a shade tree"—or a fruit tree or an animal fodder tree. It's important to gain entry and to get everybody on board and committed to the project or to the education process, that the frame of reference of the learner is as much a part of that process as is the frame of reference of the educator.

Jones's comments can be seen as highlighting Gadamer's concept of horizon. "The horizon is the range of vision that includes everything that can be seen from a particular vantage point."[52] "Horizon is another way of describing context. It includes everything of which one is not immediately aware . . . but one's horizon is also the context in terms of which the object of attention is understood."[53] "Fusion of horizons"[54] occurs when the object of attention is another's horizon. In reforestation efforts, Jones explained,

> the emphasis in Eritrea, and of course in much of Africa really, has been on exotic tree species—finding out what the environmental parameters are for the particular area of land with respect to soil, temperature, rainfall, that sort of thing—and plugging into that environment the exotic tree species about which a lot of research has been done. And what we're interested in doing is identifying those species which have clear preferences for farmers or villages, which are native species as it turns out, and working this year and next with two of those species, the commonest plants in Eritrea, juniper and olive. And so I guess the major focus of the work is looking at those plants and how to overcome the difficulties that exist with respect to germination and growing those plants, and how to produce them in large enough numbers and get them growing at an acceptable rate on the Eritrean landscape. And then when you start doing that, it is very quickly apparent that there are a few questions with respect to biology and environment that need to be addressed experimentally, but that there's a whole slew of questions to do with people, the way people organize their society and their culture that articulate at some points with putting plants on the landscape, whether it's crops or trees, or even animals. So those things have to be addressed very, very clearly.

The practical problem points to a theoretical problem:

> The question then arises, What are we doing (or rather what is happening to us) when we try to understand a horizon other than our own? We already know that the

answer that others have given—the idea that we can escape our own standpoint and leap into [another horizon]—is not the right answer. For this is impossible, and violates Gadamer's claim that we are always ontologically grounded in our situation and horizon. Rather, what we seek to achieve is a "fusion of horizons," a fusion whereby our own horizon is enlarged and enriched.[55]

I asked Jones how he would go about introducing innovations to Eritrean farmers.

SCOTT JONES: It might be to inquire about the customary activities of farmers communicating with each other. For example, a farmer who grows wheat in a particular area might choose a particular variety of seed, but then he learns by travel that other farmers use a different variety but they plant it in a different way, or they do something else that's different, so they might then make it their business as a part of their farming tradition to go and communicate directly with other farmers or ask a passing nomad, to say, "Hey, how do these guys do it down in the lowlands?" So there might be traditions of communication which are wrapped into an economic-cultural set of economic activities which farmers could get involved in that allow them to educate themselves. So in that way, as an external person not involved in the local community traditions of communication or the customary economy, you could say, well, how do they learn and develop and innovate themselves and how can I participate in that as an outsider? And the answer might be, well, instead of saying "we in North America do it like this," you could just say, "Well, we've had discussions with several farmers about this idea and it seems to us that this might work here. What are your thoughts on that? Would you like to learn more about it?" There is a point of entry that you can make as an outsider that's perhaps better if you understand a little bit about how farmers innovate themselves. And that's different from how you come at it if you just come in for two weeks in a polyester suit and a $1000-a-day pay packet, the consultant with your own preconceived ideas.

Fusion can occur because "a horizon . . . may either be narrowed or expanded. This makes possible communication at a distance between two differently situated consciousnesses."[56]

> A horizon . . . is limited and finite, but it is *essentially* open. For to have a horizon is not to be limited to what is nearest but to be able to move beyond it. Indeed the very idea of a closed horizon is a false abstraction. . . . Horizons are limited, finite, changing, and fluid.[57]

Jones's sensitivity to the language of Eritrean farmers also is worth noting. For Gadamer,

> the medium of all human horizons is linguistic . . . [T]he language that we speak (or that rather speaks through us) is essentially open to understanding alien horizons. It is through the fusion of horizons that we risk and test our prejudices. In this sense, learning from other forms of life and horizons is at the very same time coming to an understanding of ourselves.[58]

Philsophical Hermeneutics and Critical Theory

Ricoeur's hermeneutics emphasizes that the mediating function of language "takes place through the interpretation of signs, texts, and works, within which cultural heritages are inscribed and offered for our decipherment."[59] The "distanciation" of the text from the context of its inscription allows Ricoeur to overcome the persistent doubt, raised by critical theorists, especially Habermas, that philosophical hermeneutics does indeed allow us to "risk and test our prejudices."[60] Ricoeur locates "all the contradictions, all the conflicts" in this debate in the hermeneutic notion "that every culture comes to us as a received heritage, therefore as transmitted and carried by a tradition," for "[a]mong the most controversial connotations of the word 'tradition' is the idea of cultural content transmitted by a specific authority, the authority of the past."[61]

> While hermeneutical philosophy sees in tradition a dimension of historical consciousness, an aspect of participation in cultural heritages and reactivation of them, the critique of ideologies sees in the same tradition the

place par excellence of distortions and alienations and opposes to it the regulative idea, which it projects into the future, of communication without frontiers and without constraint.[62]

Habermas's theory of universal pragmatics provides "the methodological framework aimed at effecting the dissolution of constraints rooted in language."[63] Universal pragmatics is both a critical instrument "for detecting the manner in which language can serve as a source and perpetrator of unconscious restraints,"[64] and a reconstruction of the rational basis of communication, the interests and claims inherent in the speech act which can be subjected to disputatious analysis in the "ideal speech situation," "a situation in which agreement is reached simply on the basis of 'the better argument,'"[65] the possibility of which is always presupposed in human communication.

> [A]nyone acting communicatively must, in performing any speech action, raise universal validity claims, and suppose that they can be vindicated. . . . Insofar as he wants to participate in a process of reaching understanding, he cannot avoid raising the following—and indeed precisely the following—validity claims. He claims to be:
>
> a. *Uttering* something understandably;
>
> b. Giving [the hearer] *something* to understand;
>
> c. Making *himself* thereby understandable; and
>
> d. Coming to an understanding *with another person*.[66]

As the validity claims are inherent in communication, they provide both a rational basis for emancipatory critique and, in the ideal speech situation, a model for critical method.

> Whereas universal pragmatics is concerned with elucidating the formal conditions of rational discourse, critical theory is concerned with appropriating this scheme in a theory of society explicitly dedicated to a form of human life free from all forms of prejudice, self-deception and error.[67]

The discussion of universal pragmatics is pursued in chapter 6 (see *Validity Claims*, page 186). What is important to understand at this point is the difference between the goals and operations of universal pragmatics and those of philosophical hermeneutics. Hermeneutic principles recognize no Archimedean point "outside of or above history from which to view human life" where ideal speech, in practice or as model, can be situated.

> [P]hilosophical hermeneutics stresses that the interpreter of social phenomena is a member of a life-world, that the interpreter too occupies a specific historical, social, cultural position from which he or she tries to come to terms with the beliefs and practices of others. The understanding achieved is, as a result, inexorably situation-bound, an understanding from a point of view that is on the same level as what is understood.[68]

Ricoeur seeks a dialectical reconciliation of hermeneutics and critical theory. In his 1981 essay, "Hermeneutics and the Critique of Ideology," he poses two questions: Can hermeneutic philosophy account for the demands of a critique of ideology? Can hermeneutic presuppositions encompass critique?[69]

Misunderstanding

Ricoeur contends that "the concept of ideology plays the same role in critical social science as the concept of misunderstanding plays in a hermeneutics of tradition."[70] But *misunderstanding* and *ideology* are not the same. Gadamer traces the concept of misunderstanding to Friedrich Schleiermacher. Hermeneutics, in Schleiermacher's definition, is the "avoidance of misunderstanding" which arises "automatically" from the "pedagogical occasionality of interpretation."[71] In other words, interpretation that is *not* hermeneutical *always* leads to misunderstanding; hermeneutics is that universal method which voids this inevitability. Hermeneutics can do this "because there is the conviction and the confidence that the understanding which precedes and envelops misunderstanding has the means to reintegrate misunderstanding into understanding."[72]

Ideology as Distortion

Ideology, says Ricoeur, is "allegedly disinterested knowledge which serves to conceal an interest under the guise of a rationalization."[73] The key words are telling. For (in contrast to the apparent neutrality of *misunderstanding*) *allegedly, conceal, interest,* and *guise* suggest distortion within an adversarial relationship.

> In a tradition that could still be called Marxist in a very general sense, distortion is always related to the repressive action of an authority and therefore to violence. . . . The distortions do not come from the usage of language as such but from its relation to labor and power.[74]

It is, for example, "precisely for th[e] purpose" of legitimating "relations of domination and inequality which are necessary for the functioning of the industrial system but which are concealed beneath all sorts of gratifications provided by the system," Ricoeur tells us, "that the scientific-technological apparatus has become an ideology."[75] "In these circumstances," Chombart de Lauwe asks, posing critical theory's questions,

> is the faith placed in new concepts of education justified? To what extent would such education ensure respect for the diversity of cultures and self-expression for individuals and peoples? In what way could it help stop the processes of domination in world industrial civilization by liberating cultural forces that would channel technological progress, limit its harmful effects and extend its benefits to all men as a fundamental right, that is to say by fighting against inequalities[?]
>
> Is it by means of education that progress will be made? Education itself is bound up with the processes of technological, economic and cultural change. Education is a product of society. To what extent then can it help direct change and break with the processes of domination?[76]

It is well known that Gadamer's hermeneutics rehabilitates *prejudice* from the positivist "prejudice against prejudice" and rescues *authority* which, since the Enlightenment, has been "identified too quickly with domination and violence."[77] Against this precipitate anti-authoritarianism, hermeneutics "forbid[s] the elevation of the critical instance above the recognition of authority and above the very tradition reinterpreted." Alienation or distance—including critical distance—is "enveloped" by understanding.[78] Where distance is sought from which to launch critique, or methodological ground is claimed outside the universality of hermeneutics, "the struggle against methodological distanciation transforms hermeneutics into a critique of critique."[79]

In critical theory, however, "the critical instance is . . . placed above the hermeneutical consciousness for it is presented as the enterprise of 'dissolving' the constraints arising . . . from institutions." In contrast to hermeneutics, the task of the critical theory "is to discern . . . those 'ideologically frozen' relations of dependence which can be transformed only through critique" governed by our emancipatory interest in independence.[80] "The interest in emancipation is only active in the work of unmasking hidden systematic distortions."[81] This interest, according to Habermas, is exercised through self-reflection. But self-reflection "cannot be founded on a prior"—or traditional—"consensus, for what is prior is precisely a broken communication."[82] "A gulf therefore divides the hermeneutical project, which puts assumed tradition above judgment, and the critical project, which puts reflection above institutionalized restraint."[83]

Ricoeur's Reconciliation of Hermeneutics and Critical Theory

I will focus here on some (not all) of the points Ricoeur addresses to each of the protagonists in the hermeneutics-critical theory debate. To Gadamer, Ricoeur suggests a "shift" in hermeneutics so "that a certain dialectic between the experience of belonging and alienating distanciation becomes the mainspring, the key to the inner life, of hermeneutics."[84] In this revision, Gadamer's own "matter of the text" provides the model for "the moment of distanciation" which precedes appropriation. Written "work *decontextualizes* itself, from the sociological as well as the psychological point of view"—from the author's intention, the original audience, and the original social environment—"and is able to *recontextualize* itself differently in the act of reading."[85] In recontextualizing, or appropriation, what is sought is no longer an intention hidden behind the text, but a world unfolded in front of it. The power of the text to open a dimension of reality implies in principle a recourse against any given reality and thereby the possibility of a critique of the real.[86]

Here the dialectic is realized: the "appropriation of the proposed worlds offered by the text passes through the disappropriation," or distanciation, of the self, what Ricoeur calls the "playful metamorphosis of the *ego*." "In reading," he says, "I 'unrealize myself.'" The distance of the unrealized self from the self provides the ground for the critical interrogation of the self's illusions—Ricoeur uses the Marxist term "false consciousness."[87] The critique of ideology, unfolding within the tension of world and self and possible world and possible self, remains inside a hermeneutic dimension.

Can, however, hermeneutic presuppositions satisfy critical skepticism? Ricoeur, like Habermas, locates ideology in the distortion of communication.[88] Ideology both integrates and dissimulates social relations and actions: "simplification, schematization, stereotyping, and ritualization arise out of a distance that never ceases to grow between real practice and the interpretations through which the group becomes conscious of its existence and its practice."[89] In contrast to Habermas, Ricoeur sees ideology as integration as a "positive element" that supports social cohesion "not simply in space but in time."[90] Dissimulation, however, "wins out over" integration "when ideological representations are captured by the system of authority" in a society.[91] As "win" and "capture" suggest, "integration is a presupposition" of distortion[92]—it is precisely the preexisting, legitimating imprimatur of ideological integration that illegitimate authority seeks and that it hijacks.

The interest in emancipation, which is anticipatory in nature, is not different, then, from the always present practical interest in intersubjective communication. Practical interest is the sphere of "understanding meaning" communicated in ordinary spoken language and by means of the interpretation of texts.[93] The correlation of emancipatory and practical interest actually redeems the emancipatory interest from being a hopeless abstraction and mere "pious vow,"[94] for if undistorted communication cannot be exemplified in tradition, it can be exemplified in "our capacity to overcome cultural distance in the interpretation of works received from the past."[95] Again, hermeneutics provides a means for the critical project. In a final point, Ricoeur returns to "the abyss which seems to separate simple misunderstanding from . . . ideological distortion."[96]

> In modern industrial society, according to Habermas, the traditional legitimations and basic beliefs once used for the justification of power have been replaced by an ideology of science and technology. The modern state is a state dedicated no longer to representing the interests of an oppressing class, but rather to eliminating the dys-functions of the industrial system. . . . The dominant feature of the system is the productivity of rationality itself, incorporated into self-regulating systems; what is to be legitimated, therefore, is the maintenance and growth of the system itself.[97]

In modern society, rationality not only "conquers new domains of instrumental action, but it subjugates the domain of communicative action," leaving, in present communicative practices, meager inspiration for the emancipatory interest. The possibility of critique lies in the "reawakening of communicative action," based "upon what . . . if not the creative renewal of cultural heritage?" Thus hermeneutics, reintegrating misunderstanding into understanding, is the support, and hope, of critique. But further support lies in tradition itself—a tradition ignored as such by Habermas. "Critique is also a tradition." Ricoeur speaks of "the most impressive tradition, that of liberating acts, of the Exodus and the Resurrection."[98] In a similar vein, Robert N. Bellah and his co-authors of *Habits of the Heart* (1985) admire a tradition in which "Americans have often sought new visions of social life" —the "long history" of social movements in the United States, "reaching back to the agitation for independence itself."[99] Henry A. Giroux speaks of "the need to recount the narratives of those others who have become the forgotten victims of history":[100]

> Remembrance is part of a language of public life that promotes an ongoing dialogue between the past, present and future. It is a vision of optimism rooted in the need to bear witness to history, to reclaim that which must not be forgotten. It is a vision of public life which calls

for an ongoing interrogation of the past that allows different groups to locate themselves in history while simultaneously struggling to make it.[101]

In June 1992 I spoke with Issayas Tesfamariam, an Eritrean historian, who emphasized the need for Eritreans to tell their stories to each
other:

> Everybody should express how they felt during the war.
> Individual stories should come up. The most heinous
> crimes should be told, in a sense where you'll say, "Oh,
> my gosh." That kind of thing stops people for example
> from saying, "Life is too hard and I can't go on"—what-
> ever. And you hear people's stories, like heinous crimes
> done to people, and you can say, "Oh my gosh! Why the
> hell am I complaining? I'm in a better position." Because
> it gives you that frame of reference. Not necessarily the
> war, but the signatures of war have been printed on peo-
> ple's heads. They have never gotten the time to express the
> trauma of war. If 50 percent, 45 percent of the Eritrean
> population is under the age of fifteen, we should be able
> through education to teach them that the cost of indepen-
> dence was expensive, and then they should never lose
> track of it, because, like Lord Malachi in Nigeria said,
> "Tell the youth that we sacrifice our today for their
> tomorrow." So, we should be able to teach these young-
> sters that the price was high, expensive, time-consuming,
> and so forth, and then they should be able to maintain
> that, not forget it, because once they forget it, all that cost
> of lives, all that war, will be forgotten and once you for-
> get it you're disconnected from memory, and what keeps
> people moving is the memory, collective memory. So once
> you lose that you might as well be a robot or a dummy.

Ideology and Narrative

Ideology—in its functions of integrating and justifying social relations and actions (whether these reinforce freedom or oppression)—operates through stories.[102] On the societal level, says
Ricoeur, "representations are principally systems of justification

and legitimation, either of the established order or of an order likely to replace it. These systems of legitimation can be called . . . ideologies."[103] The ends toward which collective actions aim can be compared to—and more importantly may derive from—the "directedness"[104] of the plots of old stories: through "narratives, chronicles . . . the community 'repeats' in a way its own origin, commemorates it and celebrates it." Ideology, then, justifies our stories with other stories, by providing "a sort of metalanguage for the symbolic mediations immanent in collective action." Ideology readily "slips in" to the reflective distance between means (actions) and ends. Ideology operates in the "gap of 'representation'" produced by this reflective distance, filling the gap of representations with a symbolic order of reasons for acting.[105] Our reasons for acting either become a narrative plot through the symbolic order of their representation—or must take a supporting role in the movement of the plot:

> If history is . . . rooted in our ability to follow a story, then the distinctive features of historical explanation must be regarded as developments at the service of the capacity of the basic story to be followed. In other words, *explanations have no other function than to help the reader to follow further.*[106]

Ideology, then, is embodied in plots. Ideology's power to shape our actions comes from its promise, from our sense of the probability of outcomes, the "teleologically guided movement of our expectations when we follow the story."[107] "It is the function of a plot to bend the logic of *possible* acts toward a logic of *probable* narratives."[108]

"Practical reason is the set of measures taken to preserve or to establish the dialectic of freedom and institutions,"[109] institutions whose claim to legitimacy always exceeds the belief of individuals in this legitimacy. "Ideology is mobilized to fill the gap between the demand coming from above and the belief coming from below."[110]

The reflective distance wherein plausible stories link actions and ends is, as I discussed at the beginning of this chapter, a "space of play, where opposing normative claims confront one another; between these claims practical reason operates as an arbiter and judge, ending debate by decisions that can be likened to judgments in a court of law."[111] Judgment requires ideology critique. This critical function "*unmask[s]* the hidden mechanisms of distortion . . . that prevent the individual from harmonizing the autonomy of her will with the demands coming from these symbolic mediations."[112] "[T]hrough the anticipatory imagination of acting . . . I 'try out' different possible courses of action . . . I 'play' . . . with possible practices." In imagination, "I try out my power to act" in "variations on the theme 'I can'": I could, I could have, etc. Imagination also provides the ground whereon to "compare and evaluate" heterogeneous motives for acting: desires, obligations, customs, values, reasons:[113] in these imagined narratives, "I can," "I could," etc., is followed by the justifying and explanatory "if . . . ", "when . . . ", "because . . . ", "even though . . . ", etc.

This suggests that ideology critique must proceed as a hermeneutic—that is, interpretive, creative, historical, and even archaeological[114]—praxis rather than a logical procedure. The stories which legitimate oppressive power can be confronted only with different stories. Analytical and explanatory functions play a supporting role, as they do in any plot, to the work of refashioning old stories, creating new ones, and recovering (from within the community's traditions) lost or suppressed stories.

Constraints on Praxis

It is important to note that liberatory hermeneutic praxis is not the foregone result of national liberation, political revolution, or school reform movements. Thomas J. La Belle and Christopher R. Ward studied educational reforms in seven nations which had undergone "radical political and social transformation."[115] They found that "as a state activity educational reform embodies contradictory movements and that some of the state's activities in reform will be directed at establishing or maintaining its own legitimacy."

> In these countries, the post-transformation education system remained centralised with some encouragement of local participation. Given the way in which education functions as a mechanism for maintenance and selection

by those in power, the centralisation of control over the educational systems by those who successfully challenged the *status quo* in those countries is not surprising.[116]

La Belle and Ward found as well that groups who previously had the best access to education "manage to maintain favourable rules of access at the higher levels or more prestigious tracks of education."[117]

Aaron Benavot and his co-researchers found that national curricula, rather than expressing functional requirements or power relations of the society in which they were embedded (two major theories of the relationship of school learning to society), were instead

> closely linked to the rise of standardized models of society ... and to the increasing dominance of standardized models of education as one component of these general models. ... These modern models of society and education and their interrelation, are similar around the world and generate educational systems and school curricula that are strikingly similar. As a result, a new culture or set of cultures is being promulgated by mass educational institutions.[118]

Chombart De Lauwe explained this effect:

> [I]ndustrial civilization has a standardizing influence on the way we live in that it imposes the same technology on all societies. Those with the most advanced technology have power over those who are less advanced. Whether intentionally or not they impose, with their technologies, patterns of work organization and political, educational and cultural institutions. ... The new technologies made possible by scientific progress and which lead to the setting up of ever bigger and better workshops, factories and enterprises, impose on the world an industrial organization, centralization and concentration, and a new balance (or imbalance) between town and country that together tend to standardize work practices, urban development, the economy and bureaucratic administration.[119]

In agreement with Benavot et al., La Belle and Ward also found "that even a radical shift in power within a political unit may be limited by external factors associated with the larger world order"[120] through pressures that are local and immediate:

> Even as post-transformation regimes changed curricula to reflect ideological and nationalistic concerns, they had to deal with their needs for trained work-forces. As a result, many post-transformation societies placed a relatively high value on technological and scientific training.[121]

Innovations in education, Mariana Zakharieva argued, do reflect levels of national development, but "are also an expression of global economic processes and tendencies. That is why the orientation and content of innovations in different national education systems are quite similar."[122] And R. W. Niezen, studying West African Muslim schools, concluded that, even when intended as "a vehicle" for anti-hegemonic protest and social change, literacy "does not act independently to either prevent or promote" the development of a "critical approach to ideological messages."[123] Where programs are designed "to develop the critical consciousness of the illiterate so that they can understand their economic context, and to enable them to organize themselves in order to change it,"[124] efforts may be undermined by lack of financial support,[125] teachers' reversion to "mechanical application" of teaching methods,[126] and the lack of books that "constitute a response to people's needs, expectations, and concerns."[127]

Resistance to schooling may be a tradition itself, as it was in Wolde Mesghinna's village:

> When my parents decided to send me to school, friends of my parents were quite *annoyed*. They were telling my parents, "How can you send your kid to school? People who go to school are those poor people who have no herds to look after, who have no cows, no goats."

Susan T. Ferrell and Aimee Howley found two reasons why "rural residents often do not value formal education": *(a)* local economies have often required that children, as well as adults, be available for work on farms or in other subsistence and income-generating activities, and *(b)* the learning offered in schools was not seen as a means of obtaining more worthwhile forms of work or of improving productive skills.[128] Some Eritreans share these attitudes. The EPLF began a "literacy for all" campaign in 1975, but found it difficult to convince poor peasants of the importance of education.

> They are often reluctant to send their children to school because they are needed for agricultural and domestic tasks. The EPLF is finding it most difficult to reach the children of nomads, but has set up schools by the main watering places where nomad families camp for several weeks at a time.[129]

In 1992, Karen A. Hauser found the need for child labor still an obstacle, among many others, to participation in Eritrean educational programs.[130] In a study of literacy in rural areas generally, Ferrell and Howley concluded that, "Even today, when rural economies are considerably more complicated, rural residents sometimes overlook the benefits of formal education."[131] In some cases, benefits may have proven illusory. In Mali, for example,

> [a]lthough many young people have received the opportunity of education, relatively few from the countryside have achieved their higher ambitions or received the rewards expected after years of study. In addition, many students who do spend up to twelve years pursuing their education find that they are not only unable to find a place in the new society but they have also been drawn away from their traditional culture to some extent. During the past two decades, students have even come to regard the sociopolitical rewards of Western education as unattainable because they can neither continue their studies nor find work. They consider themselves members of a generation that does not have a secure position in the modern world and that has also largely lost touch with its traditional background.[132]

Wolde Mesghinna thought that appreciation of education was higher among rural Eritrean populations in EPLF-administered regions than among urban youth under the influence of Ethiopian occupation.

On the other hand, Hauser observed in 1992 a demand for education for their children by pastoralist lowlanders, who had not had schools available, a demand which Hauser described as "movement" in response to having children in school in other parts of the country. "Word spreads," Hauser explained.

Nevertheless, the Department of Education faced enormous problems resulting from four decades of Ethiopian colonial control and military occupation of the country, three decades of war, and the effects and continuing threat of famine and drought.[133] All available resources were directed toward providing schools for children. Adult education, on the other hand, remained almost entirely in the planning stage, despite acute need. These "basic problems and issues" were listed in a 1992 Department of Education document on adult education:

1) most of the people, especially in the rural areas (and here especially in the lowland areas and surroundings) didn't get any opportunity; this became a serious problem in the liberation struggle.

2) many civilians, and most of the combatants, discontinued their education due to the war and displacement; opportunities for continuing their education did not exist due to the constraints of manpower, finance, materials and the war situation itself.

3) enormous effort[s] were needed to convince peasants to be motivated and to be interested in learning.

4) many adults didn't get any opportunity for follow-up studies after the basic literacy programmes; they returned to their original situation after all the efforts invested.[134]

Constraints on Women

Women face other, particular restraints on participation in education. Lack of "time, money, strength, and endurance"[135] and weakened concentration on learning result from child-rearing, water and fuel gathering, cooking, cleaning, caring for the sick, and farming and cultivating responsibilities.[136] Agricultural extension services "given to men with the hope that they will pass the information on to their wives" may be ignored by the men since their wives are the cultivators.[137] Women's isolation in the family or on the farm may restrict their exposure to more literate environments or to languages other than the mother tongue, which may hinder their participation in literacy classes taught in another language.[138] Where women have managed to acquire elementary reading skills, sustaining literacy may be more difficult than for men: women have less access to reading material and less time to devote to it, and available reading materials often are not designed for women.[139] As well as practical constraints, women suffer social restrictions. Women are often discouraged by male family members or employers from attending classes, and by male teachers who may denigrate their abilities in the classroom.[140] Women are also the victims of domestic physical, sexual, and psychological abuse.[141] African "[l]iterature, folklore and religious texts abound with . . . beliefs reiterating the basic inferiority of women," Lalita Ramdas observed.[142] Robert Papstein repeats the "oft-quoted Eritrean proverb illustrat[ing] the traditional view of women: 'Just as there is no donkey with horns, so there is no woman with brains.'"[143] "As girls we had no right to go to school," an Eritrean woman explained to Papstein.[144] Schooling "was regarded as a waste of time and a threat to our virginity"; consequently, although "[a] few urban girls who had parents who could afford the costs went to school as an indication of status or to make them more attractive for marriage . . . the vast majority of women in Eritrea were uneducated."[145] Women, therefore, "have been the greatest beneficiaries" of the EPLF's mid-1980s literacy campaign. "Through education," Wubnesh W. Selassie asserts,

> many women in EPLF administered areas developed their ability to analyze the real causes of their marginalization, and learnt skills that facilitated their involvement in traditionally segregated work areas. Many women in these areas came to realize that equality cannot be achieved as long as they are seen as marginal to men, society and development.[146]

Since liberation in 1991, opportunities for education have expanded. Nevertheless, Hauser reported a postwar backlash among Muslim men against education for women, especially in areas of the country which were not under EPLF control during the war and where the population was not involved in a larger "social consciousness raising" process.[147]

Asseny Muro points out that educational planning and administration in Africa are largely in the hands of men.[148] Stanlie M. James reports "only one woman teaching in African secondary schools for every three men. Consequently, female and male students are often deprived of female role models."[149] Regarding a Muslim backlash in Eritrea against education for women, Paul Highfield told me that "men are denying aspirations of women. Most of the Afars say, we'll educate our daughters up to third grade or fourth grade, but after that they pull them out of school." He explained:

> Even if you can persuade them to send them to school in the first place, which is a hard job, after that they'll pull them out of school, and get them married off. They don't want them to achieve a higher level of education because they know it will make them more independent in their thinking, it'll lead to an increase in demands for their rights, and so on.

Regarding female role models in education, Highfield observed that educational planning and teacher training in Eritrea substantially ignore gender issues: "Eritrea's a very male-dominated society. Within the Curriculum Development Institute itself you've only got a tiny handful of women working as curriculum developers, as opposed to secretarial staff." I met some resistance and apathy when I raised issues of gender in writing school materials in the workshops I conducted for curriculum designers.

The Hermeneutic Project

As well as formidable technical problems—reconstructing destroyed and neglected cities and roads, feeding the population in an area of continuing drought and famine, rehabilitating devastated agriculture, and attracting investment and restarting the economy[150]—building an independent Eritrea poses a challenging, if daunting, hermeneutic "project both for the collection of men and for the single person,"[151] to apply Ricoeur's words. For, while observers and Eritrean leaders agree that the most important resource is the Eritrean people,[152] old religious, ethno-geographic, and economic divisions persist in Eritrean society, along with the newer, war legacy of a "gap . . . between Eritreans who lived under the [Ethiopian] regime and those who left to fight, between the women who became housewives and those who joined the armed struggle."[153] These are among the problems Eritreans began to address in the two-year transition period before the 1993 referendum on independence.

> During this time, the EPLF is seeking to reinvigorate public life in Eritrea after more than a quarter century when all independent civil institutions were banned. . . . While the vote's outcome is not in doubt, the EPLF views the process as essential, demonstrating that independence will actually be attained through an act of popular will, and not solely by means of war.[154]

Western observers have consistently acknowledged the EPLF's ability to unify Eritrea's diverse population in support of the independence struggle and at the same time carry out effective programs of social transformation (women's emancipation, land distribution, improved health and sanitation practices, grassroots participation in political institutions) in liberated areas, through its popular organizations of women, peasants, and workers.[155] Then, in 1992, less than a year after liberation, in

> a sharp departure from the practice of most victorious liberation movements, the EPLF has announced that the new state will not maintain control over the various popular organizations. It is encouraging people to set up organizations that will stand or fall on their own once the transition period is over.[156]

The material and technical goals for a viable, independent, democratic Eritrea depend not merely on *extending* but also on *transforming* social transformation itself into the activity of free, self-organized individuals.

Communities of Memory

A remarkably incisive and comprehensive hermeneutic analysis of culture and community is the 1985 American bestseller *Habits of the Heart: Individualism and Commitment in American Life*, by Robert N. Bellah, Richard Madsen, William N. Sullivan, Ann Swidler, and Steven M. Tipton. The crisis of values in the United States, these sociologists conclude from their studies of history and numerous conversations with middle class Americans, can only be overcome by a "transition to a new level of social integration,"[157] characterized by Jay Clayton as the cultivation of

> a new public language, a discourse of shared under-
> standings and values rather than of personal rights and
> prerogatives. . . . [T]his language of commonalty can be
> nurtured only within a tradition of shared narratives and
> practices which are national in their character.[158]

Despite the vast differences in history, culture, and current problems, I believe that, as critically as in the United States, the prescription by Bellah and his colleagues for a "transformation of the social world" is a necessity if a peaceful, independent Eritrea is to exist.

> Personal transformation among large numbers is essen-
> tial, and it must not only be a transformation of con-
> sciousness but must also involve individual action. But
> individuals need the nurture of groups that carry a moral
> tradition reinforcing their own aspirations.[159]

These groups Bellah and his co-authors call communities of memory.

> Communities, in the sense we are using the term, have a
> history—in an important sense they are constituted by
> their past—and for this reason we can speak of a real
> community as a "community of memory," one that does
> not forget its past. In order not to forget that past, a
> community is involved in retelling its story, its constitu-
> tive narrative. . . . [S]tories as collective history and
> exemplary individuals are an important part of the tra-
> dition that is so central to a community of memory.[160]

What should the community remember? *Habits of the Heart* suggests a "genuine" and "honest" community will include stories of

suffering and shame.[161] But the question of what should be remembered would not ordinarily present itself—unless the community is undergoing a crisis of identity or direction, or facing a dawn of opportunity.

Narrative and Nationalism

For Eritreans, the war created the need to examine their history and memory: "as Eritrean independence has moved from the possible, if unlikely, to the probable, Eritreans have felt the need to discover their own past."[162]

"The communities of memory that tie us to the past also turn us toward the future as communities of hope."[163] Wolde Mesghinna's statement, "We live in *hope*"[164] pointed to such a community of Eritreans. Hope is a narrative with a past and future. What do we hope for but a happy ending to the story of our lives, our community's projects, and our people's struggles? In narratives of hope, the past is a promise. History, says Ricoeur, "is less the experience of the change of everything than the tension created by the expectation of a fulfillment; history is itself hope of history, for each fulfillment is perceived as confirmation, pledge, and repetition of the promise."[165] Eritrean political independence is, as much as a military victory, the victory of Eritrean history, which has won out over the competing history of Ethiopia. In 1991, the Rev. Tewelde Beyene, Eritrean superior of Asmara's Roman Catholic Capuchin community, told Jennifer Parmelee that he could

> now teach what he regards as the "correct" version of Eritrea's past in his history classes. "I am able, for the first time, to show my students that it was Ethiopia itself that signed over Eritrea [in 1890] to Italian colonists, giving Eritrea a new and different orientation that remains to this day," he said.[166]

Nor were these contending stories merely the by-product of war. Key elements of the 30-year struggle were the competing discourses of Eritrean and Ethiopian nationalism that insistently invoked the past as national self-justification and individual inspiration, as well as propaganda, in the war; Mesfin Araya quotes a typical Ethiopian "appeal to Eritrean youth in 1985 that ended with the following conclusion: 'The history of the struggle for unity of your gallant fathers will pass judgment on you!'"[167] Each nation sought to establish its version of history as the community memory of Eritrea.

Construction of Memory

> Nationalist movements create their own mythologies, organising key incidents, real or invented, and symbols into narrative forms which evoke emotional resonance.[168]

John Sorenson argues that there are two forms of nationalist mythology: appeals to ancient history, and appeals to the recent history of nationalist struggle. The Ethiopian myth of "Greater Ethiopia" "uses antiquity as legitimation."[169] In these accounts, Ethiopia traces its descent from the Axumite kingdom of the 5th through 8th centuries; for example, in "a recent government document Ethiopia, including Eritrea, is viewed as one cultural area; indeed, Eritrea is called 'the cradle of the common culture and civilization.'"[170] This suggests, however, as Pateman points out, "that it is the Eritreans, rather than the Ethiopians, who have a better claim to be the legitimate descendants of the Axumite civilization."[171] The EPLF, however, did not push this line of argument, but pursued Sorenson's second strategy, emphasizing the history of nationalist struggle in the last 100 years, from the beginning of Italian colonialism. Pateman finds that "a persistent tradition of Eritrean resistance and opposition runs throughout the Italian period."[172]. Although "everyday forms of resistance rarely find their way into historical accounts . . . a pattern of behavior can be discerned," including "a legitimation or celebration of bandit activity."[173] There were peasant rebellions, assassinations of Italian officers and officials, and desertion of Eritreans from the Italian military.[174]

Patrick Gilkes challenges Pateman, the EPLF, and "guerrilla groupie" versions of Eritrean social, economic, political, and military history, claiming these histories have been "highjacked in the service of one element within the nationalist movement," the EPLF. Among the "myths," says Gilkes, fostered by the EPLF and its supporters are *(a)* the myth of a precolonial Eritrean national identity, *(b)* the myth of a "golden age" of economic development under the

Italians, and *(c)* the myth of "the biggest army in Africa," Ethiopia's, incredibly defeated by the EPLF.[175] Gilkes concludes that the EPLF-orchestrated mythology dissimulates the difficulties (mainly ethnic and political divisions) the country faces. But Gilkes himself acknowledges that

> [t]his is not to suggest that a realistic factual account of the past is necessarily more correct or accurate than a mythical one. History, in this sense, is created by people within a certain specific framework of time and conditions. On the individual level there are the obvious myths that appear regularly: the self-made person; the unhappy childhood; the modest origins; the successful politician. On the group level we find equivalents: the tiny guerrilla forces; the overwhelming power of the enemy; the self-reliance of the movement and the lack of outside aid; the conspiracy of opposition; the correctness of ideological choice or of strategic decisions.[176]

So,

> A mythical "golden age" is always an element of the past for any individual, and this applies equally for a state. For Eritrea it was the pre-war period of substantial economic growth as Italy rapidly built up a temporary war economy to invade Ethiopia in 1935. It lasted a mere five years, was artificial, and was never intended to be more than transitory. Now it is regarded as the bench-mark by which all subsequent economic policies in Eritrea should be compared, usually to their discredit.[177]

Other analysts[178] focus on the Ethiopia-Eritrea federation period (1952 to 1962) or on the mid-1970s emergence of the EPLF[179] as the crucible of Eritrean national consciousness. Mesfin Araya contrasts the discourses just prior to federation:

> The Unionists engaged in mobilisation *by revival and anticipatory hope.* They sought support on the basis not only of past experiences, values, and symbols, but also of imminent emancipation from [Italian] colonial bondage.... By way of contrast, the anti-Unionists

resorted to mobilisation *by revival and anticipatory fear,* albeit no less supported by concrete illustrations. They invoked their own reading of past experiences, values, and symbols, and appealed on the basis of imminent threats inherent in the demands of their opponents.[180]

In addition to the specific content, ascribing a horizon of fear to Eritrean nationalists in contrast to the pro-Ethiopia Unionists' hope, Araya's language reveals his pro-Ethiopia bias: the Unionists "engaged" in mobilization based on "past experiences" whereas the anti-Unionists "resorted" to appeals based on "their own reading" of the past. The Unionists "recalled the glorious history of Ethiopia with its Axumite civilisation and long Christian tradition, and depicted Eritrea as the geographical, historical, and cultural extension of the Empire since ancient times" whereas Eritrean nationalists "constantly stressed" a "glorified" history in which the Eritrean region had been the "centre of ancient Ethiopian civilization" that became marginalized only with the reign of Menelik (1889-1913), who built the Amhara-dominated state of the modern Ethiopian Empire. In Araya's account, the pro-Union history is true history whereas independentist history is constructed, i.e. distorted; Ethiopian history is "glorious" whereas Eritrean history is "glorified," i.e. made to seem glorious.[181] Yet Araya, in denying the existence or genuineness of Eritrean national consciousness in all previous periods, is left ascribing the undeniable fact of pro-independence sentiment to the rise of the EPLF, thereby supporting the EPLF's own cherished "myth" of a nation formed in struggle, as Sorenson points out:

> Seeking only a discourse based on symbols of antiquity, Mesfin overlooks the very expressions of national integration that he himself lists: "the songs describe the beauty and richness of Eritrea, condemn military repression by the Ethiopian regime, praise [EPLF] fighters, and long for or affirm the inevitability of national emancipation." Earlier forms of ideological mobilisation have been super[s]eded by new metaphors. To ignore developmental aspects of ideological mobilisation and focus on pre-federation forms is to fix these as timeless structures, and to overlook the transformation of symbolic

forms in nationalist texts. Whatever metaphors of revival existed before federation have been replaced by emphasis on the new society to be constructed. To dismiss Eritrean nationalism as shallow because of the absence of historical symbols is to misread the future-oriented ideology which typifies that discourse.[182]

Effective History

The struggle for the history of the Eritrean community of memory is not a struggle for truth or falsity but for identity and legitimation. "The 'nation' is precisely what Foucault has called a 'discursive formation'—not simply an allegory or imaginative vision, but a generative political structure."[183] There may be no end to the debate about Eritrea's or Ethiopia's ancient past, nor about the extent and depth of the country's economic and political transformation during the Italian period. In any case, legitimating power or policies by aiming discourse primarily at intellectuals is seldom efficacious. What works, Frantz Fanon says, "is to make the history of the nation part of the personal experience of each of its citizens."[184]

> [O]n the whole the power of effective history does not depend on its being recognized. This, precisely, is the power of history over finite human consciousness, namely that it prevails even where faith in methods leads one to deny one's own historicity.[185]

Effective history is projected into the future. Gadamer (following Martin Heidegger[186]) explains:

> The general structure of understanding is concretized in historical understanding, in that the concrete bonds of custom and tradition and the corresponding possibilities of one's own future become effective in understanding itself.[187]

The result can be historical anomalies, the meanings of which the actors may or may not be fully cognizant:

> [T]he Unionist Party, the embodiment of Ethiopian nationalism in Eritrea, which despite its persistent and

aggressive demand for unconditional union, was not prepared to sacrifice its language as a medium of official communication in Eritrea. Although the Unionists were in favour of the Ethiopian flag and the active representation of Haile Selassie in their executive body, they chose Tigri[ny]a and not Amharic as the official language in Eritrea.[188]

Recognizing the force of effective history does not simplify political problems, but it does allow political problems to be seen in a unified context of their moral dimension. *Habits of the Heart* connects the moral dimension to the communities of memory, for

[t]hey carry a context of meaning that can allow us to connect our aspirations for ourselves and those closest to us with the aspirations of a larger whole and see our own efforts as being, in part, contributions to a common good.[189]

The relationship of the national polity to living traditions embodied in everyday life and effective traditions embodied in institutions such as clans, the church, traditional healers, etc., is the barometer of legitimation of the political regime, where the weather signs of storm or calm can be read.

The [EPLF].... considers religion irrelevant, if not a hindrance to its mission and is unwilling to accommodate its claims, whether Muslim or Christian. Theoretically correct, nevertheless, this attitude has political shortcomings. In the Eritrean context, religion does have a significant political dimension that is difficult to ignore; although, let it be said again, this has little do with faith itself. The historical evidence shows how religion defines cultural attributes, and hence identity. In certain circumstances, because it represents tangible interests, this identity determines political attitudes. During the 1940s, Muslims and Christians, by and large, were moved by perceptions of their respective interests to join opposed camps, thereby playing into Ethiopia's hands.[190]

That John Markakis is right in stating the importance of religion in Eritrean society, coupled with the legitimacy of the EPLF in that society, suggests he has taken the temperature wrongly in his characterization of the EPLF's view of and relationship to religion. This is corroborated by documented examples of the EPLF's practice, such as its decade of discussion with religious leaders before promulgating new marriage laws.[191] It is in such conversations about the common good that Eritreans will have to mediate post-independence national narratives, which are the future projections of divergent traditions:

> Much more important [than ideological differences] have been the different perceptions that the main rivals have of the future for which they have been fighting. One scenario is of a society and culture based on Islamic values and the Arab language, and closely linked to the Arab world ... [reflecting] a deeply-felt need of Eritrean Muslims, especially the intelligentsia, to identify with a literate culture of historical importance and a renascent Arab world whose economic and political support would be essential for the maintenance of Eritrean independence in the shadow of Ethiopia. By contrast, the [EPLF] rejects the Arab language[192] and regards the Arab connection as artificial, even dangerous, because it highlights religion and cultivates links of dependence with conservative Arab regimes. . . . Instead, a close relationship with a reformed Ethiopia is considered indispensable to the future peace and prosperity of Eritrea.[193]

These are among the Eritrean horizons, or world views in Eritrea now. Today Eritreans' horizons include nine ancient ethnic groups and two major religions; Eritreans from the rural regions liberated long ago, those from the recently liberated cities, and returnees from refugee camps in Sudan; male and female ex-combatants from the huge Eritrean People's Liberation Army; expatriates, exiles, and refugees scattered throughout the Middle East, Europe, and North America—Eritreans who are "mentally there" (in Eritrea) and "physically here" (in the United States) and their children who are "mentally and physically here," in Issayas

Tesfamariam's words. Bringing these worlds into self-understanding and dialogue is one of the challenges faced by Eritreans, their leaders, and educational institutions.

Notes

1   Frank Hearn, "Remembrance and Critique: The Use of the Past for Discrediting the Present and Anticipating the Future," *Politics and Society* 5, no. 2 (1975): 201.

2   Paul Ricoeur, *Political and Social Essays*, ed. David Stewart and Joseph Bien (Athens, OH: Ohio University Press, 1974), 271.

3   Ricoeur, *Political and Social Essays*, 283.

4   David E. Linge, introduction to *Philosophical Hermeneutics* by Hans-Georg Gadamer, ed. and trans. David E. Linge (Berkeley: University of California Press, 1976), xii.

5   Hearn, "Remembrance and Critique," 201, 202

6   Hans-Georg Gadamer, *Truth and Method*, trans. Joel Weinsheimer and Donald G. Marshall, 2nd rev. ed. (New York: Crossroad, 1989), 102.

7   Gadamer, *Truth and Method*, 367.

8   Hans-Georg Gadamer, *Philosophical Hermeneutics*, ed. and trans. David E. Linge (Berkeley: University of California Press, 1976), 66.

9   Paul Ricoeur, *Hermeneutics and the Human Sciences*, ed. and trans. John B. Thompson (Cambridge, England: Cambridge University Press, 1981), 144.

10 Ricoeur, *Hermeneutics and the Human Sciences*, 187.

11 Ricoeur, *Political and Social Essays*, 284, 285.

12 Ricoeur, *Hermeneutics and the Human Sciences*, 144.

13 Ricoeur, *Political and Social Essays*, 256.

14 Kwame Anthony Appiah, *In My Father's House: Africa in the Philosophy of Culture* (New York: Oxford University Press, 1992), 80.

15 Paul Ricoeur, *From Text to Action: Essays in Hermeneutics, II*, trans. Kathleen Blamey and John B. Thompson (Evanston, IL: Northwestern University Press, 1991), 195.

16 Jürgen Habermas, *Legitimation Crisis*, trans. Thomas McCarthy (Boston: Beacon Press, 1975), 69.

17 Jürgen Habermas, *Legitimation Crisis*.

18 Thomas McCarthy, *The Critical Theory of Jürgen Habermas*, (Cambridge, MA: MIT Press, 1978), 369-370.

19 McCarthy, *The Critical Theory of Jürgen Habermas*, 358.

20 Colin Griffin, "Ettore Gelpi," in *Twentieth Century Thinkers in Adult Education*, ed Peter Jarvis (London: Routledge, 1987), 289-290.

21 J. E. Wiredu associates backwardness with illiteracy:

    a culture cannot be both scientific and non-literate, for the

scientific method can only flourish where there can be record-
ings of precise measurements, calculations, and, generally, of
observational data. If a culture is both non-scientific and non-
literate, then in some important respects it may be said to be
backward in a rather deep sense." "How Not to Compare
African Thought with Western Thought," in *African
Philosophy,* ed. Richard A. Wright (Washington, DC:
University Press of America, 1977), 169.

22 Eritrean Relief Committee, *News Updates,* 30 September 1991; Jennifer
Parmelee, "After 30 Years of War, Eritrea is Rebuilding," *Washington Post,*
31 July 1991, A28; Robert M. Press, "Eritrea's Women Fighters Face Difficult
Transition," *Christian Science Monitor,* 24 May 1993, 1, 4.

23 Ricoeur, *Political and Social Essays,* 291.

24 Ricoeur, *Political and Social Essays,* 272.

25 Thomas McCarthy, translator's introduction to *Legitimation Crisis,* by Jürgen
Habermas (Boston: Beacon Press, 1975), xxii.

26 Ricoeur, *Political and Social Essays,* 274.

27 Ricoeur, *Political and Social Essays,* 274.

28 Ricoeur, *Political and Social Essays,* 275-276.

29 Ricoeur, *Political and Social Essays,* 280.

30 Ricoeur, *Political and Social Essays,* 281.

31 Ricoeur, *Political and Social Essays,* 282.

32 Ricoeur, *Political and Social Essays,* 283-284.

33 Ricoeur, *Political and Social Essays,* 285.

34 Ricoeur, *Political and Social Essays,* 284.

35 Ricoeur, *Political and Social Essays,* 284.

36 Appiah, *In My Father's House,* 98.

37 Summarized in Griffin, "Ettore Gelpi," 285.

38 Ricoeur, *Political and Social Essays,* 276-277

39 Ricoeur, *Political and Social Essays,* 277.

40 Ricoeur, *Political and Social Essays,* 284-285.

41 Roy Pateman, *Eritrea: Even the Stones Are Burning* (Trenton, NJ: Red Sea
Press, 1990), 218.

42 Girmai Abraham, "Political Will, Self-Reliance, and Economic Development," *Journal of Eritrean Studies* III, no. 2 (1989): 34.

43 Eritrean People's Liberation Front, "Social Transformation in Eritrea V:
Education as a Part of the Liberation Struggle—III," *Adulis* I, no. 8 (1985): 12.

44 Richard J. Bernstein, *Beyond Objectivism and Relativism: Science, Hermeneutics, and Praxis* (Philadelphia: University of Pittsburgh Press, 1988), 146,
147.

45 Calvin O. Schrag, *Communicative Praxis and the Space of Subjectivity,*
(Bloomington, IN: Indiana University Press, 1986), 20-21.

46 Pateman, *Eritrea: Even the Stones Are Burning,* 219.

47 Eritrean People's Liberation Front, "Social Transformation in Eritrea VI: Education as a Part of the Liberation Struggle—IV," *Adulis* 1, no. 9 (1985): 10.

48 Ricoeur, *Political and Social Essays*, 285.

49 Ricoeur, *Political and Social Essays*, 292, 293.

50 Paul-Henry Chombart de Lauwe, "Technological Domination and Cultural Dynamism," *International Social Science Journal* 39, no. 1 (1986): 106.

51 Scott Jones, "Environment and Development in Eritrea," *Africa Today* 38, no. 2 (1991): 60.

52 Gadamer, *Truth and Method*, 302.

53 Joel C. Weinsheimer, *Gadamer's Hermeneutics: A Reading of* Truth and Method (New Haven: Yale University Press, 1985), 157.

54 Gadamer, *Truth and Method*.

55 Bernstein, *Beyond Objectivism and Relativism*, 143.

56 Ricoeur, *Political and Social Essays*, 258.

57 Bernstein, *Beyond Objectivism and Relativism*, 143, emphasis in original.

58 Bernstein, *Beyond Objectivism and Relativism*, 144.

59 Ricoeur, *Political and Social Essays*, 258.

60 Bernstein, *Beyond Objectivism and Relativism*, 144.

61 Ricoeur, *Political and Social Essays*, 245, 246.

62 Ricoeur, *Political and Social Essays*, 248.

63 Robert Peter Badillo, *The Emancipative Theory of Jürgen Habermas and Metaphysics*, Cultural Heritage and Contemporary Change Series I. Culture and Values, vol. 13 (Washington, DC: Council for Research in Values and Philosophy, 1991), 55.

64 Badillo, *The Emancipative Theory of Jürgen Habermas*, 55.

65 David Held, *Introduction to Critical Theory: Horkheimer to Habermas* (Berkeley: University of California Press, 1980), 345.

66 Jürgen Habermas, *Communication and the Evolution of Society*, trans. Thomas McCarthy (Boston: Beacon Press, 1979), 2, emphasis in original.

67 Badillo, *The Emancipative Theory of Jürgen Habermas*, 55.

68 Thomas McCarthy, "Rationality and Relativism: Habermas's 'Overcoming' of Hermeneutics," in *Habermas: Critical Debates*, ed. John B. Thompson and David Held (Cambridge, MA: MIT Press, 1982), 57-58.

69 Ricoeur, *Hermeneutics and the Human Sciences*, 64.

70 Ricoeur, *Hermeneutics and the Human Sciences*, 83.

71 Gadamer, *Truth and Method*, 185.

72 Ricoeur, *Hermeneutics and the Human Sciences*, 83.

73 Ricoeur, *Hermeneutics and the Human Sciences*, 80.

74 Ricoeur, *Hermeneutics and the Human Sciences*, 83-84.

75 Ricoeur, *Hermeneutics and the Human Sciences*, 98.

76 Chombart de Lauwe, "Technological Domination," 107.

77 Ricoeur, *Hermeneutics and the Human Sciences*, 66, 71.

78 Ricoeur, *Hermeneutics and the Human Sciences*, 82.

79 Ricoeur, *Hermeneutics and the Human Sciences*, 77.

80 Ricoeur, *Hermeneutics and the Human Sciences*, 82, 83.

81 Ricoeur, *Political and Social Essays*, 256.

82 Ricoeur, *Hermeneutics and the Human Sciences*, 86-87.

83 Ricoeur, *Hermeneutics and the Human Sciences*, 83.

84 Ricoeur, *Hermeneutics and the Human Sciences*, 90.

85 Ricoeur, *Hermeneutics and the Human Sciences*, 91, emphasis in original.

86 Ricoeur, *Hermeneutics and the Human Sciences*, 93.

87 Ricoeur, *Hermeneutics and the Human Sciences*, 94.

88 Ricoeur, *Hermeneutics and the Human Science*, 96; Jürgen Habermas, *Legitimation Crisis*, 27.

89 Ricoeur, *From Text to Action*, 182.

90 Paul Ricoeur, *Lectures on Ideology & Utopia*, ed. George H. Taylor (New York: Columbia University Press, 1986), 261

91 Ricoeur, *From Text to Action*, 182-183.

92 Ricoeur, *Lectures on Ideology and Utopia*, 265

93 Ricoeur, *Hermeneutics and the Human Sciences*, 81.

94 Ricoeur, *Hermeneutics and the Human Sciences*, 99.

95 Ricoeur, *Hermeneutics and the Human Sciences*, 97.

96 Ricoeur, *Hermeneutics and the Human Sciences*, 97.

97 Ricoeur, *Hermeneutics and the Human Sciences*, 98.

98 Ricoeur, *Hermeneutics and the Human Sciences*, 99.

99 Robert N. Bellah et al., *Habits of the Heart: Individualism and Commitment in American Life* (New York: Harper and Row, 1985), 212.

100 Henry A. Giroux, *Living Dangerously: Multiculturalism and the Politics of Difference* (New York: Peter Lang Publishing, 1993), 20-21.

101 Henry A. Giroux, *Curriculum Discourse as Postmodernist Critical Practice* (Geelong, Australia: Deakin University Press, 1990), 41.

102 John B. Thompson, *Studies in the Theory of Ideology* (Berkeley: University of California Press, 1984), 198-199.

103 Ricoeur, *From Text to Action*, 196.

104 Ricoeur, *Hermeneutics and the Human Sciences*, 277.

105 Ricoeur, *From Text to Action*, 195, 196.

106 Ricoeur, *Hermeneutics and the Human Sciences*, 278, emphasis in original.

107 Ricoeur, *Hermeneutics and the Human Sciences*, 277.

108 Paul Ricoeur, *Time and Narrative*, vol. 2, trans. Kathleen McLaughlin and David Pellauer (Chicago: University of Chicago Press, 1985), 43, emphasis in original.

109 Ricoeur, *From Text to Action*, 206.

110 Ricoeur, *From Text to Action*, 183.

111 Ricoeur, *From Text to Action*, 195.

112 Ricoeur, *From Text to Action*, 206, emphasis in original.

113 Ricoeur, *From Text to Action*, 177, 178.

114 For example, see Adi Ophir, "Beyond Good-Evil: A Plea for a Hermeneutic Ethics," in *Hermeneutics and Critical Theory in Ethics and Politics*, ed. Michael Kelly (Cambridge, MA: MIT Press, 1990), 94-121.

115 Thomas J. La Belle and Christopher R. Ward, "Education Reform When Nations Undergo Radical Political and Social Transformation," *Comparative Education* 26, no. 1 (1990): 95.

116 La Belle and Ward, "Education Reform," 104.

117 La Belle and Ward, "Education Reform," 105.

118 Aaron Benavot et al., "Knowledge for the Masses: World Models and National Curricula, 1920-1986," *American Sociological Review* 56 (1991): 86.

119 Chombart de Lauwe, "Technological Domination," 106; compare with Ricoeur, *Political and Social Essays*, and Ettore Gelpi, *Lifelong Education and International Relations* (London: Croom Help, 1985).

120 La Belle and Ward, "Education Reform," 105.

121 La Belle and Ward, "Education Reform," 103.

122 Mariana Zakharieva, "Studying Innovations in Education: Internationalization of Approaches," *Current Sociology* 39, no. 1 (1991): 125.

123 R. W. Niezen, "Hot Literacy in Cold Societies: A Comparative Study of the Sacred Value of Writing," *Comparative Studies in Society and History* 33 (1991): 251.

124 Nteba Bakumba and Katana Bukuru Gege, "The Experience of the Elimu Association of Zaïre," *Convergence* XXIV, no. 1/2 (1991): 25.

125 Bakumba and Gege, "The Experience of the Elimu Association," 30.

126 Elda Lyster, "Adult Basic Education in a Rural Development Project: A Micro-Level Case Study," *Convergence* XXIV, no. 1/2 (1991): 35.

127 Dianzungu Dia Biniakunu, "Regenerating African Decayed Land: Can Reading Contribute?" *Journal of Reading* 35, no. 2 (1991): 107.

128 Susan T. Ferrell and Aimee Howley, "Adult Literacy in Rural Areas," *Journal of Reading* 34, no. 5 (1991): 369.

129 James Firebrace and Stuart Holland, *Never Kneel Down: Drought, Development, and Liberation in Eritrea*, 2nd printing (Trenton, NJ: Red Sea Press, 1986), 119-120.

130 Information from Hauser and Wolde Mesghinna in this and the next section (*Constraints on Women*) are from my 1991 and 1992 interviews with them.

131 Ferrell and Howley, "Adult Literacy," 369.

132 Niezen, "Hot Literacy," 236.

133 Karen A. Hauser, *Eritrea After the War: Findings of a Trip There in Early July-Early August 1991* (New York: Eritrean Relief Committee, 1991).

134 Provisional Government, Department of Education, "Adult Education and the Future of the Combatants in Eritrea (Prepared for AALAE Workshop),″ 29 November 1992, 4.

135 Ben Wisner, *Power and Need in Africa* (Trenton, NJ: Africa World Press, 1989), 122.

136 Barbara Jackson Junge and Debebe Tegegne, "The Effects of Liberation from Illiteracy on the Lives of 31 Women: A Case Study," *Journal of Reading* 28, no. 7 (1985): 609; Agneta Lind, "Mobilizing Women for Literacy," *Literacy Lessons* (UNESCO International Bureau of Education, 1990), 7; Wisner, *Power and Need*, 122; Lalita Ramdas, "Women and Literacy: A Quest for Justice," *Convergence* XXXIII, no. 1 (1990): 32.

137 Asseny Muro, "Women Commodity Producers and Proletariats: The Case of African Women," in *Challenging Rural Poverty*, ed. Fassil G. Kiros (Trenton, NJ: Africa World Press, 1985), 67.

138 Junge and Tegegne, "The Effects of Liberation from Illiteracy," 609; Lind, "Mobilizing Women," 7; Amrit Wilson, *The Challenge Road: Women and the Eritrean Revolution* (Trenton, NJ: Red Sea Press, 1991).

139 Lind, "Mobilizing Women," 8.

140 Junge and Tegegne, "The Effects of Liberation from Illiteracy," 609; Lind, "Mobilizing Women," 7-8.

141 Stanlie M. James, "Transgressing Fundamental Boundaries: The Struggle for Women's Human Rights," *Africa Today* 39, no. 4 (1992); for Eritrean examples see Elsa Gebreyesus, "Cry Till Day: African Women Confront Violence," *Breakthrough* 25 (1994).

142 Lalita Ramdas, "Women and Literacy," 35.

143 Robert Papstein, *Eritrea: Revolution at Dusk* (Trenton, NJ: Red Sea Press, 1991), 123.

144 Papstein, *Eritrea: Revolution at Dusk*, 116.

145 Wubnesh W. Selassie, "The Changing Position of Eritrean Women: An Overview of Women's Participation in the EPLF," in *Beyond Conflict in the Horn: Prospects for Peace, Recovery and Development in Ethiopia, Somalia and the Sudan*, ed. Martin Doornbos, Lionel Cliffe, Abdel Ghaffar M. Ahmed, and John Markakis (Trenton, NJ: Red Sea Press, 1992), 68.

146 Selassie, "The Changing Position of Eritrean Women," 68.

147 Conversation with Karen A. Hauser, May 12, 1992.

148 Muro, "Women Commodity Producers."

149 James, "Transgressing Fundamental Boundaries," 38.

150 Dan Connell, "Eritrea's Path to Independence," *Christian Science Monitor*, 15 January 1992; Connell, slideshow presentation (EPLF Club, Oakland, CA, 25 March 1992); Connell, "A New Country Emerges," *Links, Health and Development Report* (National Central America Health Rights Network), Spring 1992; Eritrean Relief Committee, *News Updates*, 20 December, 1991; Jill Hamburg, "Eritrea Showing a Lot of Promise," *San Francisco Chronicle*, 9 April 1992, A16, A18; Michael A. Hiltzik, "Eritrea Reviving as an African Bright Spot," *Los Angeles Times*, 28 December 1991, A1, A12-A13; John

Stackhouse, "Fight to Make Something Out of Virtually Nothing, *London Globe and Mail*, 29 November 1991, A8; Jennie Street, "Eritrea: Building a New Economy," *New African*, November 1991, 32; Street, "Eritrea Begins to Repair Its Shattered Economy," *African Business*, January 1992, 31.

151 Ricoeur, *Political and Social Essays*, 293.

152 Hauser, *Eritrea After the War*, 11; Dan Connell, "A New Country Emerges"; Hamburg, "Eritrea Showing a Lot of Promise," A18.

153 Jennifer Parmelee, "After 30 Years of War, Eritrea is Rebuilding," *Washington Post*, 31 July 1991, A28. See also Eritrean Relief Committee, *News Updates*, 30 September 1991, and Robert M. Press, "Eritrea's Women Fighters Face Difficult Transition," *Christian Science Monitor*, 24 May 1993, 1, 4.

154 Dan Connell, "Eritrean Independence: Not By War Alone," *Guardian*, 1 April 1992, 13.

155 Firebrace and Holland, *Never Kneel Down.*

156 Connell, "Eritrean Independence: Not By War Alone."

157 Bellah et al., *Habits of the Heart*, 286.

158 Jay Clayton, *The Pleasures of Babel: Contemporary American Literature and Theory* (New York: Oxford University Press, 1993), 132.

159 Bellah et al., *Habits of the Heart*, 286.

160 Bellah et al., *Habits of the Heart*, 153.

161 Bellah et al., *Habits of the Heart*, 153.

162 Patrick Gilkes, "Eritrea: Historiography and Mythology," *African Affairs* 90 (1991): 623.

163 Bellah et al., *Habits of the Heart*, 153.

164 Susan Kalish, *Eritrea*, prod. Susan Kalish, dir. Susan Kalish, Yasha Aginsky, and John Knoop (Cinema Guild, Inc., 1697 Broadway, Suite 506, New York, NY 10019-5904), 1990, film; see p. 53.

165 Paul Ricoeur, *The Conflict of Interpretation: Essays in Hermeneutics*, ed. Don Ihde (Evanston, IL: Northwestern University Press, 1974), 405.

166 Parmelee, "After 30 Years of War, Eritrea is Rebuilding," date bracketed in original.

167 Mesfin Araya, "The Eritrean Question: An Alternative Explanation," *Journal of Modern African Studies* 28 (1990): 98.

168 John Sorenson, "Discourses in Eritrean Nationalism and Identity," *Journal of Modern African Studies* 29 (1991): 308.

169 Sorenson, "Discourses in Eritrean Nationalism," 309.

170 Jordan Gebre-Medhin, *Peasants and Nationalism in Eritrea: A Critique of Ethiopian Studies* (Trenton, NJ: Red Sea Press, 1989), 7; compare with Ethiopia, Ministry of Foreign Affairs, *Eritrea Then and Now* (Addis Ababa: Press and Information Department, 1976; reprint, New York: Committee to Defend the Ethiopian Revolution, 1978); see p. 40.

171 Pateman, *Eritrea: Even the Stones Are Burning*, 30.

172 Roy Pateman, "Eritrean Resistance During the Italian Occupation," *Journal of Eritrean Studies*, III (1989): 13.

173 Pateman, "Eritrean Resistance," 13, 21.

174 Association of Eritrean Students in North America, *In Defence of the Eritrean Revolution* (1978); Pateman, "Eritrean Resistance"; Pateman, *Eritrea: Even the Stones Are Burning*.

175 Gilkes, "Eritrea: Historiography and Mythology," 624-625.

176 Gilkes, "Eritrea: Historiography and Mythology," 624-625.

177 Gilkes, "Eritrea: Historiography and Mythology," 624.

178 e.g., Lloyd Ellingson, "The Emergence of Political Parties in Eritrea, 1941-1950," *Journal of African History* XVIII, no. 2 (1977): 261-181; and John Markakis, "The Nationalist Revolution in Eritrea," *Journal of Modern African Studies* 26, no. 1 (1988): 51-70.

179 e.g., Araya, "The Eritrean Question," and Tekle Mariam Woldemikael, "Political Mobilization and Nationalist Movements: The Case of the Eritrean People's Liberation Front," *Africa Today* 38, no. 2 (1991): 31-42.

180 Araya, "The Eritrean Question," 82-83, emphasis in original.

181 Araya, "The Eritrean Question," 82-83.

182 Sorenson, "Discourses in Eritrean Nationalism," 309-310.

183 Timothy Brennan, "The National Longing for Form," in *Nation and Narration*, ed. Homi K. Bhabha (London: Routledge, 1990), 46-47.

184 Frantz Fanon, *The Wretched of the Earth*, trans. C. Farrington (New York: Grove Weidenfeld, 1963), 200.

185 Gadamer, *Truth and Method*, 301.

186 "Everything that makes possible and limits Dasein's projection ineluctably precedes it. This existential structure of Dasein must be expressed in the understanding of historical tradition as well, and so we . . . start by following Heidegger." Gadamer, *Truth and Method*, 264.

187 Gadamer, *Truth and Method*, 264.

188 Araya, "The Eritrean Question," 94.

189 Bellah et al., *Habits of the Heart*, 153.

190 Markakis, "The Nationalist Revolution," 67-68.

191 See p. 263, note 23.

192 Arabic is a language of instruction in Eritrean (EPLF) schools for Arabic-speaking communities or any community that requests Arabic. See pp. 225–229.

193 Markakis, "The Nationalist Revolution," 68.

VI

LEGITIMATION OF LITERACY

The texts I have gathered and examined—transcriptions of conversations, my own observations recorded in notebooks or remembered,[1] documents, photographs—provide the "objects"[2] for the following interpretive analysis. This analysis is primarily but not exclusively focused on narratives emerging from the experiences of the Eritrean People's Liberation Front's national literacy campaign, 1983-1987. The national literacy campaign developed an educational praxis which informs the development of education in Eritrea today. My attention to the campaign mirrors the emphasis given it by many of the teachers and educational administrators I spoke with in Eritrea. It was, for some of them, their formative experience as educators. Then they were teenagers or young adults, eager to meet and serve the rural population. Today they are responsible for educating the whole country. Therefore, in the following discussions, I will primarily utilize the literacy campaign stories they told me. Necessarily, I will quote them at length.

A Decade's Difference

In conversation after conversation I heard the clamor for education in Eritrea.

Berhane Demoz, Planning and Programming Division, Department of Education: "Everybody, *everybody*, is pushing us to open schools. They are pushing us to open schools in almost every village. We don't have the capacity to open schools in every village."

Mohammedin Jassir, Saho Panel, Curriculum Development Institute, Department of Education: "The parents [of the Saho ethnic group] are strongly supporting the opening of the schools, and they're sending their children for education."

Abeba Tesfagiorgis, author and a director of the Regional Centre for Human Rights and Development: "The women want to get the best education now. The ones who could not get any education or got some education in the field, starting from their own daughters, I see the *thirst*, the *quest* for education."

Senait Lijam, Educational Coordinator, National Union of Eritrean Women: "For the civilians, we have already some help from an Italian missionary group, and we have opened classes in 13 stations, 13 areas around the country, in three provinces. And these are some of the photographs, over there; it will show you that these are the Muslim part of it, and they are participating in good number. We have 1,562 students already. It has only been four months since we opened it."

Solomon Ghebremariam, Office of Education, Seraye Province: "There is great need to open schools everywhere. The people are eager now to learn. They were thirsty of getting education. The demand is high; the ability of the government is less."

Woldemichael Ghebretensae, Office of Education, Senhit Province: "Those who have money, at least to pay the school fees, are learning. But there are a lot who want to learn, but they don't have anything. So desperately we need the budget for running adult education."

Kaleab Haile, director, Adult Division, Department of Education: "They pay—themselves, yes—they pay for their own exercise books, they buy blackboards, pieces of chalk. The government cannot finance them at this time, unless it gets certain aid. To run adult education program is very expensive."

Beraki Ghebreselassie, head of the Department of Education:

"The schools are either totally destroyed or damaged as a result of war. So a lot of schools have to be rehabilitated, and to meet the rising demands of the population new schools have to be constructed."

Paul Highfield, English Panel, Curriculum Development Institute: "Every single village is demanding for a school to be opened in their village."

Semere Solomon, Director, Planning and Programming Division: "They want to have a school *in their village.*"

This clamor was less than a decade old. When the literacy campaign began in 1983 farmers and herders were reluctant to spare the labor of their children, let alone their own time, for education. Social convention and religious authority barred women not only from literacy but also from leaving their homes and gathering together. Yet the literacy campaign, limited in scope and resource-poor, must in large part be credited for the postliberation enthusiasm for education. Additionally, the campaign mobilized support for the EPLF and recruitment to its ranks. Finally, through education, rural communities began to discuss, reflect on, and choose new ways of life: in health, hygiene, and sanitation practices; in diet; in agricultural methods; in new roles for women; in building local democratic and participatory institutions. But first, education had to be accepted, had to begin. How was *this* change effected?

The Literacy Campaign: Plan and Practice
During 1976 an intensive literacy campaign among rural civilians was begun, but the battles of 1978 forced the suspension of the program. In March 1983, it was restarted

> on a large scale with 599 campaigners; out of this, 451 were combatants, of course, who were grown up in the Zero School—they were in the grades of six up to grade eight. They discontinued their education for the noble cause of the literacy campaign for the Eritrean people. And we started the campaign in 183 centers or stations. And in these 183 centers, we had around 56,000 adults who were participating at that time.

These facts came from Kaleab Haile. I first learned of the campaign from Kaleab, the director of the Department of Education's Adult

Division. Although I did not record our first conversation (and some of his words were drowned by traffic noises from Asmara's busy Liberation Avenue two storeys below his office), my notes on our conversation provide a brief history and description of the campaign:

> The EPLF at that time had the upper hand in the country: three-fourths of Eritrea was liberated, and the Ethiopians were garrisoned in a few cities and towns. A national literacy campaign was mounted, but the obstacles were great: 80 percent of the population was illiterate (that is, virtually 100 percent of the non-urban population of peasant agriculturalists, agro-pastoralists, and pastoralists), and there was day-to-day terror against them by Ethiopian troops, who had, in addition, seized school buildings for their barracks. The campaign's goals were to *(a)* eradicate illiteracy and *(b)* raise the peasants' consciousness.
>
> Prior to the beginning of the campaign, the EPLF conducted a census—apparently a detailed assessment of educational needs throughout the country, and an accounting of resources needed and available, both material and human. Clearly the literacy campaign was carefully prepared: at the end of his lecture, Kaleab Haile showed me the ten or so textbooks prepared in 1983 (in Tigrinya) and still used today for the adult education program. We leafed through these page by page. They seemed carefully constructed and well-presented with drawings, maps, charts, etc. I remarked on the extent and high level of the curriculum; he told me that com-

Kaleab Haile, director of adult education. Previously he was head the Eritrean Relief Association's schools for Eritrean refugees in Sudan, and before that was head of the Zero School for six years. He joined the EPLF in 1975.

pletion of the three-year adult program was the equivalent of completing grade five of the elementary school curriculum. The math texts seemed more ambitious than U.S. first and second grade texts, if I recall these correctly.

The campaign was mounted utilizing 451 students from the Zero School who had completed grades six, seven, or eight and additional teachers from the general population, totaling 599 teachers assigned to 183 stations. [3] The teachers received an orientation in the culture and religion of the people they were to serve, as well as some training in how to present lessons. Still, they could hardly be said to "know" the people and their cultures. As well as teaching, they were supposed to be testing and evaluating the adult program, so that, based on their experiences, the program could be modified to best accomplish its objectives and meet people's needs.

The program was country-wide, in the highlands and lowlands. As part of their work, teachers engaged in the traditional labor of the people, teaching and training as they worked at midwifery, building, terracing, and gardening. They campaigned against superstitious practices in health and hygiene: for example the practice of bleeding the hands and head of jaundice victims, and the use of traditional plants for treating malaria ("They might have scientific value, but it's too early to tell," Kaleab allowed). One traditional childbirth practice, said to ease labor, was for the birthing mother to drink water that her husband had washed his feet in.

As well as midwifery and hygienic childbirth practices, the teachers taught mothers childcare and household sanitation practices. In the lowlands, they campaigned for the inclusion of vegetables in the diet of people whose conventional wisdom was that "vegetables are of the poor."

The focus on health and hygiene extended from 1983 to 1987. However, several factors intervened in the growth and, finally, the continuation of the adult program. The 1984 offensive by the Dergue narrowed the campaign to certain places. In 1985, locusts, drought, and famine limited the program to small areas. The number of stations fell to 119. Large numbers of the population were displaced, some as refugees to the Sudan, some to the cities where aid was available. "If you are unable to feed the people, you are unable to teach them."

After 1988, the campaign was confined to a few places, and the focus was on the combatants only (this is still largely true).

It should be noted that the greatest number of participants in the adult program in 1983, 1984, and 1985 were women: 60.2 percent. "Women take care of everything," Kaleab said. The program's strategy became to eradicate illiteracy among women, and then the rest of the family.

Although small in scale, the program during those years gave the EPLF the chance to try out the curriculum they had developed, in the "ups and downs of society," in the various traditional cultures. And the curriculum worked. The same curriculum worked for combatants and civilians, in the cities and in rural areas. The curriculum has remained unchanged, though future experience may indicate that changes are needed.

Ayn Alem Marcos, an administrator in the campaign, remembered the aims of the program and the chronology of its early development a little differently:

> AYN ALEM MARCOS: We didn't have such a set program, but we had a general idea what our people will need just to help them: the three Rs, and teach them some basic hygiene, and politicize them.

> LES GOTTESMAN: So you knew what you wanted to do, but you really didn't know exactly how it was going to be done—is that what you're saying? When the teachers—the graduates—went out to do the teaching, there really wasn't a program?

> AAM: Yes. We didn't have such a thorough research or documentation on the people, on the culture, on the tradition, and so forth, but we had a general thing in mind, but not in a written form, and tried to go step by step

through the programs and so forth. So we went there and started to establish centers with our students, our young students, later who became teachers, naturally. So we identified their problems, as we were trying to establish these centers, and we returned back to our base area.

LG: And you left the teachers in different posts.

AAM: Exactly—doing the three Rs: reading, numeration, and writing, at least two, three hours a day—mothers as well as men peasants. So, we got back and started to prepare a program, based on the experience that we had spent behind the enemy's lines.

LG: And how long did you spend doing your observation, before you returned?

AAM: It depends: some left early. Maybe about four to five months, and some stayed there for about six months. So we got back and started to discuss our experience with those people who stayed behind—our compatriots, teachers, our administrators, and so forth—and we were assigned to prepare a curriculum for adult education. So based on that, we happened to design a curriculum and produced materials for reading, writing, and numeration.

I have included these lengthy notes and remarks not only to set forth the campaign's history but also to highlight a dialectic *within* the EPLF's practice: a creative tension between study and planning on the one hand, and on-the-spot experimentation, the use of observation and dialogue, learning by doing on the other hand. It is by understanding the campaign within the "texture"[4] of Eritrean community life that I began to understand how education changed the communities and the communities changed education.

Communicative Praxis

Administrators can be expected to emphasize the prescribed curriculum and its successes and failures. But Ayn Alem Marcos stressed that from the beginning the campaign's intent was bi-directional learning. In this snatch of our conversation he quotes himself persuading skeptical villagers to accept a young teacher:

> AYN ALEM MARCOS: Certainly these young people are going to deal with adults, and dealing with an adult, you need to have some, you know, elements, cultural, religion, you have to speak his language. We said, "It's all right, you know. We brought these kids for two purposes. One is, we want them to learn from you. And another is, we want them to teach you what they have learned."
>
> LES GOTTESMAN: So it was two directions.
>
> AAM: Exactly.
>
> LG: They were learning and they were teaching.

Ayn Alem's simple-seeming "learning and teaching" paradigm—freighted with his understanding of the counterpoint, if not confrontation, between tradition and revolution, between laconic community elders and ardently ideological young teachers, between wise experience and youthful presumption, between lived experience and formal program implementation, between doing and instituting—reveals his confident delight in finding unity and simplicity in the complexity of Eritrean social and cultural divisions.

The general case of the operation of such unity and complexity is theorized by Calvin O. Schrag as "communicative praxis."

> [C]ommunicative praxis involves not only the texts of spoken and written discourse but also the concrete actions of individuals and the historically effective life of institutions. . . . It includes also the texture of human projects, of motivations and decisions, of embodiment, and of wider processes of social formation.[5]

The figure on the facing page is Schrag's "schematic depiction" of the "global texture of communicative praxis."[6] "Texture" denotes the dynamic relationship of elements in the "fabric of human action and social practices."[7] It is "what people 'know' as 'reality' in their everyday, non- or pre-theoretical lives," say Peter L. Berger and Thomas Luckmann in their influential 1966 treatise, *The Social Construction of Reality,* "[i]n other words commonsense 'knowledge' rather than 'ideas' . . . that constitutes the fabric of meanings without which no society could exist."[8] For Schrag this fabric is the "bonding feature" of the "sociohistorical space in which communication and praxis interplay."[9]

> The texture of communicative praxis gathers the display of meanings within the text of everyday speech and the text of the written word. . . . [I]t also encompasses the play and display of meanings within the field of perception and the fabric of human action.[10]

Analysis of the narratives of former literacy teachers is an examination of this texture. I have divided the analysis into two discussions: first, a consideration of how the rhetoric of the literacy teachers entered the textural space of community life and understanding, and how negotiation within this textural space allowed their educational project to be "threaded" (pursuing Schrag's metaphor) into the life of the community, and, second, how this changed texture, and the process of its changing, uncovered ideological ground (switching the metaphor) which served to legitimate the EPLF's larger, nationalist project.

Following Ayn Alem's cue, I began asking former literacy teachers what they had learned from the peasants they taught. I will cite many of their answers in the course of discussing negotiation. Most

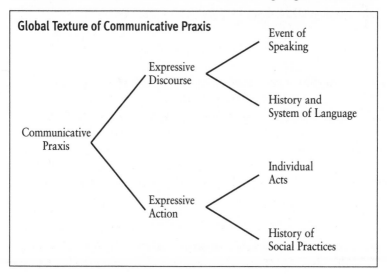

Global Texture of Communicative Praxis

Communicative Praxis
— Expressive Discourse
  — Event of Speaking
  — History and System of Language
— Expressive Action
  — Individual Acts
  — History of Social Practices

useful here, though, are the following few minutes of my conversation with former literacy teacher Abraham Bahre, who when I interviewed him was a student at the University of Asmara. His remarks encompass the major issues the campaigners faced in their project. What, I asked Abraham, had he learned from his rural adult students?

> ABRAHAM BAHRE: I myself? Well, the elementary things I learned from them is language. What I mean is, I know Tigrinya, but I was able to learn a lot of words which I was not using. Let this aside. Let me mention the bigger thing I remember: I could learn the culture of our society. Because we were brought up in an isolated place, in Sahel—we were not being in contact even with the fighters. In being as a teacher within the society, I could learn even the culture, how to speak with people, how to communicate with them. Even though they are illiterate, even though they can't write and read, they were very experienced people. They were very experienced people. And they were a *hundred* times teaching us than we were teaching them.

> LES GOTTESMAN: Really!

> AB: I can say that. They know how to do everything. And they were even knowing how to handle us.

> LG: How to handle *you*.

> AB: How to handle us. What makes us love them. We were young enough to be eager to accomplish everything we want. And they were knowing everything. And they were also teaching us *how to handle them* themselves. They were teaching us their problems. And we were convinced after a short period of time, some of their problems were—us. We can say some of us were blind enough only to look at the education: "You have to come. I told you to come; you have to come." These were our words that we were using, some of us.

> LG: And then slowly you were beginning to understand the real conditions.

AB: Yes. How they are living. What should they *do* to be able to learn. What should they have. And what should we approach and what way should we approach them. And what mistakes that we have done. Actually, what I am speaking is in a smooth thing. Or generally, since what I want you to know is what you haven't known. The good things are always known. You can say it was almost smooth. Everything was good, I can say. In order to make you aware of some problems, is why I'm telling these things. Especially culture, our culture. I didn't know that the elder ones should sit before the younger until I went there. Until I went there. I didn't know how to say even hello to the elders. We were simply calling them by their names. But we should call them by saying "Abboi Christo," which is as a word of respect.

LG: And so they were teaching you this.

AB: Yes, they were teaching us directly and indirectly.

From Abraham Bahre's comments issues of communicative praxis can be easily identified:

first, the unexpected necessity of learning a language already spoken;

second, the teacher's physical separation and reentry into "our society";

third, the strength of local knowledge and wisdom which deconstructed conventional categories, roles, and relationships of teacher and student;

fourth, the students' (peasants') strategy of teaching the teachers to teach *them*, which reconstructed a traditional Eritrean educational relationship of older and younger generations;

fifth, the construction of workable relations of authority and respect through proper symbolic representation; and

finally, the teachers' slow realization and eventual appropriation of the communities' commitment to their project, and their assuming the responsibility that commitment deserved.

Before I explore each of these as specific negotiations, it will be helpful to introduce a theoretical framework for understanding the problems of negotiation and the resources of language which make it possible. I use as a framework Jürgen Habermas's universal pragmatics, the "rational reconstruction" of "communication which is aimed at reaching understanding."[11] But a caveat is in order here. Habermas directs attention to the rational validity claims of the teachers' appeal, but not how those claims are mediated in social practice, within ordinary speech and everyday actions—as they are, since the "ideal speech situation"[12] of rational, democratic discussion wherein claims are settled never really occurs. My own discoveries and rediscoveries in examining the literacy campaign teachers' "narratives of negotiation" have played off an eclectic range of analytical concepts and frames, a range sanctioned, perhaps, by Michel Foucault's "notion of theory as a toolkit."[13] So the discussion that follows is not limited to Habermas's theory (or theories) in the argument my analysis pursues, and specifically veers into theories of the dynamics of conversation.

Negotiation

> Plato, I believe, shows insightfully that true rhetoric cannot be separated from what he calls dialectic—in the original sense, which can be understood as the art of leading a conversation. This art is really the art of agreement. Thus understanding ultimately concerns agreement and belongs to the communicative context that enforces it. That dialectic presupposes goodwill is an entirely decisive insight, one that testifies to Plato's wisdom. The Greek term is *eumeneia*. Plato thus contrasts a blindly raging argumentative rigor with the concrete situation of agreement and with the intention to agree, which first makes speech truly possible and opens the way to insight.[14]

This art of "leading a conversation," of "agreement," of "true rhetoric" was practiced, for life and death stakes, by teenage Eritrean literacy teachers in rural villages and oases "behind enemy lines" (Ayn Alem Marcos) from 1983 to 1987. The teachers had to compel the participation of each community, sometimes of each individual, in the classes, through their rhetoric. The potential for this rhetoric, "traditionally regarded as the art of bringing about a consensus on questions which cannot be settled through compelling reasoning,"[15] which for brevity I will call "negotiation,"[16] inheres in language itself. Negotiation is possible, Habermas asserts, because language, though rule-bound, has endless possibilities for new sentences. "A speaker can make use of the creativity of natural language to respond spontaneously to changing situations and to define new situations in principally unpredictable statements."[17] The sentences produced in any specific situation, however, do not once spoken disappear, but instead become part of a process of forming and developing "interpretative schemes" by which human action is planned, described, and understood.[18] Nor, as Schrag's texture metaphor means to suggest, can the sentences be entirely separated from the actions they accompany, in greater or lesser space or time.

> Communication has both a linguistic and an actional dimension. There is a rhetoric of speech and there is a rhetoric of action. The communication of messages in the impartation of objective knowledge and the disclosure of intersubjective concerns interdependently illustrates the signifying power of speech and language and the intentionality of action. Communication and praxis intersect within a common space.[19]

We experience the texture as "an interweaving of discourse and action, language and nondiscursive practices, speech and perception, yielding a holistic space of expressive intentionality."[20] Specific and cumulative speech events, the use of texts, or actions, stretch—or tighten or shred—the fabric of intersubjectively utilized interpretive schemes. Change in understanding is change in texture and is continuously occurring.

> We are consequently here dealing with practical questions which can be traced to decisions about the acceptance or rejection of standards, of criteria for evaluation and norms of action. These decisions, if arrived at in a rational process, are made neither in a theoretically compelling nor in a merely arbitrary way: they have, in effect, been motivated by convincing speech.[21]

However, within the natural unfolding of discovery and change, some speech is spoken and some acts are performed *deliberately* to accelerate or retard the pace, plot the direction, or shape the form of community understanding and action.

> A good speech which leads to a consensus about decisions on practical questions merely indicates the point where we consciously intervene in this natural-innate process and attempt to alter accepted interpretative schemes with the aim of learning (and teaching) to see what we pre-understood through tradition in a different way and to evaluate it anew. This type of insight is innovative through the choice of the appropriate word. Thanks to the creativity of natural language the native speaker gains a unique power over the practical consciousness of the members of a community.[22]

Validity Claims

But what are the conditions and ingredients of a "good" or "convincing" speech? Or action? (There are convincing actions, which we acknowledge with the cliché that they "speak louder than words." "Action," says Clifford Geertz, "like phonation in speech, pigment in painting, line in writing, or sonance in music, signifies."[23]) How does a young teacher gain unique power over the practical consciousness of the community or cause accepted interpretive schemes to be evaluated anew?

For these things to occur, as when a community accepts for the first time an educational institution, certain conditions are necessary. "Rationally motivated decisions," says Habermas, "can be arrived at only on the basis of a consensus that is brought about by convincing speech; and that means depending on the both cognitively and expressively appropriate means of everyday language."[24] These two categories, language that is both cognitively and expressively appropriate, give a rough overview of Habermas's delineation of the elements of communicative competence, "the ability of a speaker oriented to mutual understanding to embed a well-formed sentence in relations to reality."[25] Habermas finds "that the intention of arriving at practical consensus, and the human interest in a society that furthers the free communication about aims and interests, is inherent in language itself."[26] In this regard, Habermas has developed the theory of linguistic communication as a universal pragmatics, in which "norms and opinions which are 'taken for granted'" in everyday communication can be referred to a "discourse" where claims are problematized. The possibility of engaging in this "ideal speech situation" in which validity claims are freely and fairly tested underlies our trust, and our willingness to engage, in communicative acts.[27]

> According to Habermas, when one person says something to another, that person implicitly (sometimes explicitly) makes the following claims: (1) That what is said is intelligible—that is to say, that it obeys certain syntactical and semantic rules so that there is a "meaning" that can be understood by the other. (2) That the propositional content of whatever is said is true. The "propositional content" refers to the factual assertions which the speaker makes as part of what he or she says. (3) That the speaker is justified in saying whatever is said. In other words, certain social rights or "norms" are invoked in the use of speech in any given context of language-use. (4) That the speaker is sincere in whatever is said—that he or she does not intend to deceive the listener.[28]

For convenience, these four claims are known, respectively, as the intelligibility, truth, rightness, and truthfulness claims. However, certain assurances in everyday communication generally forestall the need for discursive justification of the claims. I can make this clear with a personal example.[29] Suffering from chronic nosebleeds in Asmara, I went to the central hospital, Makane Hiwot. It was my first encounter with Eritrean medical care and I did not know what to expect or how trusting to be. A nurse had me wait in a small examining room. Soon Dr. Alem entered, introduced herself, and began questioning me in English; this satisfied the first claim—what she said was intelligible and meaningful. After an examination, Dr. Alem told me I had sinusitis. Her explanation of how this conclusion was consistent with my symptoms and her observations, and the familiar ring of "sinus" and "itis" (although I do not believe I had encountered the combination before) assured me that the diagnosis was accurate—true—satisfying the second claim. The examination, which included x-rays and her looking into my nose with a lighted instrument, standard medical procedure where I come from, also convinced me that the doctor was justified—the third claim—in making an authoritative diagnosis. Finally, the doctor's attentiveness, thoroughness, and prescription for nose drops assured me that she bade me no ill-will and was sincerely, conscientiously performing her duties regardless of my gender, nationality, and the relatively minor nature of my complaint.

In my encounter with Dr. Alem, each of the validity claims was redeemed, in reference to the questions that might have been raised in—but without resorting to—an ideal speech situation. Dr. Alem validated Eritrean medicine to me—walking into the hospital was not enough. Similarly, the literacy campaigners had to justify literacy to the rural communities they had traveled to—entering the physical community was not enough. They had to enter the linguistic community and earn the right to speak effectively in it by redeeming the validity claims they presented to the people they meant to serve.

Intelligibility and Truth

In Habermas's rough division of cognitively and expressively appropriate language,[30] the former encompasses the first two validity claims, intelligibility and truth. Intelligibility must first be construed as "producing grammatical sentences"[31] in the community's language, Tigre, Saho, Kunama, or whatever it may be, and then more meticulously as using the local vocabulary. With respect to vocabulary, it may be hard to draw a line between intelligibility and other claims. The truth claim asserts that the speaker accurately represents "the" world of "experience or fact." "The competence to use language representatively is a precondition of the ability to make a distinction between a public world (*Sein:* being, that which really is) and a private world (*Schein:* illusion, that which merely seems to be)."[32] Both claims, intelligibility and truth, are seen in this "textbook" example:

> KALEAB HAILE: For example, you say this is a pen [picking up a pen] here in Asmara. So the book says, "This is a pen." And in Sahel, they call this pen with another name.

> LES GOTTESMAN: I see. So the lesson doesn't mean anything.

> KH: Yes. And sometimes, well, whether they see this pen or not, it doesn't give them any sense, because they don't use it.

LG: They don't use pens.

KH: Yes, they don't have that.

The intelligibility problem is solved by using the word by which pen is signified in the language community at hand. The truth problem—"situat[ing] the utterance in relation to external reality, i.e. 'the' world of objects and events about which one can make true or false statements"[33]—is harder to solve. Where no pens exist, and no writers, *no* word will produce them. In another example, approaching this problem has rather more drastic implications—medical, survival, and political—in the following excerpt from the "diary of a barefoot doctor" during the drought years, which appeared in an undated (probably 1986) EPLF magazine:

> Perhaps the most frustrating and agonizing part of my work was the educational part. I could never but lament the distressing situation when I had to teach a mother on what to feed her child for his proper upbringing, knowing well as I do, that there was nothing to give. This rather made the instruction not only irrelevant and academic but also absurd. I always remembered what one of my teachers used to tell me: "Never mention eggs to a woman who has never heard the word; never mention eggs when they are not accessible to those for whom the course [is] intended; you must identify and feel the way of life, the economic situation and cultural status and build an organic contact with their lives. The education you give should always be based on the surrounding reality, on what is reasonably attainable and within reach of the community concerned, and not on simple generalities which may turn out to be a disconcerting dream."[34]

While the teacher's conclusion may itself be a too-simple generality, the reflection here indicates the EPLF's attention to the linguistics of praxis and also highlights the problem of legitimating basic health and education services in a society in the midst of drought and war.[35]

What the literacy teachers had to learn, first, was a working language—for some of them, a new form of their own mother tongue.

SALEH MAHMUD: When I went to the campaign I was almost sixteen or seventeen years. I have not any experience of life. But from the adults I came to understand some problems of the life. I learned how to speak in front of a crowd. The first times, I wasn't able to speak in front of the people. But from the adults, I learned how to speak, how to communicate with adult people, how to communicate with children.

LES GOTTESMAN: You *learned* that from working with them.

SM: Yes, the manner of speaking.

LG: Did they help you learn it?

SM: Yes. Yes.

Sometimes a teacher had to learn a second language. Zecarias Tedros, a Tigrinya speaker, learned Tigre; more than that, as an artist and teacher of art to Tigreans, whose own art is decorative but not representative, he learned a new language of art.

Zecarias Tedros went to the field at age 11, studied at the Zero School, and became an artist and art teacher. He taught in the national literacy campaign, 1983–1987.

ZECARIAS TEDROS: Because I know Asmara —I went to the field from Asmara—at that time I could draw so many things which I remembered from Asmara, like the cars, special cars, the Palace. But there I had time to make an exhibition for the parents, and I had to show my works to my students. So if I draw a car or a palace, something which I can find in cities, they can't understand that. So, taking

Decorative household containers on a prayer rug, Bilen nationality. Watercolor by Zecarias Tedros. (Photo by Frank Duhl.)

this into consideration, my plan was to take the drawings or pictures from that society, things we can find there easily and that they know.

LES GOTTESMAN: So you drew things that they were familiar with.

ZT: Yeah. Well, sometimes when they studied science in second grade, our book had the *fishes, marine*—something like these words—but they don't have any idea about fish. Then at that time, I as an art teacher, I was preparing teaching aids, for all the teachers. But now I want to tell you about this; we'll come back later about the teaching aid materials.

LG: That's fine.

ZT: But at that time because we were dealing with the spirit of the people, with their situation, with their phenomena, they were interested about the arts. And as they observe the exhibition, they can find some popular figures from the society. So they wondered how with this pencil and a paper, how can he make this. They were interested.

LG: What were some of the favorite subjects? What did they like to see in drawings?

ZT: They were interested in animals —like camels, goats—and the materials, the objects of the marriage.

LG: Like which objects of marriage?

ZT: Like for perfume, it has its own container. This is a bottle of perfume

Young Tigre woman from the highlands of Senhit Province. Watercolor by Zecarias Tedros. (Photo by Frank Duhl.)

Tigre mother from Nacfa. The beaded headpiece is a charm against infant mortality. Watercolor by Zecarias Tedros. (Photo by Frank Duhl.)

[he draws it], let's say, and if a lady is preparing for marriage, she has to make a container, she covers it with seashells. With colorful materials, she prepares very nice, like this [he draws]. And the Tigre nationality is rich with such materials. So I go to the marriage occasions with the peasants, and I take the materials separately, I try to paint it with colors, something attractive, so they were very interested in these materials. And the animals. And the decorations.

LG: From the marriage.

ZT: Yeah.

LG: So in a way you were learning from them, about their culture.

ZT: Indeed.

LG: And then you were making pictures of it for them.

ZT: Indeed. I want to tell you, I am of the Tigrinya nationality, but in that area I am able to speak Tigre as much as my mother tongue. First when I went to that area, I was completely a Tigrinya man. I didn't know even a single word in Tigre. But I became a teacher there, so I can learn so many things from them, as I have said, cultural, language, oh, many things.

LG: So do you think that your experience there has had an effect on your own art?

ZT: Yeah, indeed. Because if I were in Asmara, I couldn't have like such works, because this area of Asmara, as you have seen, is a town. You can't find the original or the core of the culture here. If you want to study about Tigre, you have to go there, and you have to take something original or typical from that area. Even the appearance of Tigre, they have here [he indicates his cheeks]—

LG: The scars.

ZT: Yeah, and hairstyle, shoes, clothes, so many things. You can't do that in this area. So I think it was helpful for me.

LG: So you feel you have more cultural experience.

ZT: Yeah.

In both the Tigre language and the language of art, Zecarias Tedros became intelligible to the Tigre people and "true" to the world they live in.

Rightness

The "elementary things" that Abraham Bahre picked up from his students—"language . . . a lot of words I was not using"—and the "manner of speaking" that Saleh Mahmud had to learn included but went beyond intelligibility, that is, speaking Tigre or Tigrinya with the accent of the village, or using the local vocabulary; and beyond truth, learning or refamiliarizing themselves with the common objects and activities, and their names, of village or pastoral life. "The bigger thing" that Abraham Bahre remembered was learning "the culture of our society" and how to communicate with its members in order to "accomplish" his educational and political mission. This cultural knowledge was imparted by the community. The teachers were slowly initiated into the forms of communication in which the informal assurances of rightness and truthfulness forestall an ideal speech situation (which is, anyway, culturally if not theoretically unavailable) indefinitely, while still bringing the participants into meaningful communication.

In Habermas's general formula "convincing speech" depends on "both cognitively appropriate"—that is, intelligible and true—"and expressively appropriate"—right and sincere—"means of everyday language."[36] To justify the rightness claim, a speaker has to show, first, that a proposition is "legitimate and appropriate"[37] in "the *normative context* that gives the speaker the *conviction* that his utterance is right,"[38] and second (if challenged), that the norm itself is valid. We can see the rightness claim, challenge, and response, with mixed results, in the shaky beginnings of Eritrea's national literacy campaign. The campaign at its outset faced a population on the edge of survival:

> AYN ALEM MARCOS: What we did, just, first, as a program, we wanted to have public meetings, trying to politicize the people through seminars, telling them why we were there, and what we want from there, and the importance of the program itself. And then tried to take some questions and, you know, their views on the things that we came up with, the new idea, of the literacy program. We had quite a substantial number of people totally refusing to participate in the program, for certain reasons. First, the time we left— the time we embarked on this program—was a critical time economically because it was the drought of 1983, 1984, and people were saying, "Look, we don't have anything in our stomach; how dare you ask us to come and attend classes." And some people were saying, "Look, we cannot get engaged in such things because we are going to go away from this village."

> LES GOTTESMAN: Because they couldn't survive there.

> AAM: Exactly. Either go to the Sudan or to Ethiopia or to other villages where conditions are, they think, better. So this was the problem that we had.

> LG: How did you answer them? When people said that, what could you offer?

> AAM: *We-e-l-l-l.* The first thing, those people who were on their way to leave the village, there's nothing you can do; they can leave.

In fact, it was drought and desperation that furnished the campaign's initial discourse of appeal:

> AYN ALEM MARCOS: But for those people who were staying behind, we were just trying to convince them that, if he doesn't have anything to do, he cannot till the land, he's not engaged in other economic activities, but still he stays at home and eats whatever meager material that he

has. So if he just spends an hour or an hour and a half a day attending our class, *maybe* that will be helpful for him to improve his life eventually, when time comes. So we had some people, really wanted to come; we didn't force them. So we started with a very limited number of people.

The discourse acknowledged the truth of the severe conditions, and offered for consideration an analysis of the situation, that is, a normative view, which admits of a previously unconsidered (and unavailable) possibility for action: literacy. The rightness claim was fragile, so promises were tentative, minimal: "maybe" literacy would "help" improve life "eventually." Disaster has often, in human events, been recorded as providing an opening for people to grasp new solutions. When I presented this proposition to Paul Highfield—

> LES GOTTESMAN: Well, it's easy to understand how you could introduce the idea, over time, that a clinic would be very beneficial to people. It's harder to understand how you introduce the idea that a school is beneficial when people's traditional way of life and being successful within that way of life, however that's measured— being secure and safe and prosperous or whatever—had never depended on schooling.

—his rejoinder was quick:

> PAUL HIGHFIELD: They weren't. The maximum majority of the population in the 1980s wasn't successful and wasn't secure. I mean because of the drought and the famine—plus the war. Taken together, the situation was catastrophic.

> LES GOTTESMAN: So you think that gave education an opening to provide some solution? Or the hope of some solutions?

> PH: I'm sure it did.

> LG: How?

Highfield went on to explain the long process of the EPLF's establishing the rightness of claims for social transformation among semi-pastoralists. In the process of negotiation, new situations establish new norms, opening up new possibilities:

> Well, you see, once people have accepted—and we're talking about different cultures within Eritrean society; if you're talking about semi-nomads, once they begin to see in concrete terms that their children aren't dying anymore, by providing them with basic health facilities, once the women begin to start learning how to read and write in adult literacy classes, and their consciousness begins to be raised, and the men as well in a different way—once people's consciousness is raised to that extent, then they can begin to see beyond the next month or whatever, which traditionally people saw as, you know, is there going to be enough pasture down where I have to take the sheep and goats, or up to the mountain, has it rained enough in the past month, this sort of thing. And once a school *is* established, and then it becomes regularized, just the fact of students going to school regularly on a daily basis, that sort of routinization of school has a very big impact on the consciousness of the people, once it's accepted as a natural thing for people to go to school. It took me a while to realize that: this very basic thing of setting up a school, and the fact that students have to go to school every day involves a certain routine. Okay, the education was rather passive in a lot of ways, it was very teacher-centered and so on, but just the very fact that education was being provided, that they were learning with other children, that they were relating to other children in a formal framework which was in a settled situation, day to day, month to month, year to year, had an enormous impact on their way of looking at the world. And children are very open to new ideas and to change. It's the parents who are less open to it. And, you see, there was an adult literacy campaign going on at the same time. Because of the drought and famine there were a lot of problems associated with it, but the basic concept of adult literacy was accepted quite well by then by the most conservative part of the society.

In this narrative Highfield telescopes a complex process that begins with Eritreans facing the inevitability of change understood as a limited number of options: severe privation and possibly death, or migration. Whatever hope—or lowered resistance to cultural innovation born of despair—remains is enlisted in a new project by the EPLF's offers of help, beginning with addressing people's material needs—"If you are unable to feed the people, you are unable to teach them" (Kaleab Haile)—and proceeding to the introduction of new social routines whereby people can better organize to provide for themselves.

Looking ahead to a later discussion, it is worth noting here that in being enlisted to the literacy project, or other social innovations, the people are engaged to a narrative built on a pre-existing happy ending; "traditional religious theory," says Kwame Anthony Appiah,

> in certain respects . . . shares the purposes of modern natural science, which we may summarize in the slogan "explanation, prediction, and control." . . . [R]eligious beliefs of traditional peoples constitute explanatory theories and . . . traditional religious actions are reasonable attempts to pursue goals in the light of these beliefs—attempts, in other words, at prediction and control of the world.[39]

The norm of desiring babies to live, not die, was traditional.[40] The means to health, inoculations or sanitation, was new. Highfield suggests that the pastoralists carefully evaluated results—from the standpoint of traditional goals or values. In that context, the EPLF's rightness claims, for the efficacy of scientific health care and literacy in achieving traditional goals, were won against competing claims.

Woldemichael Ghebretensae charted the changes that were possible in some areas over time, when the immediate drought and famine threats to survival had passed:

> The school is a means for changing the society. In the late '80s, we had some kind of campaign. For example the nomads drink from the stream; it's very dirty water, with some kinds of disease. So, in the science of hygiene, we teach the children to drink clean water. If they want to get clean water, they have to dig a well. So for every village,

we set the children in groups. Every group has to dig a well for his village. They have to dig to get clean water. So this way they educate the parents. Another way of getting interested about education is, the nomads are not clean: they don't wash their clothes, they don't wash their kitchen utensils, they don't wash their hands. But every morning the students or the children get clean—in the school. They have to wash. Not only for themselves, they have to get clean their house also, they have to clean the surroundings around their house. So this hygiene helped the society, and little by little, after five or six years, people see the changes. Now, the ones who have children who are students are different from the ones who haven't been students: their clothes are clean, they get combed, they clean their fingernails. Anybody who walks around there can pick out whether he is a student or not. That way at least the society was changed little by little. And, in addition to that, when the students finished the elementary school, sixth grade, a nomad has to see something economically in order to get interested about education. When a person gets educated, he gets money. Practically, they haven't seen this before. So when you get your child educated, when he finishes his education, he gets money, he gets a salary, he can help his parents—they don't understand this: they haven't seen it before. So when the students finish the fifth grade, we were recruiting them as teachers—not because they are

Woldemichael Ghebretensae began teaching at the Zero School in 1977. He was head of the school for three years, then worked in the district educational offices in Barka and Danakil provinces. He now heads the district office in Senhit Province.

qualified, but in order to change the society we are recruiting them as teachers, as barefoot doctors. They are the only ones who are educated in that society. We give them money. They are getting paid. This way they realized. And the youth of the nomads who wanted to be married were choosing one of the students, because she is advanced; she is clean, she knows how to hold the household. He prefers a student rather than an uneducated girl. So their interest, the ones who wanted to be married, focused on these students. So every summer when these students finish elementary school, every summer we give them a semester course. Then after two summers he gets one grade up. So we give them make-ups every summer. And now some of them are tenth grade, at this time, the ones who were recruited at that time. They are directors. They are administrators of the schools around there. They are the best teachers. There is a success in the community. Now the community has been changed. The one who knows that area in 1982 will be embarrassed when he sees the society now. It's completely changed.

Woldemichael's account focuses on children and details significant changes in social attitudes realized between generations. At the same time, it is clear that change was a material force, posing compelling claims society-wide and intergenerationally.

The EPLF Subculture

The former literacy teachers told many stories of the negotiations which brought adults into education or won approval of education for their children, and I will examine a few more of these in detail. But first, it is necessary to understand the obstacles to literacy teachers being accorded "power over the practical consciousness of the members of a community."

There is . . . another side to this power: the specific lack of power of the speaking subject *vis-à-vis* habitualized language-games; they cannot be modified unless one participates in them. This in turn can be successful only to the extent that the rules which determine a language-game have been internalized. To enter into a linguistic

> tradition necessitates, at least latently, the efforts of a
> process of socialization: the "grammar" of language-
> games has to become part of the personality structure.[41]

The literacy teachers had, in fact, been socialized to a unique and
self-conscious subculture and its language-game, which was shared
by no other Eritrean social group. Significantly, Abraham Bahre
notes the social division in terms of language:

> First of all, when we were assigned to go to our people,
> especially, we were eager to get out of Sahel, and to face
> our people. That was because we were in that secret
> place under the valleys, the mountains. We'd been sepa-
> rated, isolated there. We were eager to know, even to
> communicate with the people, to know how the people
> looked like and what do they say. Since we were ambi-
> tious to find them, we were eager and we went.

The students' eagerness came, in part, from their complex relationship to the population they essayed to serve—their own people,
from whom they had been separated, geographically, culturally, and
had grown apart. Their interest was familial—note Abraham
Bahre's repeated inclusive pronoun, "our people"—and at the same
time almost anthropological: the project was to "find" and to
"know" "them." They were "ours" and, at the same time, others.
The EPLF subculture, in the mountainous base area, was unlike any
natural culture in Eritrea. Paul Highfield told me:

> The EPLF has built up its own culture, which is very, very
> different from traditional culture. Things that went on in
> the base area were unheard of before. People didn't do
> work collectively, women and men didn't sleep in the
> same room, as a normal thing. The whole thing about the
> relationships between the sexes had to be handled very
> carefully. In fact, in the beginning, when the EPLF was
> first established, it was forbidden for fighters to have sex
> with each other, for quite a few years, to protect women
> basically because the men would see it as a normal thing
> if they were sleeping in the same area as a woman that
> would be for sexual reasons. So many, many barriers
> were broken down.

The Zero School (also called the Revolution School) was marked by a studied egalitarianism: the EPLF had always eschewed titles, military ranks, stripes, badges, medals, or salutes.[42] In the Revolution School, Solomon Woldmichel said,

> teachers and students were cooperative, they learned together, they worked together, they lived together, they ate together, because they all are fighters. They're comrades. Yes. And no teacher, no student: we only remember we are students and they are teachers when we are coming to class only. And a sort of discussion—hot debate sometimes—was going on in class.

EPLF culture also dispensed with linguistic forms of respectful address:

> BERHANE DEMOZ: As a sign of respect for elderly people, the pronouns as a sign of respect—we have them in Tigrinya.
>
> LES GOTTESMAN: I see. Like *tu* and *vous* in French.
>
> BD: Yes, *tu* and *vous* in French. We have that in Tigrinya. Now, the students who stayed longer in the Revolution School were addressing us—even us, their teachers—directly: they were saying you-*tu*.
>
> LG: So they were familiar.
>
> BD: Yes. Now, when they come back to the society, they were calling the older people just like us. The older people were not happy about this. Some of the people. Of course, some of them understood that. But some weren't happy.

Revolution School codes of speech, modes of dress, hairstyle, and behavior clashed with the proprieties of rural Eritrean peoples. "These people do not know these youngsters," Ayn Alem Marcos told me. "They've been away from their cultural niche for so long period of time, and they are now new: they have to *relearn*; they can*not* function. You see?" To be sure, the campaigners had been given "orientation courses"[43]:

BERHANE DEMOZ: What we did was to give them an orientation on the program of the literacy campaign, on
the social setup of Eritrea in general, and mostly we
were stressing the psychology of adults—of course, we
were not telling them we were dealing with the psychology of adults, but we were telling them how they
should approach adults, what they should do, what cultures should the students consider when they teach the
adults. For example, whenever you approach an adult,
you have to be courteous, you have to be polite, you
have to know that he has a lot of experience in life, he
knows a lot better than you, except for writing and
reading. Therefore, you have to respect, and you're
going to learn from him. Also we were dealing with the
culture of all the nine nationalities, because we have to
be with them all.

And we were also dealing with the sexual differences in our country. We have to deal with that because,
for example, if you go to the lowlands, and if you happen to be the teacher of, let's say, the Afar, the women
come to class with veils on their faces. So what do they
have to do to jump over these obstacles? These were the
things we were telling them.

Nevertheless, youthful arrogance and missionary zeal could not be
suppressed:

ABRAHAM BAHRE: Actually, we were very critically oriented, and the aim that we had to with us to accomplish
or to teach our people, we were really eager to teach the
people, and we were thinking about how to take the
people from this illiterate darkness, from the darkness.

And they were young—half the age, in many cases, of their
youngest students. Most societies don't take youthful speech seriously. Some deny speaking rights altogether on the basis of social
status, age, or gender. For example, Senait Lijam explained,

traditionally, there was a committee in a village, but it
was made up of men only. And this assembly, when they
just sit and discuss, if a woman happens to come by, she

was forbidden to pass when the assembly was sitting, discussing the fate of the village.

Saleh Mahmud faced these attitudes in recruiting students to literacy classes:

> SALEH MAHMUD: If I tried to speak, and I tried to gather the village, and I tried to speak to them what is the benefit of the school, of the education, and they have to learn, they have to send their children, some of the adults were not listening to me. They were calling to me, "You are a child. You have to learn still. You have no right to tell us what is education and what is our benefit. We are fathers. We know how to run our lives. You are a child." They were saying me like that.
>
> LES GOTTESMAN: So what did you do?
>
> SM: Anyhow, I was trying to convince them, and sometimes leave them speak as they do, as they want.

It is clear, returning to Schrag's schema, that Saleh Mahmud's and all the teachers' first project was to constitute themselves as effective speakers and actors within the texture of communicative praxis, as "subject[s] whose mode of being in discourse is essentially that of being able to speak with other subjects." This subject, however, cannot be self-constituted. "A speaker/hearer intertexture limns the space in which the speaking subject is implicated."[44] In this space,

> I am able to say "I" only because of an acknowledgment of you as my interlocutor within the dynamics of the dialogic encounter. The "I" and the "you" are as it were coconstituted, sharing a common, intersubjective space. . . . I lend you a thought-experiment, a possible way of seeing things, and you respond. Your response is one of incorporating what I have said, by either acceptance, rejection, or modification.[45]

The constitution of the self, where one's speech is goal-oriented, is tied to the outcome of the dialogue. The rejection out of hand of the rightness claim, when the rejection occurs for extra-dialogical reasons—"You are a child"—leaves no verbal space in which the speaker can defend other claims. A remedy to this blockage, however, lies in action, not in words.

Truthfulness

Habermas argues that truth and rightness can be "'discursively redeemed': the speaker can elaborate upon why a given claim is true, or is normatively satisfied."[46] Intelligibility and truthfulness, however, must be demonstrated. Intelligibility is fulfilled "immanently to language"[47]: a sentence itself "must be grammatical, it must conform to an established system of recognized rules for the use of language."[48] But truthfulness is redeemed by acts. "A speaker can only show himself or herself to be sincere by demonstrating sincerity in action (fulfilling promises, honouring commitments, and so on)."[49] This does not mean truthfulness is redeemed only when fulfilling acts follow specific promises, *post hoc ergo propter hoc.* Acts exhibit "propositional content" and "'illocutionary' traits," Paul Ricoeur says,[50] and the latter is of interest here. Illocution is what we intend to *do* in saying something[51]: promise, praise, command, request, beg and so on.

> [T]he use (selection) of linguistic devices is in the concrete act of speech determined by the *purpose of the utterance*; it is directed toward the function of the act of speech. We can see a considerable difference in linguistic devices, according to whether it is, for instance, a matter-of-fact everyday communication or the occasional (solemn) recital of an event, or . . . whether it is a conversation among contemporaries or speech to children or to one's elders.[52]

Among actions, gestures comprise the clearest recognizably illocutionary vocabulary; intent is clear because gestures follow rules—a cupped palm begs, a scooping arm motion beckons, and so on. Complex and cumulative acts are read by rules, too, by which witnesses interpret their propositional content and illocutionary force.

> If we enter into a ceremony but do not know the rules of the ritual, then all the movements are senseless. To understand is to pair what we see with the rules of the

> ritual. . . . We *see* the movement *as* performing a mass, *as* performing a sacrifice, and so on.[53]

The *seeing as* persists. "Like the speech act, the action event . . . develops a . . . dialectic between its temporal status as an appearing and disappearing event, and its logical status as having such-and-such identifiable meaning."[54] The act disappears, but its meaning is inscribed in the texture of communicative praxis.

In communicative acts, truthfulness is informally assured when words, actions, or physical gestures or aspects, to the participants' understanding, complement or tropologically stand in for each other. Habermas notes:

> In non-deformed language-games there exists a congru-
> ence of expression on all three levels of communication;
> those utterances symbolized linguistically, those that are
> presented in actions, and those embodied in physical
> expressions do not contradict but complement one
> another metacommunicatively. Intended contradictions,
> which themselves contain a message, are, in this sense,
> regarded as normal. It is a further aspect of the normal
> form of everyday communication that a part of extra-
> verbal meanings, which varies with its socio-cultural con-
> text but which remains constant within a language com-
> munity, is intentional, i.e. in principle verbalizable.[55]

Incongruence—an apparent inconsistency of speech, deed, gesture, and expressive aspect, as, say, when a wink accompanies a verbal pledge—suggests hypocrisy, emotional ambivalence or mental insta-bility, cultural insensitivity or naïveté, or any number of other inten-tional or unintentional insincerities. Social norms, as we have seen, find certain juxtapositions incongruous—extreme youth and wise words, for one example—and will not legitimate them.

Behavior Change

In the face of a blanket rejection for status, such as the one the "child" Saleh Mahmud met, a generalized truthfulness or sincerity claim had to be advanced. The literacy teachers had first to win hearers in order to defend the truth and rightness claims of their proposals. In the teachers' narratives, four classes of actions emerge which served to establish truthfulness. First is behavior change, evident in narratives already examined above: learning language, observing a sitting order, using respectful forms of address, and any number of ways in which the teachers acknowledged and conformed to community norms. Such conformity may not alone guarantee sincerity; conformity can be merely opportunistic. But I detected no cynicism, no mere expediency, in the teachers' accounts of these changes—they always described them as *learning*.

Work and Risk

The second set of actions expressing the teachers' sincerity encompasses the dangers they faced and the hard work they did. Administrators I asked were vague regarding the number of teachers killed.[56] "We have paid. Some were captured; some were killed. It's an undeniable fact," Ayn Alem Marcos acknowledged. "We were lucky. We were lucky enough. But we had some martyrs. We had some martyrs," said Berhane Demoz. In any event, "the people were seeing what the teachers were doing to teach them, and what risks they were taking," Berhane noted. The teachers themselves painted vivid pictures:

SALEH MAHMUD: Always we were exposed to the enemy attack. Most of our schools were located in a distance less than ten kilometers away from the enemy camps. So at any time you can be attacked by the enemy.

SOLOMON WOLDMICHEL: It was a very hard and tough time for me. First of all, most of the students, the teachers, were very youngsters, thirteen, fourteen, fifteen, sixteen years old. And the enemy was chasing us almost every night then. We teach with our guns, without putting them aside. There are only the guns on our shoulders. And we teach the whole day. After the night is coming, we left the village and go to the bushes to hide ourselves to be safe from the chasing of the enemy because totally there was not any military post of the EPLF. The only military post is the teachers.

SALEH MAHMUD: We were facing a shortage of school supplies and so many things. Firstly, an acute shortage of school supplies, an acute shortage of teachers. Let me tell you one example of our timetables at that time. In 1982, in a school having more than 200 students, daily students, and 300 adult students, there were only two teachers. We were working four shifts. From eight a.m. to eleven p.m. Four shifts. Fortunately, this area was semi-liberated. We were sleeping at our school. But we had a turn to guard at night, one hour, also, as a fighter.

ABRAHAM BAHRE: We were not only school teachers. We were participating in their productions. We had regular time that we participated in their work, especially in the work of the poor people, especially in the work that is done by the whole village. We were a part of the village. We were not only separate teachers. And also some of us were people helping in maternity. And some of us were also dressers for the doctors, dressing wounds. And we were helping them in all these things. And this led us to be *mixed* with them and to learn and to teach them.

The teachers' sincerity was redeemed by acts of joining "normal" community activities—such as they were or were adapted to the pressures of Ethiopian military occupation and war. To say that "the people were seeing" the hard work the teachers did and the risks they ran is not to say that these factors were seen as exceptional, outside of, or different from the toil and danger which formed the texture of community life in a war zone.

Innovation

A third set of actions, educational innovations, often developed in collaboration with students, expressed dedication to the community and to teaching. Ayn Alem Marcos recounted several innovations. I will quote him at length, interrupting with some comments:

AYN ALEM MARCOS: Another experience that we gained from this campaign was, we just went there empty-handed. We said to our young teachers, use your initiative, your creativity, and create something. We cannot supply you with blackboards. We cannot supply you chalk. We can't supply you with exercise books. Said, just go there and do things. It's amazing: in certain areas we had a lot of—how should I put it?—educational innovations. For example, every cottage or house has got a grinding stone. So one of our guys in a certain village happened to say, "Okay, we are teaching them how to read and write in classes; but how can we reinforce this? Because we don't have posters. We don't have any other printed materials that our students can take home." So they created something—through discussion, of course: there is always discussion. One of the guys said, "Look, we have charcoal, and most of the houses are whitewashed. And about 60 or 50 percent of the time the mothers, or even the young girls, are spending their time grinding. And in most cases, the stone is put in the corner of a room or a house, so they face the wall as they are grinding. So just write slogans and letters and everything with the charcoal on the wall." That was one of our pedagogical innovations. And it did a really good job. And the amazing thing, some of the written materials were really funny, saying, "My name is"—it's her name. "I have two children. And I have a patriot husband who is in the militia" or "is a farmer" or "is a member of the mass organization of the EPLF. And we have to work hard in order to keep the enemy out of our country." Such things! When I returned back after a year or so, in every house you see such things. And I was amazed.

It is worth remarking on the probable effect of this innovation. "Fixing" elements of a woman's identity—in an explicitly political configuration of "facts" of her life—in writing, and the display of that writing in the home, goes farther than building her reading skills. The wall itself becomes a proposed "map" of "social reality"[57] and "variation of the *ego*"[58] of the individual woman, reappropriated on a daily basis:

> By "appropriation," I understand this: that the interpretation of a text culminates in the self-interpretation of a subject who thenceforth understands [her]self better, understands [her]self differently, or simply begins to understand [her]self.[59]

As the social space and its meaning are transformed by the "written self," so her life is transformed in the repeated and renewed encounter with this version of self at a reflective distance.

AYN ALEM MARCOS: Another thing: we didn't have black-boards. So our teachers used to convince mothers, some mothers, to take turns bringing their cooking pan—it's a pan where they bake local bread[60]—they bring it to class. They clean it up, bring it to class, and then the teachers use the pan as a blackboard. And another thing is, they used to make blackboards out of skins and hides. And they also used to make their own chalk by looking for white limestone, they'd grind it, and they'd bring flour, and then mix it and bake it and make chalk out of that. We were not supplying them with chalk. This was one of the things that they took initiative to create. Another thing, we had shepherds, a lot of shepherds, young kids of sixteen, seventeen, eighteen, nineteen; in fact, the adult education program starts from fifteen onwards. Their parents are having a regular day class, but the kids are not having this opportunity. So, in one area, they discuss this. "We have to force these young people to come and attend day class." And some of them say, "Look, unless they are looking after these sheep and goats and cattle, the family cannot exist." And so they said, "Okay, why shouldn't we conduct class in the evening?" And some-body said, "Where the hell can you get the kerosene and petromax?"—'cause there's no electricity there. So they said, "Okay, we'll try our best by using a bonfire." So they say, "Okay, where can you get the wood from?" Because, as you may see, the environment is completely destroyed. Said, "Well, we'll insist that"—because since they are shepherds, they roam around—"they pick up pieces of wood, of firewood, and bring it over. And try to use it as economically as possible." So they started with that, and they didn't go too far, and the shepherds them-selves, since they were extremely motivated, suggested that, why shouldn't they start early, early in the morning, right before they leave, that is six o'clock in the morning, before they take the flocks, because they leave eight, eight-thirty, or nine. So they said, we will have a good two hours or an hour and a half. So the teachers started their class—six o'clock. So things were going on like that.

These examples—using bread pans as blackboards, and integrating classes with the shepherds' work schedule—highlight the collaborative and dialogic process which fosters both innovation and trust. The problem-solving process itself, the educational outcomes which the process supported and made happen, and the objects and aspects of daily life—the shepherd's redivision of daytime, the enlarged "meaning" of a bread pan doing double-duty at home and in class—were inscribed in the texture of communicative praxis; responsibility for the educational project was generalized among the students, their families, and within the community at large; and the teachers and other community members were increasingly interimplicated in converging practice.

Other innovations came from the teachers' reflections on culture and pedagogy. Two innovations mentioned by Berhane Demoz are interesting for the fusion of horizons they reveal—the transposition of *oneself as oneself* into someone else's shoes.[61] The first innovation revises a reading lesson. The teacher imaginatively reaches inside the students' epistemic horizon for guidance:

Berhane Demoz worked on curriculum materials for the national literacy campaign, taught at the Zero School for 12 years, and was a member of the Planning and Programming Division of the Department of Education when I spoke with him.

BERHANE DEMOZ: In the Sahel, one of the teachers was teaching the first letter, in Tigrinya, which is *beh.* Now, he was trying to show the adults a sheep. He was trying to show the picture of a sheep because the first letter of sheep is *beh.* He was trying to tell them, "What is this?" They told him that it was a sheep, in

Tigrinya, of course, *begeyexh*. Now, what happened was, "sheep" has three letters, in Tigrinya. All right? The second letter and third letter come in at least the third or fourth months. Now, after he told the class, he came to me and told me, "The way that we are teaching is not effective, because we are asking them only a third of the letters, which is the first letter, but we're making it complicated because we're adding three other letters which come late in the third or fourth months; therefore, we have to change our method." He was very creative, and you know what he told me? It's better if we use *door*. And he told me that he's not going to use letters, but the shape of the door. It's like this [drawing the sides and top of a door in the air]. The door's like this, and the letter looks like that [drawing same shape]. He was very creative. I can give you a lot of examples. But this was the way they were improving the teaching.

The second innovation revises arithmetic instruction: the teacher's transposition to the student's horizon, as Gadamer insists, "involves rising to a higher universality that overcomes not only our own particularity but also that of the other"[62] and, in this case, of Eritrean cultures altogether:

> BERHANE DEMOZ: I can tell you: very creative teaching materials. I remember hearing, in Barka one of the teachers was preparing *abacus*. He used to cut the bamboo, put them in a ring, and he was teaching adults to count. It was not part of the culture of the people. It was his own idea. They were very creative. In fact, they really had a big role in improving and developing the material.

Here is a fusion of horizons that crosses the world in search of pedagogical resources that will solve local problems.

Coercion

Finally, the sincerity of the teachers' intentions was expressed through coercion. The teachers, and EPLF policy, forced some community members to learn to read and write. From my interviews, I gathered that coercion was applied to illiterates elected to village assemblies, to members of agricultural and small cottage industry cooperatives the EPLF encouraged in some areas, and to small town merchants. Ayn Alem Marcos provided the fullest account of this practice and its rationale:

> We didn't have even such a lot of objections, but there was some challenge. Anyway, we tried our best to convince them and to get engaged in the activities. For example, I want to mention an anecdote for you. This woman, who is from a certain small town, who was selling local beer, she used to have a very small bar, a very traditional small bar, and we asked her to go and register for this literacy campaign. She refused. She said, "Look, I am living by selling this locally-made beer, and my income is so low, and I have two children, no husband, so who is going to take care of my children when I go, and who is going to feed my children if I don't make some money?" And we said, "Well, the two hours that you are spending at the literacy center will not have such an effect on your income. And moreover, we'll let you come to the center with your children, because many mothers are coming to the center with their children, so the children will get with each other to play, to get used to each other, and so forth." And she just insisted, "No, no, no, no." And so we said, "Well, we'll take an action, disciplinary action." So she started going. One day we happened to drop by her place. And we were just discussing. And there were also other people drinking the local beer. And the woman said, "What time do you have?" And we said, "About two o'clock." "Oh," she said, "I have to go"—this is after two months or so— "I have to go to my school." And we just looked at each other. And what amazed us was, she just brought her robe—her *netsala*—and she picked up her exercise book and she said, "You guys, you know how much you have drunk. Put the money on this table, and there is the lock: lock the door and put the key in such-and-such area." And she said, "I'll be back in about two hours' time, okay? But in case you want to leave earlier, please do that for me," and she just left. You know what? This woman

could have stayed behind, collected her money, and let her customers leave, and come late to school. But we felt that she had understood the importance of the program, how much it will help her. So after a year, in 1984, I had the chance to go to the same area. Believe it or not, this woman was instructing her children how to read and write—one of the small kids. So there are a lot of such things really taking place. Sometimes you try to persuade them to go. Sometimes you just insist that you'll take an action unless this person goes to school.

At first thought, a truthfulness (and rightness) claim vindicated under a condition of coercion seemed to me contradictory. Certainly Ayn Alem's account is self-justifying, as were similar narratives from other literacy campaign workers. But my second thought turned toward a consideration of the transformative function of education—a recognition, that, in some instances and literacy is one of them, the promise of education cannot be understood, and therefore cannot be appropriated, until the promise is fulfilled. Compulsory education is based in part on the same rationale that is evident in Ayn Alem's narrative, that children will later be grateful for what they are compelled to learn now. Applied to newly-literate adults, it's likely to prove even more quickly true: they will become advocates of literacy—and, indeed, the bartender in the story turns around and makes literacy compulsory for her children.[63] Resisters become supporters, endorsing not only the benefits of reading and writing but, in this case, the rightness of compulsory education and the truthfulness of the EPLF's claim to be working in the best interests of the Eritrean people—and to know what those interests are.

The Praxis of Negotiation and the Promise of Literacy

In addition to the activities and discourses of the literacy teachers which led to their acceptance in the communities in which they taught, they had the task of recruiting communities, and individuals one by one, to the classes. I want to examine a few recruitment narratives that provide examples of the operation of promise in the literacy campaigners' negotiations.

Saleh Mahmud "joined" the EPLF at age eleven. Since he "wasn't strong enough to fight in the front lines" he was sent to the newly-opened Zero School, where he completed grade four before being assigned as a literacy campaigner to work with the Muslim population in Semhar Province, the coastal plains along the Red Sea. At age fifteen, he faced the task of convincing Muslim women to join literacy classes.

> SALEH MAHMUD: Most of the husbands were working outside the country in Saudia. So we were telling them, for example, "You, you will write your letters to your husband yourself. And if your husband sent to you a letter, you will not expose it to others, your mystery; that means you will read it yourself. But now look: for example, your husband sends to you a secret; you have no way to take it for yourself; you will go to other people and tell him your secret. So teaching is beneficial for you." And we were doing such things.

Saleh Mahmud, of the Tigre nationality, joined the EPLF in 1977 and was a student at the Zero School. He served in the national literacy campaign. This photo was taken at the Teachers Training Institute, where Saleh was training teachers in the Tigre language.

LES GOTTESMAN: That's great! [Both laugh.] So people understood that, and they got interested.

SM: Gradually all of the people understood the benefit and started, even the Muslim women also, started to learn, and some of them completed the three years' course, some of them only one year. They were able to write and read.

My reflection here begins with my original response ("That's great!") to Saleh's negotiating stratagem. The promise of protected marital privacy (a minor one relative to the potentially wide application and transformative effects of reading skills) seemed to me to be a mere trick to lure the naive wives to literacy class. "That's great!" applauds Saleh's cleverness. On second thought, the tacit endorsement, in Saleh's ploy, of women's traditional segregation in rigidly confined social spaces and discourses seemed to me, frankly, reactionary. Eventually, however, I saw in Saleh's promise to the women his ability to enlist and encompass personal and cultural concerns into the vision of educational promise, though certain of the empowering possibilities of that promise go beyond current cultural (or personal) concerns. Stewart R. Clegg writes:

> A theory of power must look to the field of force in which power arrangements are fixed, coupled and constituted so that, intentionally or not, certain "nodal points" of practice are privileged in this unstable and shifting terrain. Better to think of power not as having two faces or three dimensions but as a process that may pass through distinct circuits of power and resistance. How these channels or circuits of power are fixed and reproduced is the crucial issue. A radical view of power thus would consist not in identifying what putative "real interests" are but in the strategies and practices by which, for instance, agents are recruited to views of their interests that align with the discursive field of force that the enrolling agency can construct.[64]

In another story, Saleh reveals the "unstable and shifting terrain" of power within a family when literacy became an issue:

SALEH MAHMUD: There was a woman whose husband was strictly religious, so he refused to let her go to the school. But she was having a great desire to learn. At the end, she decided to divorce from her husband, and she divorced. Before she was divorced, she was learning by her son. He was teaching her while the father was out. The son was going to school.

One time the husband came and he caught them. But she divorced, and got her freedom to learn, and learned. After that, she married another man. Unfortunately, the other man was also not in a position to leave her to learn and to exercise what she learned. So again she started the process with her son. But at this time, the process was not difficult, because she knew how to read and write, and her son was sending to her letters. And she told me this after she became grade four. She told me, "Look, since I was with my first husband, I was not able to communicate with my son unless he will come. But now, even though my husband is like that one, I am able to communicate with my son with letters."

Saleh told these women the truth. Now that they do read and write letters, they can and do acknowledge that Saleh's promise has been fulfilled; they recognize the rightness of his promise and of literacy, that is, its appropriateness to their concerns:

> SALEH MAHMUD: And the previous example that I gave you, the one who sent a letter from Saudia to his wife, also were told me by another woman. Previously, we were telling *them*, but after they learned they told *me*, "See. Three years ago you were telling us about this fact. But now it happened really."

As with compulsory education, the promise cannot be appropriated until it is fulfilled. Each subsequent act of literacy, by enlarging fulfillment, extends and redefines promise. When the women perform further, varied acts of reading and writing, then promise along with fulfillment will enlarge and change also. In the case of the woman who unluckily chose two anti-literacy husbands, literacy promised and fulfilled the desire not only to read and write but also for power to be redistributed in the family: literacy both strengthened and justified the literacy alliance between the mother and son.

These anecdotes also reveal the two sides of Schrag's formulation of communicative praxis. "Communication and praxis intersect within a common space. Communication is a qualification of praxis. It is the manner in which praxis comes to expression"[65]—in Saleh's narrative the concept of "literacy" which is communicated is the specific practical benefit of literacy the women are won to. "But praxis is also a qualification of communication in that it determines communication as a *performing* and an *accomplishing*"[66]—

so the *expressed promise* of literacy—letter reading and writing—was not appropriated by the women until they had accomplished the competence and performed it as specific acts they valued; then they appropriated the whole: promise and fulfillment, meaning, competence, and acts of literacy. When these women discover and engage in new applications of their reading and writing skills, then the meaning of these competencies will broaden. I can illustrate this by amplifying the personal example I have already used, my hospital visit for nosebleeds in Asmara.[67] As I explained, the validity claims of Dr. Alem were vindicated informally, her language and symbolic acts were congruent with my expectations of what medical care should be like, and I accepted her diagnosis and treatment. But even this was tentative. One thing more had to happen for me to appropriate this as competent medical practice: my nosebleeds had to stop. After a few days of nose drops, they did. Only then did I appropriate the entire episode as "a positive experience of the Eritrean health care system" (as I now characterize it).

Negotiation tales abound in my research transcripts. Here a small bribe reveals the elasticity (or hypocrisy) in "religious" tradition:

SENAIT LIJAM: There are some religious values that women should veil their face and should not go out. We [the National Union of Eritrean Women] have, for example, opened an adult education in Gash and Barka areas where most of the people are Muslims, especially in Barka. So the first time they say, "Hey, my woman is not going to go out, she should veil her face, and she's not going to go out from the house to go to the adult education classes." But we insisted. We said, "Why? Why?" We are not going to tell them to go against their religion. We don't care what religion they profess. But it is a must that a woman should liberate herself from the burden of illiteracy. She should be literate to start with. Otherwise, if she does not have the skill of, at least, writing and reading, she is not going to progress in any kind of skill training for the future, to make herself acquainted with some kind of skill that will lead her life. So we insisted, and finally they accepted it. And now they are going to school. And sometimes we also try to convince them by giving the women some

incentives. Those who attend the adult education program, we try to give them some kind of sugar at the end
of the week—a half kilo or a quarter of a kilo—so they
can take it home and then use it for coffee or tea for the
family. So the man becomes convinced, because she's
bringing at least something. So you see here, it was not his
deep religious faith that he wanted to hinder or stop his
wife from school. It was an excuse. So when we give some
incentive, he will say, "Okay, so go." He even tries to send
his daughter: "And you also go!" Because she also is
going to bring some sugar or something else.

Power not only shifts and adjusts, but may also display paradoxi-
cal qualities. A cultural restriction may structure alternative free-
doms for expression or action. The thick texture of communication
and praxis, in Schrag's formula, or the integrative function of ideology, in Ricoeur's,[68] may explain the unexpected accommodations which culture makes with irresistible or inevitable innovation—so that economic opportunities are seized, so that castes can
meet and conduct their business. The same child status which pre-
vented his being taken seriously in the public forum allowed Saleh
Mahmud a surprising entrée to sheltered Muslim women—and
them access to literacy:

Especially in the Muslim region, if I weren't a child, they
weren't coming to the school. Because they don't expose
their face to strong enough man. But since I was a child,
there is no matter to oppose my teaching. They were
treating me as their child. So it helped me. Even in their
homes, the grownups can't enter the room of the
women, but we, as children, we can get in and speak
with them. Even with the bride, with the newly married
girl. It doesn't get out until three or four years. We were
entering to their rooms, to their homes, and we were
communicating with them—because society was looking
at us as children.

The instability of power is both sobering and comic, and is precisely the point, in one of the literacy campaign's propaganda skits
Zecarias Tedros described:

They can understand the use of education because we were preparing some theaters which invites them to, makes them conscious about school. For example, it is a fable, like a children's story, but it makes an impression on them. Let's say I am an Ethiopian officer, and you are a citizen in X town. You do something, and I say, "Oh, what's-your-name, I wrote this paper, and give this paper to Mr. X." And you don't know what is written here, because you have not an idea about reading. But what is written here is, "Kill this one because he is a member of *shabiya*, of the EPLF. So kill this one." I write it, and you give it to the police officer. And when he reads this paper: "Oh, you are a member of the EPLF. You are going to be killed now" or "You are going to be sentenced to 14 years." He says so. And the peasants, the audience, can understand from this, if this guy had an idea about reading, about education, how to read, he can save himself from death or from something like that.

Here literacy offers the possibility to turn the tables on the arrogant oppressor: if the hapless Eritrean could have read the note, then it would be the Ethiopian officer who plays the fool for assuming that "Eritrean" equals "illiterate." Solomon Woldmichel analyzed colonial power and the teaching strategy it called for:

> LES GOTTESMAN: There's a lot of interest and enthusiasm for education everywhere in the country. Why? How do people think? They think education is important, but what do they think will happen?

> SOLOMON WOLDMICHEL: The main thing I think that they interrelate their ignorance with their subjugation. The main cause for their subjugation under colonialism is their ignorance. Most of the time when we are politicizing the people, we just interrelate ignorance with the subjugation. And this made them very keen to see their problems, because they don't really know what subjugation or what colonialism means.

> LG: They just know that they are having a hard time.

SW: Yeah. They don't know, really. They don't understand because they don't have any knowledge of—they are ignorant. The main thing the colonialists exploit is the ignorance of the people. To subjugate. They cheat the people with *simple* things. We are always relating, when we are teaching them, what the colonialists are doing when they are subjugating the people, how they exploit the ignorance of the people. We don't only fight—at the same time when we are fighting we have to learn to know what they are doing. Our backwardness is our main problem. And to solve our backwardness, to be equal to our colonizers, we have to fight at the same time we have to learn. That's what we teach the people.

LG: And they understand that.

SW: Yeah. They understand that.

The skit appealed to the desire to resist, encouraged resistance, and posed literacy as resistance and as a means to greater resistance. It so sure-footedly portrayed colonial relations that the main thrust of its caricature served not to indict Ethiopian injustice but to criticize the audience. In the skit, illiteracy adds insult to injury. The shame of ignorance, worse than being merely public—exposed to the audience—is collective and shared by them, yet, embodied in a play—in play—is empowering because it frees the imagination to discern alternative possibilities. "Games of freedom," says Frank Hearn, "by temporarily liberating people from the coercion of the 'real' world, provide a vision and an experience of autonomy and community which, when sustained, make the unresponsiveness of society unbearable."[69] Power shapes rationality—Ethiopian power makes it rational, in the absence of means to resist, not to do so. The imaginative variation of the self in play supplies the critical distance on the self that opens into the interest in emancipation.

For Habermas, the hermeneutic understanding described here is not merely reflective, but "action-oriented"—"designed to guarantee, within cultural traditions, the possible action-oriented self-understanding of individuals and groups. . . . It makes possible the form of unconstrained consensus and the type of open intersubjectivity on which communicative action depends"[70]—and the emancipatory interest in freedom from domination, according to Christopher Broniak, "*is* communicative action, living both actively and reactively, critically and creatively, thinking as well as feeling."[71] The "ground of this interest," Robert P. Badillo adds, is in the power of critical inquiry to "detect, oppose and eradicate whatever does not favor the well-being of the social unit taken as a whole or in terms of its constitutive members."[72]

There may be, in the literacy campaign skit, an additional cultural-characterological dimension from which the protagonist's predicament gains dramatic power, and the message motivational potency, and that is its reading of Eritreans' (the audience's) "cultural personality," if Sister Mary Thomas Johnston is right:

> I find sometimes as a matter of fact I make more of a thing about my not having known something, or having made a mistake, just to try and be the example to students that there's nothing wrong in making a mistake. Because here—I don't know if it's a cultural thing but certainly students have told me—it's bad to say you've made a mistake. You never say you make a mistake. You're always right—even when you do realize you have made a mistake.

While such a trait of face-saving bravado, or denial, may provide, in Clegg's terminology, a "nodal point" ("intentionally" or not) for a propagandistic appeal within the "field of force" of power arrangements[73] the skit describes, I hasten to add that no Eritreans, only Europeans (of thirty and eight years' residency in Eritrea, to be sure), spoke to me of this "cultural" "bad" "habit," in both cases as a problem education could and should take on:

> PAUL HIGHFIELD: The Tigrinya are very shy people, afraid to speak, partly because they're afraid to make mistakes: if they make mistakes, then people laugh at them. That's a very bad cultural habit which everyone, when you point it out to them, people are aware of it, but on a deep level, you can't do much to change it. Amongst our students in the Revolution School we were changing that. A lot of them were bold and confident. We did find that a difference. Including young women as well. It was a remarkable change.

Although the alleged personality trait remains insufficiently documented for me to designate it a nodal point where Eritreans can be enlisted to transformative practice, significantly both Zecarias Tedros, regarding the effect of the pro-literacy parable on audiences, and Highfield, regarding a change in students' self-presentation, pronounce the negotiation successful.

Students as Teachers, Teachers as Students

Teacher-student and teacher-community relationships are also nodal points of power. Teachers traditionally have *power over* students and *standing in* the community. But the literacy teachers' self-assumed power, and their own belief in it, derived from nontraditional sources: technical expertise, book learning, modern social practices, scientific method, and revolutionary cause. Further, they understood that their project could not be literacy only: "In many cases the young people [of the literacy campaign] do not limit themselves to being teachers, but become social 'animators.'"[74] They had valuable skills and knowledge to offer, but they were outsiders, and they were young.

Although the teachers' youthfulness gave some groups and individuals reason for resisting the proffered classes, other communities utilized the category of youth to reestablish traditional generational relationships of authority, such as Sister Mary Thomas Johnston described:

> The parents, mother and father, were the first educators. The schoolhouse, the teacher, was well respected, and they learned. The church, the priest taught, and their fellows in the school—and the street. When they were in the street playing, they learned. If you did something wrong, you were scolded by *any* grownup around.

Many teachers described themselves as having been adopted, as being treated as the sons and daughters of villagers. Their relationships with younger community members had the characteristics of older to younger siblings:

> LES GOTTESMAN: What motivates a shepherd to want education?

AYN ALEM MARCOS: First of all, the type of teachers we managed to use were almost of their own age—as young as they were. And seeing them, kids of the same age, speaking English, writing on the blackboard, and having good, clean—although not expensive—clothes, this and that. The cultural level of the young teachers really attracts them and motivates them. And, besides, this young teacher jokes with them, he plays football with them, and helps them even tilling the land whenever there is a collective tilling of land. They psychologically completely identify themselves. And later, after three or four or five months, parents started to complain about their children. The complaint was, the children were so much motivated that they sometimes forget their main duty: they lose maybe a kid or sheep because they go under a tree and start to study their lessons, or even getting engaged in playing a new game that's been introduced by the teachers—football, volleyball, so forth. So, this was the experience we had. Later, even, most of these shepherds happened to join the People's Liberation Army. That was another step.

The villagers provided guidance not to, or not only to, the teachers personally, but to their project, and that "ma[de] us love them," Abraham Bahre explained.

ABRAHAM BAHRE: We were being informed by them in achieving that aim or in the things we were doing. In talking we may do some mistakes, and we may be in a hurry. These were the things they were informing us. They were communicating with us. And we had also a committee from the people, the committee which takes care of the education. It punishes the mistakes of the people, the people who didn't abide by the regulations. It also informed us, it is better to do these things, it is better not to teach them on these days because they are interfering with religion—so many things that we don't know.

LES GOTTESMAN: In order for the education to succeed,

the teachers have to learn from the students, particularly when the students are adults.

AB: Yeah, that's true.

Despite arrogance and obtuseness, the campaigners did, indeed,
seek this instruction and cultural knowledge, and social initiation
by the rural people, sometimes systematically:

ABRAHAM BAHRE: In some villages, we had to take one
hour in order to finish that village.

LES GOTTESMAN: You mean just to go from house to
house.

AB: Yeah, to go. One house here with its plot of land,
another place there. To go to know what they want, and
what their feeling is, what problems they face, and on
the other hand to learn, so we can learn from them.

In part, the teachers' cultural openness was a result of the EPLF's
"training":

KALEAB HAILE: What we did was, we give introductory
courses for the campaigners. We armed them through
community development programs, what is the social
aspect of the reality of our people, what are the beliefs
they have, whether it can be a superstitiousness or a traditional belief, and what are the ethics of the people, what
is their religion, and what are the social conditions in general of the people. And then we gave agriculture courses,
in which we helped the people in improving their life conditions, gardening, planting vegetables, and so forth.

And the teachers doggedly pursued learning wherever it was available:

SALEH MAHMUD: I had to work fifteen hours a day.
Sometimes I had to go two hours away from the camp
to sleep. Therefore, the chance to improve yourself is
very few, very few. But I was trying to do something.
Even if I had half an hour, I was reading. Even if I had
got *anyone* who had better knowledge than me, I ask
him. And in the summer, we were having summer cours-

es. But the summer courses were not simple. I was in the Semhar province on the Red Sea coast, but the courses were given at Gash. You have to travel two weeks. And sometimes, since we had no way to cross Eritrea directly from east to west, we were forced to go through Tigray, so the way takes one month. Because of the enemy, we couldn't pass, cut directly through Eritrea. So we were forced to go through Tigray. So the way takes one month. And the course takes one month. Another month for returning. In this way, I attended three courses in the Gash province and three courses in Sahel province in the north, the far north of Eritrea. And I was coming from far southeast Eritrea.

These factors, the community's tutelage and the teachers' desire to learn, fed into the process of configuring the "proper" relationship of the teachers to the community. In this way the teachers were, rather than marginalized, validated for the unique, useful educational function they served.

Postliberation Negotiation: Language of Instruction

The negotiated issues of the literacy campaign in the 1980s have now become long-settled questions. But negotiations continue, between the educational policy-makers and the diverse communities of the nation. What has not changed is the personnel: the same educators whose campaign stories amazed me face the new issues with, I believe, some wisdom and justifiable confidence.

Following liberation, negotiation mainly revolved around the question of language. The government wants primary education to be in the mother tongue of each community. For "[t]hose nationalities, whose vernaculars are not written, the EPLF has ad[o]pted the curriculum system of transliteration, [wherein] the [L]atin alphabet is used as the medium of reading and writing."[75] That, Girmay Haile said,

> has resolved a lot of the problems, being able to supply elementary level education in their own mother tongue. It has made it much more easier for students and also for teachers to communicate, to transfer the necessary knowledge for that level.

But another issue had surfaced. Girmay, a member of the Planning and Programming Division of the Department of Education, explained that the language policy of the government prescribed that

> any nationality has the right to use its own language as the medium of instruction—its own language or any other language that it chooses as a medium of instruction at the elementary school level. So sometimes instead of using their mother tongue, in some areas they prefer some other language, they prefer Tigrinya, or they prefer Arabic because they think that since these two languages are more widely used in many parts of Eritrea and everybody knows this language so our children could benefit more from this, and so on.

Of non-native languages, most requested, apparently, was for instruction to be in Arabic.

> PAUL HIGHFIELD: Some ethnic groups, or some communities within some ethnic groups, are saying, "Well, we want to learn in Arabic and not in Tigre or Afar because we spend all our time trading with the Yemenis and the Saudis. We use Afar amongst ourselves, so why do we need to learn Afar anymore?" Well, also for religious reasons: "We want to know Arabic more so that we can study the Koran and so on—but also so we can further ourselves through trade."

The Department of Education saw pedagogical and political liabilities, and cultural loss, in non-native-language instruction. "First of all," Tesfamicael Gerahtu, head of the Department's Curriculum Development Institute, explained, "educationally, taking into consideration the psychology of the children, it won't be an easy matter to study in a second language. So there are certain pedagogic and psychological constraints in using a second language." Further, Highfield observed, some groups

> don't recognize the importance of developing their own language—linguistically and from the point of view of having it as a written language. They don't recognize

that that's a key part of their identity and their culture that needs not just to be preserved but developed.

In Gerahtu's analysis, the pedagogical and cultural issues are intertwined with the government's interest in national unity and reconstruction:

> Second of all, if you use your mother tongue, or if the mother tongue is used in educating a certain nationality, what you are actually doing is, you're trying to develop the pride, nationality pride, of the community, so that they could be motivated and interested to promote their culture, to participate equally in the nation's overall reconstruction strategies, so that they could play their part in the national unity of the country. So it has this advantage. So one of the basic points that we have been stressing during the armed struggle was, we have to strive for equal participation of all the nationalities in the national liberation struggle. If we are to assert this equal participation of all these nationalities, they have to be educated, and the easiest way to educate these people is through their own culture and language. Of course, just because sometimes they don't realize these objective arguments, sometimes simply from superficial and emotional attitudes or sometimes also from some religious influences, they say, for example, "We would prefer Arabic," "we would prefer Tigrinya," or "we would prefer another thing."

Negotiation of the language issue takes place in the community itself, in a participatory process:

> LES GOTTESMAN: So if a community wanted a language other than the mother tongue, there would be something that would be worth discussing, and continuing to try to make them see the advantages of the mother tongue?
>
> TESFAMICAEL GERAHTU: Yes, of course. Because there is the parents' committee; in the people's council there is a section for social and educational services. So through the people's council, through the parents' committee, and through the community at large, at various times

various discussions pertaining to such policies are made. It's only by convincing the people that you try to gear the development or direct it to the desired way.

But, of course, traditional authority is a forceful voice in the debate:

> PAUL HIGHFIELD: Some of the ethnic groups are saying now that they want to learn in Arabic rather than their own language because they can't see that in order to be able to preserve their identity and so on they should learn at the elementary level in their own language. And they say the Muslim religion and the Muslim people are Arabic; therefore, we have to learn in Arabic rather than our own language—we can take our own language as a subject but not as a medium of instruction. How do you begin to change people's attitudes on that? It's very difficult if the elites are demanding that: then the ordinary people won't be able to argue against that. Well, you have to try to argue against it, but you can't force the people, you see. Of course, we try and argue against it when they're making that decision, try and point out the advantages and so on, but if they say "We want to learn in Arabic rather than in Tigre," if they say "No, we'll learn in Arabic," then basically we can't do anything about it.

The language discussion is not confined to villages in isolation, but is also regional. Highfield pointed to the proactive Tigre population of the Maria Tselam area of Senhit Province,

> one of the areas which says, "No, we do want to learn in Tigre, not in Arabic." They are now arguing against other people in the province, in Senhit province, who do want their schools to go Arabic, and they say, "No, no, we don't want that to happen to ours."

Many educators mentioned Maria Tselam to me. It is clearly an EPLF success story, where the population embraced education, and where social and material change ensued:

> TESFAMICAEL GERAHTU: There are areas, completely semi-nomadic, and we started to teach them in their

mother tongue in 1981, and in the last ten years we have produced many, many youngsters who finished their middle school and took some short training courses in various occupational areas, in health, in agriculture, to be teachers, and many other things, and also mechanics, in handicrafts, and they're serving the community now in this semi-nomadic area called Maria Tselam. So in ten years, we have been able to effect a significant social, cultural, and economic change in this area. The education has been completely the instrument for effecting this change. So, for example, in this area we have been using the mother tongue as a medium of instruction and still continue.

Promulgating native languages will continue to be difficult. In 1993, the Department of Education was laboring to produce written versions of some of the languages, training teachers—and desperately seeking teachers to train—in the minority languages. An adequate number of native speakers teaching would, Highfield thought,

change attitudes towards the local language, and then therefore towards their own culture and their own sense of self-identity, which is important. But you'd still need other external factors to develop the language; otherwise it would tend to die out. You would need to have, say, a regional newspaper and more books produced in minority languages that were read outside of the classroom, documents translated, and documenting discussions held at the assembly level produced in that language rather than in the two languages, Tigrinya and Arabic, that are—even though it's not been officially announced— these sort of official languages. Unless those sorts of policies are adopted, then you're going to be fighting a losing battle from the point of view of trying to preserve some of the smaller ethnic languages. I don't know if the government is aware of what needs to be done from that point of view. I've discussed it informally with the people in the Education and Information Ministries, and they say, "Yeah, that sort of thing is important, but"— you know—"the resources don't exist at the moment."

Legitimation

All of the negotiations discussed so far led to education being accepted and integrated into the social practice of the community. But not all negotiations were successful. Woldemichael Ghebretensae considered literacy work among the Afar a total failure:

> That Tigre area was successful but in the Danakil area, the Afar, we were not successful. We were not able to get student education. Their work is attached with the sea. They always go and come. They don't care about education. If a child is about ten or twelve years old, he gets on the boat. They go fishing, they go as a merchant marine from Eritrea to Saudi Arabia or somewhere else. They are just involved in the sea. They don't care about their education. So in that area we were not successful.

I was surprised to learn that the population surrounding the Zero School steadfastly spurned education:

> PAUL HIGHFIELD: The area where we were was much more conservative than other areas. The nomads who were in the area where the Revolution School was never sent any child to the Revolution School.

> LES GOTTESMAN: It was open to them if they wanted access?

> PH: Yeah. Yeah. In fact I think the last year we were there before liberation, we got two nomads attending classes—two nomads themselves but not the children. They were afraid of their children learning a different culture and growing up and then joining the EPLF and then being killed. Or leaving. Another thing, they thought it was maybe too radical for them, altering this traditional way of life: they didn't want it.

> LG: Were there any ways in which the Front tried to introduce education to that particular group?

> PH: The teachers and the people's administration in our area, they tried it constantly, but they refused. I mean,

little kids every day used to wander in and out around the classrooms, because the classrooms were under the trees and so on, with their goats, seeing the education process going on.

LG: But they never joined?

PH: No.

Yet, Highfield added, contact with the EPLF "did influence them in other ways. They became much more organized in a way, more settled in one area"—a major change in their way of life. It is clear that *(a)* the pastoralists accepted and resisted change consistently as a community and *(b)* acceptance and rejection were not expressed as such, abstractly, but were embodied in specific patterns of action that observers "read" as symbolic of these decisive concepts.[76]

In another example, Eritrea's referendum on independence was a broadly symbolic (or multi-concept) assertion to the world of Eritrea as a nation and "Eritrean" as a national and cultural identity. At the same time, everybody knew, the referendum was an act of legitimating a specific government, its policies, and a leader, Isaias Afwerki—none of which were on the ballot.

What runs through these examples are concepts—cultural preservation and adaptation, individual identity and legitimation of authority, the force of tradition and the ideology of mass democratic choice—manifested in symbols that are understood by their participation in systems of symbolic expression: people voting with ballots and "with their feet." Thought, says Geertz,

> consists of the construction and manipulation of symbol systems, which are employed as models of other systems, physical, organic, social, psychological, and so forth, in such a way that the structure of these other systems—and, in the favorable case, how they may therefore be expected to behave—is, as we say, "understood."[77]

Because the behavior of these "other systems" and the course of human events unfold in time, the symbolic systems that humans construct, manipulate, and understand generally take, or participate in, narrative forms. "The understanding of action," says Ricoeur, "in effect, is not limited to a familiarity with the conceptual network of action and its symbolic mediations. It goes so far as to recognize in action temporal structures that call for narration."[78]

> Human action occurs within cultural settings that maintain symbolic narrative forms for use in the articulation of action. These symbolic forms have a public character and are not the private understandings of a particular actor. Thus, an act is undertaken with the knowledge of what it will mean to the community in which it takes place.... The communal significance of actions confers an initial "readability" on them. The manners, customs, and other social agreements also supply an evaluation of actions in terms of their conformity to moral norms, and they define which actions are good or bad, better or worse.[79]

Performing this evaluative function, then,

> representations are principally systems of justification and legitimation, either of the established order or of an order likely to replace it. These systems of legitimation can be called, if one likes, ideologies, on the condition that ideology not be too quickly identified with mystification and that ideologies be recognized as having a more primitive and more fundamental function than that of distortion—that of providing a sort of metalanguage for the symbolic mediations immanent in collective action. Ideologies are first of all representations that repeat and reinforce symbolic mediations, investing these mediations, for example, in narratives, chronicles, through which the community "repeats" in a way its own origin, commemorates it and celebrates it.[80]

Ideology inherently supposes that different narratives are possible and available. Ideology stands at the fork in the "narrative path"[81] pointing to right or left as *the* way to a happy ending. That is how, in Geertz's account, ideology "makes an autonomous politics possible" and why, where divergent narratives are discovered or emerge, it must: ideology provides

the authoritative concepts that render [politics] meaningful, the suasive images by means of which it can be
sensibly grasped. It is, in fact, precisely at the point at
which a political system begins to free itself from the
immediate governance of received tradition, from the
direct and detailed guidance of religious or philosophical canons on the one hand and from the unreflective
precepts of conventional moralism on the other, that
formal ideologies tend first to emerge and take hold.[82]

Chapter 5 discussed two aspects of ideology: ideology as distortion
and ideology as integration. As distortion "[t]he word 'ideology,' of
course, has a somewhat bad name."[83] For example,

[i]t is Habermas's contention that in every communicative situation in which a consensus is established under
coercion or under similar types of condition, we are likely to be confronting instances of systematically distorted
communication. This is, in his view, the contemporary
formulation of ideology.[84]

In this definition authoritative concepts and claims are ideological
that maintain their legitimacy despite the fact that they *could not* be
redeemed by ideal discourse.[85] However, for Ricoeur, "[t]he model
that sets ideology in opposition to reality is inadequate because reality is symbolically mediated from the beginning."[86] "[B]efore being
constraining, norms organize action, in the sense that they config-
ure it, give it form and sense."[87] So,

if we separate off the other two layers of ideology—ideology as distortion and as the legitimation of a system of
order or power—the integrative function of ideology, the
function of preserving an identity, remains.... [N]o
group and no individual are possible without this integrative function.[88]

On this last point, Ricoeur turns to Erik H. Erikson's analysis of
identity formation. Ideology, says Erikson, "harnesses the young
individual's aggressive and discriminative energies" to a group
identity.

[I]dentity and ideology are two aspects of the same

process. Both provide the necessary condition for further individual maturation and, with it, for the next higher form of identification, namely the solidarity linking common identities in joint living, acting, and creating.[89]

In this function, ideology is integrative *through* distortion, which Erikson denotes nonpejoratively as formula, structure, creed, simplification, and the like:

> More generally . . . an ideological system is a coherent body of shared images, ideas, and ideals which, whether based on a formulated dogma, an implicit *Weltanschauung*, a highly structured world image, a political creed, or, indeed, a scientific creed (especially if applied to [humans]), or a "way of life," provides for the participants a coherent, if systematically s[i]mplified, over-all orientation in space and time, in means and ends.[90]

Ricoeur concurs:

> the concept of integration is a presupposition of the other two main concepts of ideology—legitimation and distortion—but actually functions ideologically by means of these other two factors.[91]

In other words, ideology integrates social life *by* systems of distortion—providing "templates for the organization of social and psychological processes"[92]—and *by* legitimation of authority: "It is not by chance that a specific place for ideology exists in politics, because politics is the location where the basic images of a group finally provide rules for using power."[93] The negative connotation of distortion, Ricoeur maintains, should be reserved for distortions that mask "frozen" relationships, that limit possibility in the interests of preserving power only.[94] But the integrative function of ideology, as well as constraining, makes dynamic social action possible:

> [I]t is . . . the attempt of ideologies to render otherwise incomprehensible social situations meaningful, to so construe them as to make it possible to act purposefully within them, that accounts both for the ideologies' highly figurative nature and for the intensity with which, once accepted, they are held. A metaphor extends language by

broadening its semantic range, enabling it to express meanings it cannot or at least cannot yet express literally, so the head-on clash of literal meanings in ideology—the irony, the hyperbole, the overdrawn antithesis—provides novel symbolic frames against which to match the myriad "unfamiliar somethings" that, like a journey to a strange country, are produced by a transformation in political life. Whatever else ideologies may be—projections of unacknowledged fears, disguises for ulterior motives, phatic expressions of group solidarity—they are, most distinctively, maps of problematic social reality and matrices for the creation of collective conscience.[95]

At this point I will turn to two dramatic stories in which Eritrean communities faced problematic social reality during the national literacy campaign, and in which inseparable concepts of integration and legitimation were embodied in dynamic, symbolic social action. The storyteller is Ayn Alem Marcos, whose gift for narrative richness makes detailed analysis particularly enjoyable.

Story number one:

AYN ALEM MARCOS: One day these youngsters came to this village, and they were teaching. It was the rainy season, sometime in July or August, and there was torrential rainfall. So the youngsters were told by the adults, the community, to spend the night in that village—because most of our intermittent rivers are flooded, and you cannot cross them, and it was dangerous. There are certain areas where you just only teach and go back to your camp. In this area they were not supposed to spend the night. So, because of the condition, and they were told that the enemy had not visited this village for a *long* period of time, so the kids were convinced to spend the night. Guess what! About four o'clock in the morning, the enemy came and surrounded the village. [Long pause.] And the village informers came and knocked at this house and said, "The enemy's here." So the kids said, "Okay, you guys relax—we have our Kalashnikovs with us."

LES GOTTESMAN: So they were planning on trying to shoot their way out.

AAM: Shoot their way out. If they are shot, it means that's it, and if they are—I mean, you don't have any other choice; if you are captured, still you will be, after interrogation, you'll be killed. And if you just try to break through, it's luck: it's 50-50. So the villagers insisted. In the evening, they got together a priest, a village elder, mothers got together. "What can we do with these kids?" So the priest said—there were four youngsters, I think— "I will take two and put them in my church and dress them like deacons and conduct services." So immediately—it didn't take them time—they took these guys, the chosen two guys—the third one was a girl—took them there, and immediately they brought a razor blade and shaved their hair, 'cause it's an Afro, with curls and so forth, and everybody can tell that they're—they shaved their heads and put deacon clothes and the priest started to do his ritual. And the two, a girl and a boy, a certain father said, "I'll take care of these youngsters." He went home, he undressed them and changed their clothes with peasant clothes, and just kept them at his place. And they threw away their—this is our sandal [indicating his own EPLF plastic sandals]—and their clothes and everything was hidden; their gun was hidden in a very faraway place, and about seven, seven-thirty in the morning, the enemy called a village meeting. So they

Ayn Alem "Joe" Marcos at the Teachers Training Institute.

gathered. The father who promised to take care of the two youngsters brought these youngsters with him to the meeting—the fighters. So they sat there, and the enemy gave a lecture, and one of the topics they were discussing was that we were—I mean EPLF's people were—coming to the village and giving them political education and academic stuff. [Laughs.] And they told them that this is a drug! [Laughs.] And they shouldn't take it seriously. And anybody who is really taking it seriously, now—this is the time—expose these people who are collaborating with these people. And everybody got quiet. They said, "Come on, come on." The whole village was there. Believe it or not, they stayed until two o'clock, if I'm not wrong. Two o'clock in the sun. In the open air. And then, eventually, they didn't expose anybody, and mothers were shivering who knew that these young people were in the meeting itself, and the priest with his deacon was in his church—he didn't come, although the church was searched. And then by the end of the day, the enemy left, and the youngsters returned back to their base area. And nobody, nobody said a word.

The second story:

AYN ALEM MARCOS: Another time—the village was surrounded. Okay, this is another village. That one was in a Christian area in Sahel, the highlands. This was in a dry, hot area, a Muslim area, in Senhit. The enemy as usual came, at daybreak and surrounded the village. So the teachers—there were about five or six of them—they were told that the enemy was there. So they didn't have any other choice: just to hide themselves. So there's this plant—it grows dense; usually it grows in a desert area. So they said, we have two choices. One is to go and hide in that plant; and the plant is actually in the center of the village. And then with their arms, like their hand grenades and so forth, if anything happens, to throw two or three of the grenades that they have at the enemy, and then use the rest for themselves. All right? So they sat there. So the enemy, as usual, gathered the villagers and started to politicize them, this and that and that. But in the meantime—since the period was so extended—in the meantime, the soldiers used to come and piss on that plant. They were urinating—and the fighters, too, they had to do it right there, in front of their comrades. And that took also—what?—four hours or five hours, something like that. They stayed there. And the villagers didn't—they knew that they were there—and nobody said a word.

In these stories, physical, social, and imaginative reintegration of the community occurs through symbolic acts and transformations.

> The concept of symbolic action is notable because it emphasizes description of social processes more by tropes—stylistic figures—than by labels. Geertz warns that if we do not master the rhetoric of public discourse, then we cannot articulate the expressive power and the rhetorical force of social symbols.[96]

Integration and transformation are comprehensive: both physical and imaginative. In the first story, the crisis results because the teachers stayed too long, at the villagers' urging, as though a tentative integration demanded an immediate test of its most dangerous implications.

> The concept of integration precisely has to do with the threat of the lack of identity. . . . What a group fears most is no longer being able to identify itself because of crises and confusions creating strain; the task is to cope with this strain.[97]

In any event, the teachers dropped, if only temporarily, their itinerant relationship to the village and made it their home. Alerted to danger, village authorities and "mothers" meet—a family model. The crisis brings a confluence of collective and individual decision—consensus. The process is one of discovering possibilities that can be neither only collective nor only individual, for no group decision or vote could safely compel an unwilling priest or father to take responsibility for the teachers, and no individual action to protect them could be carried out without the entire community's conspiracy—a conspiracy of silence, at least. Now the teachers' conformity to village norms (e.g.,

speech and manners, discussed earlier in this chapter) must take physical form. Their hair—the guerrillas affected a long "Afro" style—is
cut, their trademark EPLF-manufactured sandals and their military
fatigues are hidden, and their weapons are taken to a "faraway
place." They don the clothing symbolic of customary village roles:
peasant youth and church deacon. The teachers who had been physically *in* are now physically *of* the village; survival of all depends on
their *invisible* presence. Similarly, the fabric of village life must undergo a change, while appearing not to. The fabric of communicative
praxis, in Schrag's metaphor, is stretched to admit new meanings. The
most patterned of village institutions, the church, is opened to a new
social function. A church service is started, outside the scheduled rou-
tine of rituals, and with the new "deacons." The peasant father
adopts two children; they are transported, transformed—he brings
them to his home, changes their appearance, and then brings them to
the compulsory meeting where the (ironic) "truth" of the transformation will be tested. Simply, it is shown to be possible and is actually experienced that the teachers can be physically integrated into the
village. They are *more of* the village than *not of* it.

Physical space is transformed, actually and imaginatively. The
church in the first story and the bush in the second become actual
hideouts and potential sites of battle and certain death.

In the second story, the teachers hide in the actual and symbolic
center of town. But the center displays a liminality parallel to their
own. They are of the "bush" (the "field," the rural terrain of war)
and in the town, just as the bush is of the desert and in the town.
Then, in the act of becoming *of* the town, the teachers inhabit the
bush. This desert plant anomalously urbanized is a space of transformation, an in-between space so prominent, so imposing it renders
the easily identifiable teachers invisible. In both stories the teachers
are, as it were, hiding in plain sight, where they will not be looked
for, where "the trees cannot be seen for the forest," as though the
social and political gulf between the soldiers and the Eritreans is also
a cognitive gulf. The Ethiopians can't even see whom they are urinating on, and the very unpleasantness of being urinated on is, for
the teachers, a reproach of their foes.

Just as space is transformed, time is altered. Village activities are
interrupted, and at a strange hour. For the villagers lined-up at gun-
point in the center of town, the hours (one imagines) seem endless.

But, as well as the actual transformation of identity, space, and time, there is also the imaginative transformation of physical surroundings and social narrative. In a vivid, imaginative narrative that had to have been replayed with variations over and over in the minds of the assembled villagers, the church in the first village and the bush in the center of the second village became deadly battlefields. Imaginative social roles and consequences were unavoidably offered for consideration, in a process that can be compared to play. Hiding the young teachers in the church, in the family, or in the bush in the center of town is a form of play—no less so because the game is deadly—encompassing familiar elements of children's games: costuming, concealment, imposture, bluffing, waiting out, and so on. It is helpful here to recall Hearn's assertion that the "freedom" of play is vital to "discredit . . . the present order [and] legitimate resistance."[98] In this play, role possibilities are actually as well as imaginatively extended, in, Ricoeur maintains, "the transformation of everything into its true being."[99] The priest becomes a fighter—he is certainly endangered as such. The family becomes the family of a fighter, subject to persecution as such. Children become responsible members of the community whose understanding of the situation must be depended on if they are not, innocently, to give away the game. The center of town becomes the site of a (real) battle of nerves and (an imagined but potentially real) one of bullets and hand grenades should the fighters be discovered—and thus forever transformed in memories which themselves transform the rememberers and their possibilities for future acts.

Similarly, these situations and actions, and the decisions they result from, are indelibly inscribed in the history and praxis of the communities. The villages assembled at these meetings become metaphors for themselves in an ideal state of unity, solidarity, gravity, resistance, intelligence, cunning, and performance under stress. The villages live their most dangerous and demanding possibilities and survive. As history, the collectively scripted accounts of these events that later emerge are ideological because in them new levels and patterns of community integration are performed and accomplished. As praxis, these events become a model of preparedness and action for self-protection. As for the teachers, they will grow their hair and otherwise readopt the signs of their identity as liberation fighters—not the deacon, not the peasant's daughter—but with the added dimension that they have played these roles, could play them again, and that possibilities known and unknown forever abide. Finally, for the EPLF and Ayn Alem, the storyteller, these stories are self-endorsing: in them a worked-for integration of the teachers into rural Eritrean communities is enacted.

But this still leaves a final issue to be answered. What is the ideology that legitimated the teachers, that integrated them into the community, both in the long process of negotiation and in these dangerous baptismal moments? What is the ideology's name?

The answer is important. These acts of protecting the teachers by integrating them into the village metaphorically legitimated not only their authority to teach, not only literacy and education as a way of life, but legitimated also the liberation movement. The teachers were fighters. They were armed representatives of the revolutionary nationalist movement. They had a revolutionary program for social change that made authoritative demands on the community. In protecting the teachers, the villagers protected this. What legitimated the teachers' demands and their "right" to make them?

> The very structure of legitimation itself ensures the necessary role of ideology. Ideology must bridge the tension that characterizes the legitimation process, a tension between the claim to legitimacy made by the authority and the belief in this legitimacy offered by the citizenry. The tension occurs because while the citizenry's belief and the authority's claim should correspond at the same level, the equivalence of belief with claim is never totally actual but rather always more or less a cultural fabrication. Thus, there is always more in the authority's claim to legitimacy than in the beliefs actually held by the group members.[100]

What Ricoeur here calls the tension to be bridged he has elsewhere called a "gap of representation" in which ideology provides "a sort of metalanguage for the symbolic mediations immanent in collective action."[101] Ideology fills the gap of representations with a symbolic order of reasons for acting. What, for the villagers surrounded by Ethiopian troops, filled this gap? What filled it every day? Says Geertz:

> It is when neither a society's most general cultural
> orientations nor its most down-to-earth "pragmatic"
> ones suffice any longer to provide an adequate image
> of political process that ideologies begin to become
> crucial as sources of sociopolitical meanings and atti-
> tudes.[102]

The gap was not, in these rural communities, filled with empirical
data—a higher infant survival rate, a garden's greater yield of pep-
pers—or even the pleasure of reading and writing one's own letters.
A recognizable pattern of symbolic expressions characterized the
villagers' reception and day-to-day relationship with the teachers.
These are acts which "performed" and "accomplished"[103] the ideological function of social integration:

    1. Villagers institutionalized care of and concern for the teach-
ers in collective structures:

> ABRAHAM BAHRE: What I remember is, in the village I
> told you, Hadamu, the first day that we entered the peo-
> ple were in an assembly. And at that time, in that assem-
> bly, they contributed a lot of things for our living condi-
> tions. And they contributed money and a *lot* of things.
> And they elected a committee which takes care of us,
> and the committee was coming to our house regularly
> and checking on everything, what we eat and what we
> need, what problems we were facing in our education,
> what help they could do for us, which house was appro-
> priate for us to live, and for security matters, everything,
> they were checking us. So I can say that they were treat-
> ing us as their sons and daughters.

    2. The villagers wanted to be with the teachers:

> ABRAHAM BAHRE: They were blushing whenever we entered
> the class. They were eager to see us in front of them.

> ABRAHAM BAHRE: And we were invited so many times in
> their houses. While we had a form to fill in about the vil-
> lage, in order to know how many children had the vil-
> lage and how many of them should we take by force to
> the school because some of them are meant to be shep-

herds. And while we were studying and taking the study of the whole village, we can't fill the form of three or four houses in an afternoon. Why? Because they were preparing coffee or everything. "Chat with us!"

ABRAHAM BAHRE: Another things what I remember is when we were leaving from the village that we were teaching, we were leaving in the village in night, by night, without being seen by the students and by the villagers, because a lot of children—young, young, very young—would follow us; even if we went to the Sahel, they were following us.

3. Villagers risked their lives to protect the teachers:

SOLOMON WOLDMICHEL: They—first of all, they search the areas before we enter the town, the village, from the bushes. They make sure whether the enemy is not keeping themselves in the village or not. And sometimes they hide us in their homes, and they guard the whole night— the man who is in his home, guarding us the whole night while we are sleeping inside the house. Yeah. They are very cooperative, the people. That's why we are still alive—because of the people's protection.

PAUL HIGHFIELD: People were very protective toward them. There's a lot of stories how when the Ethiopian soldiers came to the villages, 'cause they knew that in certain villages this was going on. Some of them were killed. But in other cases they might have disguised them as local people, when roll call was made. They used to hide one of them in a haystack—things like that.

AYN ALEM MARCOS: This was a place where I went to, and while the teachers teach, older people and very young ones will guard, will just sit in every corner, east, west, north, and south, with their cattle; if something happens, if they see a strange movement, they run to the school, tell the teacher to abandon this class and run away.

ABRAHAM BAHRE: I can mention so many things that they have saved us—our lives from the enemy. We are also proud of them and we were confident of them. We couldn't be handed to the enemy because of them. The enemy couldn't find us because of them.

AYN ALEM MARCOS: Tried to protect them like he's protecting his property, his *valuable* property.

4. Villagers treated their relationship with the teachers as one of mutual obligation and concern:

ABRAHAM BAHRE: So they are, I can say that, especially in the first time, they loved us very much, and they made us work harder than what we anticipated.

AYN ALEM MARCOS: But it didn't take them too long to learn from these adults' way of life. So what I'm trying to point out here is, the adults and the community fell in love *literally* with these teachers, *literally* .

ABRAHAM BAHRE: Some of them tell you their personal problems. They were cultivating us as their sons and even, *even* their problems with the administration [i.e., the village assembly]. The administration was elected by them from the people, and sometimes they came—have some conflicts. Even that thing—which we do not, which it doesn't belong to us—they used to tell us.

5. They recreated traditional generational relationships:

SALEH MAHMUD: For example, women, while I was teaching them mathematics, sometimes they become fed up or I don't know, they start to chat with themselves, they say anything about their husbands, about anything. Then, at the last, "Oh, the child is—" [knocks on table] they said. "The child is—stop talking." [Laughs.]

ABRAHAM BAHRE: They protected us a lot. So I think the question is, what were they thinking about us? They were looking at us as their sons and daughters.

What is the ideology that, comprising these symbolic expressions, was "mobilized to fill the gap between the demand coming from above and the belief coming from below"?[104] What is its name?

Ayn Alem Marcos said, "Ah, forget about this, saying it's for the revolution. This is *something else.*"

In regard to the literacy teachers, the gap of representation was filled with the symbolic expressions for many concepts that, gathered together, recognizably compose the concept of love.

Notes

1 "The ethnographer always ultimately departs, taking away texts for later interpretation. (And among those 'texts' taken away we can include memories—events patterned, simplified, stripped of immediate context in order to be interpreted in later reconstruction and portrayal)." James Clifford, "On Ethnographic Authority," *Representations*, 2 (1983): 131.

2 Clifford Geertz, *The Interpretation of Cultures* (n.p.: Basic Books, 1973), 15.

3 A 1986 Eritrean Relief Association report, *Developing a National Education System for Eritrea: The Beginnings* (Khartoum), reported the division of teachers as follows:

> Some 451 students attending grade six and above in Zero School were made available to serve as teachers, health workers and campaigners. . . . However, these alone were not sufficient numbers, so more had to be recruited from the villages. Some 148 such teachers were obtained from the various people's associations, such as the National Union of Eritrean Peasants.

4 Calvin O. Schrag, *Communicative Praxis and the Space of Subjectivity*, (Bloomington, IN: Indiana University Press, 1986).

5 Schrag, *Communicative Praxis*, 24.

6 Schrag, *Communicative Praxis*, 41.

7 Schrag, *Communicative Praxis*, 30.

8 Peter L. Berger and Thomas Luckmann, *The Social Construction of Reality: A Treatise in the Sociology of Knowledge* (New York: Anchor Books, 1966), 15.

9 Schrag, *Communicative Praxis*, 23.

10 Schrag, *Communicative Praxis*, 30.

11 Jürgen Habermas, *Communication and the Evolution of Society*, trans. Thomas McCarthy (Boston: Beacon Press, 1979), 8, 1.

12 Josef Bleicher, *Contemporary Hermeneutics: Hermeneutics as Method, Philosophy and Critique* (London: Routledge and Kegan Paul, 1980), 163.

13 Michel Foucault, *Power/Knowledge: Selected Interviews and Other Writings, 1972-1977*, ed. Colin Gordon, trans. Colin Gordon, Leo Marshall, John Mepham, and Kate Soper (New York: Pantheon, 1980), 145.

14 Hans-Georg Gadamer, *Truth and Method*, trans. Joel Weinsheimer and Donald G. Marshall, 2nd rev. ed. (New York: Crossroad, 1989), 348.

15 Jürgen Habermas, "The Hermeneutic Claim to Universality," trans. Josef Bleicher, *Contemporary Hermeneutics*, by Josef Bleicher (London: Routledge and Kegan Paul, 1980), 183.

16 "ne•go•ti•ate . . . *v.* . . . *intr.* 1. To confer with another or others in order to come to terms or reach an agreement: '*It is difficult to negotiate where neither will trust*' (Samuel Johnson)." *American Heritage Dictionary of the English Language*, 3rd ed.

17 Jürgen Habermas, "The Hermeneutic Claim to Universality," trans. Josef Bleicher, in Bleicher, *Contemporary Hermeneutics*, 184.

18 Habermas, "The Hermeneutic Claim to Universality," 184.

19 Schrag, *Communicative Praxis*, 22.

20 Schrag, *Communicative Praxis*, 31.

21 Habermas, "The Hermeneutic Claim to Universality," 183.

22 Habermas, "The Hermeneutic Claim to Universality," 184.

23 Geertz, *The Interpretation of Cultures*, 10.

24 Habermas, "The Hermeneutic Claim to Universality," 184.

25 Habermas, *Communication and the Evolution of Society*, 29.

26 Bleicher, *Contemporary Hermeneutics*, 152.

27 Bleicher, *Contemporary Hermeneutics*, 163. Universal pragmatics is also discussed in chapter 5; see page 141.

28 Anthony Giddens, "Jürgen Habermas," in *The Return of Grand Theory in the Human Sciences*, ed. Quentin Skinner (Cambridge, England: Cambridge University Press, 1985), 128.

29 I am appropriating Giddens' explanation in "Jürgen Habermas," 128-129, substituting my example for his.

30 Habermas, "The Hermeneutic Claim to Universality," 184.

31 Thomas McCarthy, *The Critical Theory of Jürgen Habermas* (Cambridge, MA: MIT Press, 1978), 280.

32 McCarthy, *The Critical Theory of Jürgen Habermas*, 280, 281.

33 Robert Peter Badillo, *The Emancipative Theory of Jürgen Habermas and Metaphysics*, Cultural Heritage and Contemporary Change Series I. Culture and Values, vol. 13 (Washington, DC: Council for Research in Values and Philosophy, 1991), 61.

34 Zahra Ibrahim, "From the Diary of a Barefoot Doctor," *Adulis*, III, no. 6 (1986): 12-13.

35 Schrag's circumscription, that "praxis is . . . a qualification of communication," applies here. *Communicative Praxis*, 22. See p. 216.

36 Habermas, "The Hermeneutic Claim to Universality," 184.

37 David Held, *Introduction to Critical Theory: Horkheimer to Habermas* (Berkeley: University of California Press, 1980), 333.

38 Habermas, *Communication and the Evolution of Society*, 64, emphasis in original.

39 Kwame Anthony Appiah, *In My Father's House: Africa in the Philosophy of Culture* (New York: Oxford University Press, 1992), 120.

40 As the picture on p. 192 suggests.

41 Habermas, "The Hermeneutic Claim to Universality," 184.

42 Dan Connell, *Against All Odds: A Chronicle of the Eritrean Revolution* (Trenton, NJ: Red Sea Press, 1993), 30; James Firebrace and Stuart Holland, *Never Kneel Down: Drought, Development, and Liberation in Eritrea*, 2nd printing (Trenton, NJ: Red Sea Press, 1986), 43; Glenys Kinnock, *Eritrea: Images of War and Peace*, photographs by Jenny Matthews (London: Chatto and Windus, 1988), 40.

43 Eritrean Relief Association, *Developing a National Education System for Eritrea: The Beginnings* (Khartoum, 1986), 25-26. The literacy teachers I talked to never mentioned the orientation courses; the literacy administrators never failed to mention them.

44 Schrag, *Communicative Praxis*, 125.

45 Schrag, *Communicative Praxis*, 125; compare with Clifford, "On Ethnographic Authority," 133.

46 Giddens, "Jürgen Habermas," 130.

47 Habermas, *Communication and the Evolution of Society*, 28.

48 Held, *Introduction to Critical Theory*, 334.

49 Giddens, "Jürgen Habermas," 129-130.

50 Paul Ricoeur, *Hermeneutics and the Human Sciences*, ed. and trans. John B. Thompson (Cambridge, England: Cambridge University Press, 1981), 205.

51 Douglas Robinson, "Speech Acts," in *The Johns Hopkins Guide to Literary Theory and Criticism*, ed. Michael Groden and Martin Kreiswirth (Baltimore: Johns Hopkins University Press, 1994), 684.

52 Bohuslav Havránek, "The Functional Differentiation of the Standard Language," in *A Prague School Reader on Esthetics, Literary Structure, and Style*, ed. and trans. Paul L. Garvin (Washington, DC: Georgetown University Press, 1964), 3.

53 Paul Ricoeur, *Lectures on Ideology and Utopia*, ed. George H. Taylor (New York: Columbia University Press, 1986), 257, emphasis in original.

54 Ricoeur, *Hermeneutics and the Human Sciences*, 205.

55 Habermas, "The Hermeneutic Claim to Universality," 195.

56 Solomon Woldmichel was more explicit:

> LES GOTTESMAN: So the enemy knew that the teaching was going on.
>
> SOLOMON WOLDMICHEL: Yeah! They know that. They were chasing us! Some of our comrades were killed, were executed while they were teaching. A *lot* of teachers, I think.
>
> LG [subdued]: Yeah.
>
> SW [subdued]: Well.
>
> LG [subdued]: Huh.

SW: Some of them were captured when they were teaching. The enemy surrounded them and captured them. Youngsters—twelve, thirteen years old.

LG: So the enemy was really determined to find and kill the teachers.

SW: Yeah! A lot of programs that were *designed* to kill the teachers. Special military units were assigned to do such things. Whenever a soldier captures a teacher and brings a captured a teacher to the town, the Dergue was giving him some special gifts or some special prizes, money, something else.

LG: So they were very motivated to find you.

SW: Yeah, they were motivated.

57 Geertz, *The Interpretation of Cultures*, 220.

58 Ricoeur, *Hermeneutics and the Human Sciences*, 94.

59 Ricoeur, *Hermeneutics and the Human Sciences*, 118.

60 A large circular griddle, called *mogogo*, made of clay or metal.

61 Hans-Georg Gadamer, *Truth and Method*, trans. Joel Weinsheimer and Donald G. Marshall, 2nd rev. ed. (New York: Crossroad, 1989), 305, emphasis as in original.

62 Gadamer, *Truth and Method*, 305.

63 This does not necessarily work in the opposite generational direction, as attested to in Woldemichael Ghebretensae's account of the EPLF giving salaried jobs to pastoralists who completed fifth grade in order to win their parents' approval of schooling; see p. 198.

64 Stewart R. Clegg, "Narrative, Power, and Social Theory," in *Narrative and Social Control: Critical Perspectives*, ed. Dennis K. Mumby, Sage Annual Reviews of Communication Research 21 (Newbury Park, CA: Sage Publications, 1993), 28. Clegg follows Michel Foucault; see, for example, Foucault, *Discipline and Punish: The Birth of the Prison*, trans. Alan Sheridan (New York: Vintage Books, 1977), 23-24; and Foucault, *Power/Knowledge*, especially 109-133.

65 Schrag, *Communicative Praxis*, 22.

66 Schrag, *Communicative Praxis*, 22.

67 See page 187.

68 Schrag, *Communicative Praxis*; Ricoeur, *Lectures on Ideology and Utopia*,; and see discussion beginning on p. 233.

69 Frank Hearn, "Remembrance and Critique: The Use of the Past for Discrediting the Present and Anticipating the Future," *Politics and Society* 5, no. 2 (1975): 224-225.

70 Quoted in Badillo, *The Emancipative Theory of Jürgen Habermas*, 40.

71 Quoted (with emphasis) in Badillo, *The Emancipative Theory of Jürgen Habermas*, 40.

72 Badillo, *The Emancipative Theory of Jürgen Habermas*, 43.

73 Clegg, "Narrative, Power, and Social Theory," 28.

74 Research and Information Centre on Eritrea (RICE), "The Educational System in Liberated Eritrea," *Eritrea Information* 9, no. 8 (1987), 14.

75 Provisional Government of Eritrea, Department of Education, *Basic Information on Education in Eritrea*, November 1991, 1.

76 "I use 'symbol' broadly in the sense of any physical, social, or cultural act or object that serves as the vehicle for a conception." Geertz, *The Interpretation of Cultures*, 208, note 19.

77 Geertz, *The Interpretation of Cultures*, 214.

78 Paul Ricoeur, *Time and Narrative*, vol. 1, trans. Kathleen McLaughlin and David Pellauer (Chicago: University of Chicago Press, 1984), 59.

79 Donald E. Polkinghorne, *Narrative Knowing and the Human* Sciences (Albany, NY: State University of New York Press, 1988), 144.

80 Paul Ricoeur, *From Text to Action: Essays in Hermeneutics, II*, trans. Kathleen Blamey and John B. Thompson (Evanston, IL: Northwestern University Press, 1991), 195-196.

81 Peter T. Kemp and David Rasmussen, eds. *The Narrative Path: The Later Works of Paul Ricoeur* (Cambridge, MA: MIT Press, 1988).

82 Geertz, *The Interpretation of Cultures*, 218-219.

83 Erik H. Erikson, *Identity: Youth and Crisis* (New York: W. W. Norton, 1968), 190.

84 Held, *Introduction to Critical Theory*, 256.

85 Held, *Introduction to Critical Theory*, 256.

86 George H. Taylor, editor's introduction to *Lectures on Ideology and Utopia*, by Paul Ricoeur, ed. George H. Taylor (New York: Columbia University Press, 1986), xxxi.

87 Ricoeur, *From Text to Action*, 195.

88 Ricoeur, *Lectures on Ideology and Utopia*, 258.

89 Erikson, *Identity: Youth and Crisis*, 189.

90 Erikson, *Identity: Youth and Crisis*, 189-190.

91 Ricoeur, *Lectures on Ideology and Utopia*, 265.

92 Geertz, *The Interpretation of Cultures*, 218.

93 Ricoeur, *Lectures on Ideology and Utopia*, 259.

94 Ricoeur, *Lectures on Ideology and Utopia*, 266.

95 Geertz, *The Interpretation of Cultures*, 220.

96 Ricoeur, *Lectures on Ideology and Utopia*, 11.

97 Ricoeur, *Lectures on Ideology and Utopia*, 261.

98 Hearn, "Remembrance and Critique," 201; and see pp. 125–127.

99 Ricoeur, *Hermeneutics and the Human Sciences*, 187; and see pp. 125–127.

100 Ricoeur, *Lectures on Ideology and Utopia*, 13.

101 Ricoeur, *From Text to Action*, 195-196; and see p. 148.

102 Geertz, *The Interpretation of Cultures*, 219.

103 Schrag, *Communicative Praxis*, 22.
104 Ricoeur, *From Text to Action*, 183.

CONCLUSION

RETURN TO THE SOURCE

Hermeneutics is the study of interpretation as a fundamental human experience and activity. Hermeneutics tries to answer the question, what does it mean to "understand"? Once an arcane sub-specialty of Biblical studies, concerned with the problems of interpreting ancient texts, hermeneutics in the last thirty years has quietly influenced anthropology, sociology, history, literary studies, science, and politics, and even business.

The job of hermeneutics, according to Josef Bleicher, is to identify how this process of understanding is possible, how it takes place, and how the purpose of understanding is realized. Bleicher identifies that purpose as "the emergence of practically relevant knowledge in which [human beings are] changed by being made aware of new possibilities of existence and [their] responsibility for [their] own future."[1]

In Bleicher's definition, hermeneutics walks an ambiguous boundary between description and prescription. On the descriptive side—in the sense that the work of hermeneutics, to quote Hans-Georg Gadamer is "to clarify the conditions in which understanding takes place"[2]—humans always already do hermeneutics. But the question, "How do new possibilities of life emerge?" easily slides into a question of how this can be made to happen.

Certainly when Paul Ricoeur writes of the "tasks of the political educator," we expect prescription, and he obliges. The political educator, says Ricoeur, must prepare the people for the "responsibility of collective decision" by making apparent the moral implications of decisions. The task is twofold: the educator "should make apparent the ethical significance of every choice appearing to be purely economic. Secondly, he ought to struggle for the erection of a democratic society" whereby the exercise of collective choice is possible.[3] Ricoeur identifies "an *ethos*, an ethical singularity which is a power of creation linked to a tradition, to a memory, to an archaic rooting" that is the wellspring of creative change for each "historical group."[4]

It is, however, a "truncation" of the "common *ethos*"—a legacy of colonialism—that Tsenay Serequeberhan identifies as the problem of postcolonial African liberation:[5] the problem of "the concrete actualization of [Africa's] present chimerical 'independence.'"[6] This truncation persists in the failure of Westernized, urban Africans, invariably including revolutionary leaders and cadres, to (using Amilcar Cabral's formula), "return to the source":[7] "The process of 'return,'" says Serequeberhan, "is a cultural and political recovery of the suppressed historic possibilities in the existence of the colonized."[8] Serequeberhan's book, *The Hermeneutics of African Philosophy* (1994), is a theoretical discussion, with few practical or historical examples and none from Eritrea; but Serequeberhan is an Eritrean and dedicates his book to the EPLF. Serequeberhan's discussion illuminates the Eritrean situation, and the situation of much of postcolonial Africa. He brings together the philosophical hermeneutics of Gadamer with the liberation strategies of Frantz Fanon and Cabral.

The western press often cites Eritrea as Africa's "bright spot," "a model for Third World development," "Africa's 'miracle' nation," "an African nation that works," and similar soundbites.[9] Unstated, but implicit, are the questions, What is the secret of the EPLF's success? and, Can this model be applied elsewhere? These questions, however, are also voiced beyond the usual self-serving Western rhetoric of development; those Western observers of Eritrea who yet remain deeply distrustful of Western motives and aims

(such as Basil Davidson and Dan Connell and including myself[10])
are aware of a profoundly promising mood and process in Eritrea.
The EPLF is emphatic on the point: Yemane Ghebreab, Deputy
Secretary of External Affairs, told me, "It is our experience that
experiences really cannot be replicated. Each country is unique, and
the idea that you can export some form of experience to other countries we don't think is really possible."

Yet Cabral's notion of a return to the source is maximally gen-
eralizable. Serequeberhan recasts Cabral's return, and Fanon's idea
that the "encounter of the urban militant and the rural mass" is
"essential . . . to the promise of African liberation,"[11] as a
hermeneutic "fusion of horizons":[12]

> The Westernized native is appreciated for [his] skills and
> wider horizons. . . . Simultaneously, in daily interaction
> in the midst of dire hardships and struggle, he comes to
> fully appreciate and value the resilience and elas-
> ticity . . . of the indigenous history and culture. . . .
> European values and skills are thus absorbed into a new
> synthesis.[13]

In regard to Eritrea, Asmarom Legesse has pointed out:

> On the whole, African nations are governed by urban
> elites with little first-hand knowledge of the countryside
> and the traditional roots of their society. The EPLF, how-
> ever, spent most of its career amidst the herding and
> farming populations of Eritrea. That gave the Front inti-
> mate familiarity with the rural population to a much
> greater extent than is true of other parts of Africa.[14]

In this framework we can consider the Eritrean experience not as a
model but as a case study. The narratives I recorded represent
Eritrean educators' earliest encounters with rural communities,
behind enemy lines in the midst of Eritrea's independence war, during the mid-1980s' national literacy campaign. The difficulties and
successes of the campaign exposed these educators, many of them
teenagers at the time, to the nation's trove of cultural wisdom, in
non-literate but structured symbolic forms, in the social practice of
rural Eritrean communities.

As the teachers worked to advance their projects of mass literacy, social change, and national liberation, they developed a reflective praxis in which they became students of the communities as well as their teachers. The campaign exemplified a model of collaborative learning that at its heart is a fusion of cultural horizons, with positive educational, social, and political effects. First, the campaign contributed to creating a national thirst for education that today is expressed in a nationwide demand for education which (unfortunately) outstrips the government's ability to provide it. Second, the acceptance of education into rural life, even in the limited areas the campaign reached, provided a process for social change to be considered and adopted, transforming, in some cases, rural health and sanitation practices; introducing democratic local government; advancing the status of women in many aspects of life; and improving agriculture. Third, rural people's participation in the campaign was a means to legitimate the liberation movement, this legitimation taking the form of a psycho-social "adoption" of the young teachers by the communities in which they taught. The rural population in great measure took responsibility for the well-being of the teachers, and protected teachers' lives at risk to their own. Most important, the communities deconstructed the assumed hierarchy which puts teachers over students, then reconstructed their relationship to the young teachers along traditional older-younger generational lines. The aim and the result of these inversions was the validation of teachers as legitimate voices in educational, social, and political matters, so as to make their teaching ability most effective and their knowledge most useful.

This bi-directional learning is the essential process of decolonization, according to Serequeberhan.

> It is in and out of this fusion of necessity that the urban and rural native *encounter* each other, *for the first time*, as possible co-protagonists in a process of political struggle and originative history. As Fanon notes . . . the "meeting [or fusion] of revolutionaries coming from the towns [Westernized natives] and country dwellers [peasants/ nomads]" is the dynamic locus out of which unfolds the dialectic of African self-emancipation.

In being "stranded in the county districts" the Westernized urban "revolutionaries," for whom politics is both a calling and a passionate vocation, find the human actuality whose needs and situation their radical discourse has thus far only abstractly articulated. The "people," the "masses," become very concrete in this encounter, in all of their cultural complexity and material misery.[15]

Colonialism "establishes itself . . . by violently negating indigenous cultures,"[16] cultures whose inherent characteristic "is to be open, permeated by spontaneous, fertile lines of force."[17]

This culture, once living and open to the future, becomes closed, fixed in the colonial status, caught in the yoke of oppression. Both present and mummified, it testifies against its members. It defines them in fact without appeal. The cultural mummification leads to a mummification of individual thinking. The apathy so universally noted among colonial peoples is but the logical consequence of this operation. The reproach of inertia constantly directed at "the native" is utterly dishonest. As though it were possible for a man to evolve otherwise than within the framework of a culture that recognizes him and that he decides to assume.[18]

Recent historians have dispelled the notion common in older, European-authored histories that Eritreans displayed near-total passivity in the face of Italian rule, despite 50 years of demographic, economic, and class dislocations. Roy Pateman has traced a history of active resistance, Jordan Gebre-Medhin of incipient political opposition.[19] But certainly there is truth, if not the whole truth, in Richard Sherman's assessment that,

under Italian rule, the Eritreans were, at best auxiliaries. And yet, despite this subordinate social and economic position, there was little or no Eritrean discontent. Food and consumer goods were always cheap and plentiful; taxation was at a token rate. Under this system of control, even co-optation, Eritreans . . . "remained content, docile, and obedient."[20]

This was no less true of Ethiopian occupation than of Italian colonialism. Gebre-Medhin characterizes the Haile Selassie years as ones of "stagnation, paralysis, regression, and restoration of feudalism"[21] Semere Solomon, head of the Planning Division of the Department of Education, painted this picture of education under the Dergue:

> One of the things that we have inherited from the Dergue's system, by having the whole education system destroyed, there existed for at least the last six, seven, eight years the attitude of hopelessness, the attitude of being desperate: what will be our future? We can see so many of our colleagues, having graduated, standing idle, doing nothing, unemployed, even losing what they have already accumulated in their 12 years of education. And there was, to a certain extent, an attitude of hate towards the Dergue's education. They didn't have a chance to enter and pursue their studies at the university, they didn't get to go abroad, they didn't have the chance to get employment. So this has created a state of hopelessness amongst the ranks of the student population. We have to work hard in order to change this kind of attitude.

With the end of the war and the achievement of independence, Eritrea is poised to make great leaps in its material conditions and speed up the social transformation process—yet must also face a backlash against social changes already made.

> [I]t does not suffice merely to expel the colonizer in order to effectively decolonize. It is further necessary to destroy a parasitic and ossified inert and residual Being-in-the-world of the colonized and to institute the "practices of freedom" within the culture and historical context of the decolonizing society, in the process of self-formation.[22]

Paul Highfield outlined the situation:

> The thing now is, in so-called normal society, which itself has been totally distorted and changed in the past seventeen years by the Ethiopian regime destroying the culture, and by the oppression of the regime—in fact, people living in the cities and towns became *more* con-

servative during the Dergue's regime, really I suppose trying to cling onto traditional values—so, now you've got the situation where conservatism is very strong.

But the EPLF has faced conservatism and resistance before, and, eschewing imported and imposed solutions, used conservative institutions to authorize change, as shown in the praxis of the literacy campaign teachers, and in such examples as the Front's careful, consultative process in land reform and in rewriting marriage and inheritance laws.[23] In the process, traditions and institutions are themselves moved and transformed: "the arrested heritage of native society is vitalized in discarding and appropriating that which is necessary for survival."[24]

The return to the source is not a return to the inert past. Decolonization, by reopening the effectualness of a people's history, reestablishes their ability to appropriate a future.

> A noncolonized society grows, transforms, and, in all of this, constantly evaluates and re-evaluates its past in light of the future exigencies of its existence. . . . Colonized society, on the other hand, is not free to evaluate its past in terms of a possible future. It is a society without a future precisely because this is what colonialism negates and grounds itself on.[25]

Frank Hearn describes such a process as

> a restructuring of the present in accordance with the organizing principles exhibited in the idealized portrayal of the past. Thus, the future society, the society which "ought to be," represents a synthesis of the mythical past and those features of the present society which are necessary for the actualization of the "good life."[26]

In the "*encounter* of the urban and rural native," says Serequeberhan, "the standpoint of the present is put in question and what is appropriated is not the inert past but the effective historicity of the fusion of these two elemental and dynamic forces."[27] In Fanon's directive to revolutionaries,

> It is not enough to try to get back to the people in that past out of which they have already emerged; rather we

must join them in that fluctuating movement which they are just giving a shape to, and which, as soon as it has started, will be the signal for everything to be called in question. Let there be no mistake about it; it is to this zone of occult instability where the people dwell that we must come; and it is there that our souls are crystallized and that our perceptions and our lives are transfused with light.[28]

It was this practice, what Arnold Krupat has called the "dual directionality of cultural contact,"[29] between rural Eritreans and the progressive subculture of the liberation movement, that the EPLF enjoined in the national literacy campaign.

[The] process of fusion does not happen as a result of official and formal proclamations or affirmations. It occurs out of *cohabiting* the same historical, political, and existential space in the midst of the most concrete and ultimate of human possibilities—death. It occurs by osmosis and diffusion—the way an exile assimilates the mannerisms and language of his hosts.

Just as the urban militant is cultured into the values and concerns of the rural native, conversely, in this context, the peasants/nomads reclaim their human existence and cultural heritage not as a frozen relic of a dead past, but as the living culture of an actuality—historical and political—in the process of self-institution.[30]

Ayn Alem Marcos told me,

What occurs to you [as a teacher] is, now teach, make them feel that they're Eritreans, you know. That's a very difficult thing, to make a person feel that he is—his identity, his national identity being an Eritrean. Very difficult thing. People can learn a skill—how to write, read, or gain some knowledge. But psychologically to change him, to create self-concept in him, is very difficult. The basis of identity is like anywhere else, your nationality, your culture, your traditions: this is where it begins. But as a nation, it's through politicization, and through sharing common experiences. For example, let's say that you came from the southern part of Eritrea and I came from the northern part of Eritrea and others came from east and west—different cultures, different languages. But coming together, sharing experience, of living, of working, of acting, will create sort of a national identity, wouldn't it?

This principle is active in educational planning and administration in Eritrea today. The EPLF's practice is to draw all sectors of society into the discussion from which policies emerge. So, for example, the curriculum revision process (see page 101) begins with community consultations, but, Highfield told me,

> it's not just going around talking with local assemblies and local leaders in different areas and political representatives and that sort of thing; once that's happened, we'll come back to Asmara and then have a wide-ranging discussion with other ministries, other social bodies, religious leaders, and so on, to discuss these questions—and that's where *their* input will come in because they might have different views, different priorities from what the people have. It's going to be quite a complicated process.

The EPLF has encouraged a national *style* of reflection. In two conversations (a year apart) Highfield described what he called the EPLF's "flexibility," a result, partly, of the Front's 20 years of responding to sudden changes in the military situation:

> One good thing about the EPLF is always this thing about something that's new is always being tested, not imposed for all time, and it's seen as a trial thing, and I think that is, you know, pretty well established in people's minds, and there's always the need to see how relevant it is, to see the reaction, and so on, from different angles, and then—and then to adapt it. It's never seen as something that's implemented for the first time as being the finalized thing.

The EPLF proved resistant to the ideological currents and temptations of superpower rivalry. At the same time the front's practicality—experimentation, discussion, reflection—has equally resisted internal ideological hardening or excess.[31] Yemane Ghebreab told Connell

> of an emotional encounter he had with Isaias [Afwerki, EPLF secretary-general] in 1978 after the Soviet intervention in Eritrea forced the front to retreat the mountains: "We were discussing the nature of the Soviet Union. I tried to prove my point by quoting Lenin—saying Lenin said this, and Lenin said that—and Isaias said, 'So what? Lenin could be wrong.' For me that was a shock. Everybody was questioning Stalin, Mao, whoever, but no one was questioning Lenin. What this showed was that no one was an absolute authority, and there were no models for our struggle."[32]

Ten years later, Australian novelist Thomas Keneally asked Isaias Afwerki how a post-war administration would avoid becoming a bureaucracy dissociated from the people.

> Afwerki shrugged. "We're going to be empirical," he said. . . . "It's unrealistic to think this will be the same after independence. Our only criterion for a policy is whether it works for people. Nothing's carved in stone. I hope we've learned that much from the mistakes of other revolutions."[33]

Now, with the difficulties and necessities of war removed, a national *moment* of self-reflection is at hand, in which it is possible, perhaps, for Eritreans to speak of the "good life"—despite the obstacles they still face—without irony. Paul Ricoeur writes:

> [I]t is in unending work of interpretation applied to action and to oneself that we pursue the search for adequation between what seems to us to be best with regard to our life as a whole and the preferential choices that govern our practices. . . . [B]etween our aim of a "good life" and our particular choices a sort of hermeneutical circle is traced by virtue of the back-and-forth motion between the idea of the "good life" and the most important decisions of our existence. . . . This can be likened to a text in which the whole and the part are to be understood each in terms of the other. Next, the idea of inter-

pretation adds to the simple idea of meaning that of a meaning for someone. For the agent, interpreting the text of an action is interpreting himself or herself.... Interpretation ... provokes controversy, dispute, rivalry—in short, the conflict of interpretations—in the exercise of practical judgment. This means that the search for adequation between our life ideals and our decisions, themselves vital ones, is not open to the sort of verification expected in the sciences of observation. The adequation of interpretation involves an exercise of judgment which, at best, can aspire to plausibility in the eyes of others.[34]

Saleh Meki, Secretary of Marine Resources and Inland Fisheries, echoes Ricoeur from deep within the Eritrean situation. He told me:

I mean this literally: everybody has paid for his independence, so everyone has to have a share. In whatever way we do it, everyone has to have a share, in both developing this country, securing its peace, and helping its progress. Now, the system we come through, of course, has to be done in consultation with our people. The EPLF has certain views of how things should be done. And the EPLF at the appropriate time will express itself on how other things ought to be done. But I think, as I said earlier, since everybody has paid a price for this independence, everybody has a right and an obligation and a responsibility to bring the state that all of us want and require: justice, the peace of our people, the development of our country, all of these things are sometimes easier said than done. How do you do it? How do you really have full participation of the people? By voting every four years? I don't know. Is having political parties, fifty or a hundred political parties as we have in some African countries, suddenly supposed to bring us freedom? I don't know. We have to debate these things. What we do know is that people will be free to express themselves as they wish. People will have all the right to association. These are basic rights that nobody is going to handle, is going to interfere with. So this freedom of association and freedom of expression—freedom

comes with responsibility, and the responsibility to actu-
alize these things for the benefit of all our people would
be what we theoretically envision. How we do that practically—of course there are steps one has to go through.
Unity is done slowly, carefully, always addressing the
basic needs of your people and the people around you.
You just can't think of your own interests because your
interest is totally tied to the interests of other people. If it
controverts the interests of your neighbors, then it's not in
the interest of your people. And there are no mutually
exclusive interests, anyway. And this is the general perception, anyway, of how we look at it.

In the moral imperatives Saleh Meki finds in Eritrea's history and in
the commitments and acts, sacrificial and heroic, of Eritreans, the
promise of liberation is fulfilled and renewed, and the hermeneutic
descriptive becomes, finally, prescriptive.

Notes

1   Josef Bleicher, *Contemporary Hermeneutics: Hermeneutics as Method,
    Philosophy and Critique* (London: Routledge and Kegan Paul, 1980), 3; see
    p. 33.

2   Hans-Georg Gadamer, *Truth and Method*, trans. Joel Weinsheimer and
    Donald G. Marshall, 2nd rev. ed. (New York: Crossroad, 1989), 295.

3   Paul Ricoeur, *Political and Social* Essays, ed. David Stewart and Joseph Bien
    (Athens, OH: Ohio University Press, 1974), 284-285.

4   Ricoeur, *Political and Social Essays*, 281.

5   Tsenay Serequeberhan, *The Hermeneutics of African Philosophy: Horizon
    and Discourse* (New York: Routledge, 1994), 105.

6   Serequeberhan, *The Hermeneutics of African Philosophy*, 8.

7   Amilcar Cabral, *Return to the Source: Selected Speeches* (New York: Monthly
    Review Press, 1973).

8   Serequeberhan, *The Hermeneutics of African Philosophy*, 105.

9   For example Jill Hamburg, "Eritrea Showing a Lot of Promise," *San Francisco
    Chronicle*, 9 April 1992, A16, A18; Joshua Hammer, "Eritrea: Back From the
    Ruins," *Newsweek*, 26 February 1996, 40; Michael A. Hiltzik, "Eritrea
    Reviving as an African Bright Spot," *Los Angeles Times*, 28 December 1991,
    A1, A12-A13; Scott Jones, "Planting the Seeds for Success," *The Oregonian*,
    30 June 1991, P1, P4; Charles F. Laskey, "A Model for Third World
    Development?" review of *Never Kneel Down: Drought, Development and
    Liberation in Eritrea*, by James Firebrace and Stuart Holland, *Africa Today* 40,

no. 2, (1993): 94-96; George W. Shepherd, "Free Eritrea: Linchpin for Stability and Peace on the Horn," *Africa Today* 40, no. 2 (1993): 82-88; John Stackhouse, "Fight to Make Something Out of Virtually Nothing, *London Globe and Mail*, 29 November 1991, A8; Jennie Street, "Eritrea: Building a New Economy," *New African*, November 1991, 32; Street, "Eritrea Begins to Repair Its Shattered Economy," *African Business*, January 1992, 31.

10   Basil Davidson, *The Black Man's Burden: Africa and the Curse of the Nation-State* (New York: Random House, 1992); Dan Connell, *Against All Odds: A Chronicle of the Eritrean Revolution* (Trenton, NJ: Red Sea Press, 1993); Connell, "An Island of Stability in Strife-Filled Africa," *Christian Science Monitor*, 20 November 1994, 10-11; Les Gottesman and Frank Duhl, "Eritrea, Dawn," *Breakthrough*, 18, no. 1 (1994): 3-9, 59.

11   Serequeberhan, *The Hermeneutics of African Philosophy*, 96.

12   Serequeberhan, *The Hermeneutics of African Philosophy*, 100.

13   Serequeberhan, *The Hermeneutics of African Philosophy*, 108, emphasis and brackets in original; the internal quotes are from Frantz Fanon, *The Wretched of the Earth*, trans. C. Farrington (New York: Grove Weidenfeld, 1963), 68.

14   Asmarom Legesse, "Traditions and the Constitution in Eritrea," *Eritrea Profile*, 24 September 1994, 3.

15   Serequeberhan, *The Hermeneutics of African Philosophy*, 94, brackets in original.

16   Serequeberhan, *The Hermeneutics of African Philosophy*, 58.

17   Frantz Fanon, *Toward the African Revolution (Political Essays)*, trans. Haakon Chevalier (New York: Grove, 1967), 34

18   Fanon, *Toward the African Revolution*, 34.

19   Roy Pateman, *Eritrea: Even the Stones Are Burning* (Trenton, NJ: Red Sea Press, 1990), 47-66; Jordan Gebre-Medhin, *Peasants and Nationalism in Eritrea: A Critique of Ethiopian Studies* (Trenton, NJ: Red Sea Press, 1989), 56-69. See also Association of Eritrean Students in North America, *In Defence of the Eritrean Revolution* (1978).

20   Richard Sherman, *Eritrea: The Unfinished Revolution* (New York: Praeger, 1980), 14; the internal quote is from G. K. N. Trevaskis, *Eritrea: A Colony in Transition* (London: Oxford University Press, 1960), 17.

21   Gebre-Medhin, *Peasants and Nationalism*, 61.

22   Serequeberhan, *The Hermeneutics of African Philosophy*, 81.

23   Amrit Wilson, in *The Challenge Road: Women and the Eritrean Revolution* (Trenton, NJ: Red Sea Press, 1991), 116-120, describes a 3-year process of "working from the concrete experiences of the people in putting [the EPLF's anti-feudal] aims and methods into practice" before actual redistribution of land began in the Labca valley, and Pateman, in *Eritrea: Even the Stones Are Burning*, 162, describes a similar, 4-year effort in a northern mountain village near Afabet that culminated in 120 landless peasants gaining land and former (Ethiopian) "government" land being "shared out."
   Starting in 1977, the EPLF began discussing changes in marriage laws. When, through discussions, people "were convinced that changes were needed, they

were involved in making them" (Wilson, *The Challenge Road*, 136). Thus, changes were specific to a given area and often different in some details from new laws in other areas. The reforms allowed for gradual change, for example allowing parents to arrange a marriage with the couple's consent. An EPLF member interviewed by Wilson described the process of reform in mid-eastern Eritrea:

> First the EPLF cadres and the representatives of the People's Assembly had a meeting and discussed the customary laws of Muslims and Christians; they chose the most important ones. They fixed [the minimum] marriage age at 17, and decided to prohibit forced marriage and infibulation. [They] allowed divorce by women, [and] laid down a maximum for the amount of gold given at weddings and the amount [of] food prepared. They came to agreement on these changes. Then they had a bigger meeting with EPLF cadres, People's Assembly and religious leaders—Muslim, Protestant, Catholic and Orthodox. They agreed on all these points. For infibulation they passed the law, and for clitoridectomy they passed a law saying that the family had to report to the People's Assembly who would ensure that there was no infibulation performed at the same time as the clitoridectomy. Then the laws were read to the people. There was some opposition from them but since the religious leaders supported the laws, the opposition was easily overcome. (137, brackets in original)

For this account to be properly understood, it must be noted that the process described here took ten years.

24 Serequeberhan, *The Hermeneutics of African Philosophy*, 100.

25 Serequeberhan, *The Hermeneutics of African Philosophy*, 80

26 Frank Hearn, "Remembrance and Critique: The Use of the Past for Discrediting the Present and Anticipating the Future," *Politics and Society* 5, no. 2 (1975): 201.

27 Serequeberhan, *The Hermeneutics of African Philosophy*, 100.

28 Fanon, *The Wretched of the Earth*, 227.

29 Arnold Krupat, *Ethnocriticism: Ethnography, History, Literature* (Berkeley: University of California Press, 1992), 15.

30 Serequeberhan, *The Hermeneutics of African Philosophy*, 99.

31 See Ruth Iyob, *The Eritrean Struggle for Independence: Domination, Resistance, Nationalism, 1941-1993* (Cambridge, England: Cambridge University Press, 1995), 135.

32 Connell, *Against All Odds*, 274. In *The Hermeneutics of African Philosophy* Serequeberhan writes:

> In [the] inter-implicative dialectic between armed groups and their popular mass base, daily life is not defined by its indifference to politics/history but becomes that which makes for its possibility. In this context, the urban militants stranded in the interior have to learn to "make do" with the mass among whom they find themselves. Political engagement loses its

abstract replicability (Marxist-Leninist formulas?) and becomes the constant attempt to be relevant to lived experience. (98–99)

33 Thomas Keneally, "Let Eritrea Live," *Adulis* IV, no. 3 (1987): 15, first published in the *Sydney Morning Herald*, 20 June 1987.

34 Paul Ricoeur, *Oneself As Another*, trans. Kathleen Blamey (Chicago: University of Chicago Press, 1992), 179-180.

INDEX

Abebe, General Abbiye, 47

Abraham, Girmai, 91, 132

action, 185, 186, 195, 204–205, 220, 232

Adashi, 92

Addis Ababa, 46, 52, 56, 59, 81, 82; Treaty of, 41; University, 84

Adi Teclesan, 73

Adwa, 41

Afabet, 50

Afar: language, 226; people, 101, 155, 202, 230;

Africa, 27, 30, 31, 39, 40, 41, 43, 45, 46, 47, 51, 53, 54, 69, 70 89, 115, 253, 261; economy of, 114–117; European colonialism in, 40, 41, 42, 69, 255; liberation of, 120, 253, 254; postcolonial, 120, 252; precolonial education in, 69–70, 71

Afwerki, Isaias, 231, 260

Agordat, 73

agriculture, 76, 77, 94, 135–140, 152, 154, 155, 175, 254; education, 77, 94, 224, 229

All Ethiopia Trade Union, 50

Allied powers, 45

American University (Beirut), 78

Amhara (people), 41, 57, 59, 161

Amharic (language), 46, 47, 69, 80, 81, 83, 88, 163

Angola, 54

anthropology, 14, 200, 251

Appiah, Kwame Anthony, 32–33, 51, 69, 127, 132, 197

appropriation, 14, 16, 17, 19, 20, 21, 208, 216–217, 257; and distanciation, 16, 140, 144–145

Arab: nations, 51, 52, 164; people, 47, 228

Arabic (language), 69, 79, 80, 81, 89, 164, 226, 227, 228, 229

Araya, Mesfin, 158, 160–161

Aristotle, 133–134

Arreza, 97

art, 190–193

Asmara, 1, 3, 6, 7, 8, 44, 46, 48, 50, 56, 58, 59, 67, 74, 77, 81, 84, 88, 97, 99, 100, 104, 105, 128, 176, 187, 188, 190, 192, 217, 259; liberation of, 27, 56, 84–85

Assab, 44

authority, 69, 140, 143, 144, 145, 183, 233

Axumite kingdom, 40, 159, 161

Badillo, Robert P., 220

Bahre, Abraham, 7, 182–183, 193, 200, 202, 207, 223–224, 242–244

Bakhtin, M. M., 71

Barentu, 73, 74

Barka Province, 30, 89, 99, 211, 217

Basic Needs Approach, 92, 111–114, 117–118

Bellah, Robert N., 4–5, 146, 157

Bello, Walden, 115

Benavot, Aaron, 150, 151

Berger, Peter L., 180

Berkeley (California), 8, 53

Bernstein, Richard J., 133

Beyene, Rev. Tewelde, 158

birth attendants. See midwifery

Bleicher, Josef, 33, 34, 251

British Labour Party, 52

Broniak, Christopher, 221

Burgess, Doris, 117

Cabral, Amilcar, 252, 253

Cairo, 83

Castro, Fidel, 49

Challenge Road, 56

Chombart de Lauwe, Paul–Henry, 135, 143, 150

Clayton, Jay, 157

Clegg, Stewart R., 215, 221

Cliffe, Lionel, 117

Clifford, James, 15

Cohen, Herman, 51–52

Cold War, 31, 39, 51

Comboni Sisters, 6, 81

Connell, Dan, 31, 57, 253, 260

conversation, 12–15, 17, 33, 126, 173, 184, 204. See also dialogue; research

Coptic Church. See Orthodox Christian Church

"Creating a Popular Economic, Political and Military Base" (EPLF document), 117

Crites, Stephen, 19–20

critical theory, 140–142, 143, 144–147, 149

Cuba, 49

curriculum, 115, 151. See also education in Eritrea

Curriculum Development Institute (Department of Education), 4, 6, 11, 99, 155, 226; English Panel of, 6, 175; Saho Panel of, 6, 174; Science Panel of, 68, 78, 80

Danakil, 230

Davidson, Basil, 31, 51, 253

democracy, 2, 20, 23, 29, 30, 46, 47, 54, 91, 119, 120, 132, 133, 175, 252, 254

Demoz, Berhane, 6, 12, 174, 201, 202, 206, 210–211

Department of Communication (Provisional Government of Eritrea), 91

Department of Construction (Provisional Government of Eritrea), 91

Department of Education (Provisional Government of Eritrea), 1, 3, 5, 6, 7–8, 91, 92, 95, 101, 102, 152, 174, 226, 229; Adult Education Division, 6, 90, 101, 174,

175; Planning and Program Division, 6, 96, 103, 174, 175, 226, 256; Provincial Office of Education, 6, 99; Teacher Training Institute, 4, 99. *See also* Curriculum Development Institute

Department of External Affairs (Provisional Government of Eritrea), 8, 253

Department of Health (Provisional Government of Eritrea), 91

Department of Marine Resources and Inland Fisheries (Provisional Government of Eritrea), 8, 261

Department of Transportation (Provisional Government of Eritrea), 91

Dergue, 48–50, 51, 67, 83–86, 177, 256

development. *See* literacy and development

dialogue, 1, 12–17, 102, 126, 146, 203, 210. *See also* conversation; research

Dien Bien Phu, 50

distanciation. *See* appropriation

Djibouti, 30, 58

drought, 2, 30, 34, 57, 90, 102, 153, 155, 177, 189, 194–195, 196, 197. *See also* famine

Dulles, John Foster, 46

education in Eritrea: administrators of, 4, 6, 7, 8, 10, 11, 27, 29, 34, 179; adult, 7, 30, 32, 98, 100–101, 118, 119, 122, 137, 153, 176, 177, 202; agricultural, 76, 77, 79, 90, 93; under British rule, 78–80; and communities, 8, 9–10, 86, 92, 93–94, 95–96, 102, 103, 104–105, 119, 179, 181, 183, 184, 197–199, 222–225, 227–228, 254; curriculum of, 7, 10, 58, 70, 76, 79, 88, 92, 93, 118, 134, 176–177, 178, 179; curriculum

designers for, 1, 34, 155; curriculum revision of, 101–103; demand for, 10, 79, 80, 81, 98, 105, 254; under the Dergue, 83–86, 100, 129, 153, 256–257; English language in, 6, 28, 79, 82, 89, 130; Ethiopian teachers in, 80–83; by example, 69–75, 86; during Federation, 80–81; of fighters, 28, 87–88, 101; for girls, 72, 77, 79, 80, 154; under Haile Selassie, 80–82; history of, 29, 67–105; under Italian rule, 75–78; languages of, 58, 76, 77, 79, 80–81, 82, 88, 118, 154, 190, 225–229; by missionaries, 75, 78; and Muslim people, 155, 174, 214–218; and parents, 86, 98, 103–105, 198–199, 227; political, 29, 75, 77, 117–118; postliberation, 58, 68, 74–75, 95–105, 175; precolonial, 68–70; promise of, 19, 20, 27, 32, 34, 213–217, 219; for self-reliance, 92–93, 118–119; and social transformation, 9–10, 12, 17, 18, 19, 22, 23, 32–34, 72, 74, 87, 103, 119, 143, 213, 254; textbooks for, 79, 80, 81, 90, 99, 176; vocational, 75, 77, 80, 91, 93, 100, 132; of women, 88, 89, 153–155, 175, 202, 221, 254. *See also* health; national literacy campaign

effective history. *See* historical consciousness

Egypt, 40, 53, 80

Eisenloeffel, Frits, 88

ELF. *See* Eritrean Liberation Front

Endalal, 92

EMAC. *See* Eritrea Material Aid Campaign

English (language), 28, 69, 74, 79, 82, 89, 130, 223

EPLF. *See* Eritrean People's Liberation Front

Erikson, Erik H., 233–234

Eritrea (film), 28, 47

Eritrea Material Aid Campaign (EMAC), 2–3

Eritrea: agriculture in, 2, 18, 29, 32, 43, 57, 155, 135–139; ancient, 40, 162; annexation by Ethiopia, 46–47, 81; British occupation of, 42, 44–45, 78–80; Christians in, 30, 48, 163, 237; development in, 8, 10, 30, 32, 155–156; economy of, 8, 33, 57, 58, 155–156; Ethiopian colonialism in, 219–220, 256–257; ethnic groups in, 30, 48; federation with Ethiopia, 45–47, 80–81, 160; feudalism in, 42–43, 45; geography of, 30; Government of, 28; history of, 39–61, 158, 159–161, 262; independence of, 2, 3, 27–28, 30, 39, 40, 41, 45, 52, 158; independence war in, 11, 21, 27–28, 30, 31, 47–48, 50–52, 56, 90, 95, 103, 130, 147, 158, 189, 253; international aid to, 52, 57;

Italian colonialism in, 39, 40, 41–44, 45, 69, 75–78, 130, 153, 158, 159, 160, 162, 255; Italian racial laws in, 42–44, 76; land reform in, 20, 28–29, 32, 156, 257; languages of, 30, 46, 69, 162–163, 259; liberated areas of, 2, 28, 58, 88, 90, 103, 176; manufacturing in, 42–43, 44, 46, 57; as model of development, 30, 31, 252–253; Muslim people in, 30, 47, 48, 59, 68, 69, 163, 164, 174, 214, 228, 237; national service in, 58; people of, 30, 42, 43, 44; political isolation of, 3, 29, 39, 46, 49, 58, 119; political parties in, 39, 44, 46; ports of, 40, 43, 44, 56; postliberation, 8, 21, 56–61, 103, 156–157; precolonial, 41; Provisional Government of, 1, 5, 28, 34, 56–58, 59, 85, 95; referendum on independence of, 1–2, 30,

52, 57, 58–61, 156, 231; refugees of, 2, 53, 57, 58, 89, 98, 164; religion in, 30, 31, 45, 48, 68, 69, 156, 163–164, 175; self–reliance in, 28, 30, 31, 57, 91, 119, 129; Soviet troops and advisors in, 50; taxation in, 42, 52; trade unions in, 44, 46; transportation in, 43, 57; Unionist Party of, 45, 160–161, 162–163; urbanization of, 43

Eritrean Assembly, 46–47

Eritrean Health Service, 56

Eritrean Liberation Front (ELF), 47–48, 52, 59, 82; civil war with EPLF, 48, 87, 88

Eritrean Medical Association, 53

Eritrean People's Liberation Army, 27, 49, 54, 56, 57, 164, 223; and literacy, 87; postliberation service of, 57–58. *See also* Eritrean People's Liberation Front

Eritrean People's Liberation Front (EPLF), 2, 3, 6, 28–29, 34, 47, 48, 50–60, 68, 117, 129, 130, 133, 159, 160, 161, 175, 176, 178, 181, 189, 195, 213, 219, 230, 231, 236, 237, 239, 241, 252, 253, 257, 258, 259, 260, 261; civil war with ELF, 48, 87, 88; culture of, 29, 179, 200–201, 258; demobilization of fighters, 74–75, 100; documentation of experiences, 12; education programs for fighters of, 87, 100, 178; environmental policies of, 121; factories and workshops of, 54–56, 87; financial support for, 51, 52–53, 58; fighters of, 8, 10, 53–54, 200–201; leaders of, 2, 231, 260; mass organizations of, 53, 92, 134, 156, 208; medical capability of, 56; military victories of, 50–51; programs of, 2, 48, 86–105, 152, 173, 197, 224, 225;

public works of, 56, 57–58; and religion, 163–164; self–effacing style of, 11–12; self–reliance of, 3, 28, 39, 51, 53–56, 57; and social transformation, 195–199, 211–213; strategic withdrawal of, 49, 89, 175, 260; at war's end, 87, 156. *See also* Eritrean People's Liberation Army; national literacy campaign

Eritrean Relief Association, 53

Eritrean Relief Committee, 6

Erota, 92

Espinoza, César Picón, 112

Ethiopia, 30, 31, 39–40, 41, 45, 45, 46, 47, 48, 49, 51, 52, 56, 57, 59, 61, 70, 80, 81, 82, 83, 84, 158, 163, 164, 194; ancient, 40, 159, 161, 162; Italian invasion of, 43–44, 160; Workers Party of, 49; education in, 80, 81, 82, 84. *See also* Eritrea

Ethiopian Airlines, 58, 73

Ethiopian military. *See* military

Ethiopian Orthodox Church. *See* Orthodox Christian Church

Ethiopian Peoples Revolutionary Democratic Front, 56

Europe, 8, 31, 40, 53, 120, 164, 253

European colonialism. *See* Africa; Eritrea

famine, 2, 30, 34, 153, 155, 177, 194–195, 196, 197; relief, 3, 41, 51. *See also* drought

Fanon, Frantz, 162, 252, 253, 254, 257–258

Ferrell, Susan T. 151, 152

Festa, Andrea, 76, 77

Firebrace, James, 52, 54, 87

Foucault, Michel, 162, 184

Frankfurt School, 120

Freire, Paulo, 120

fusion of horizons, 71, 135, 138–140, 210, 211, 253, 254. *See also* Gadamer, Hans-Georg

Gadamer, Hans-Georg, 1, 13, 15, 16, 17, 33, 126, 138, 139, 140, 142, 143, 144, 162, 211, 251, 252. *See also* fusion of horizons

Gash Province, 217, 225

Gebre-Medhin, Jordan, 45, 255, 256

Gebreyesus, Elsa, 7, 73

Geertz, Clifford, 12, 13, 14, 16, 186, 231, 232–233, 238, 241–242

Gelpi, Ettore, 133

Gerahtu, Tesfamicael, 6, 11, 226, 227, 228–229

Ghebreab, Yemane, 8, 253, 260

Ghebremariam, Solomon, 6, 96, 174

Ghebreselassie, Beraki, 6, 11, 87, 91, 95, 100, 101, 103, 174–175

Ghebretensae, Woldemichael, 6, 99, 174, 197–199, 230

Ghinda, 60

Gilkes, Patrick, 159–160

Giroux, Henry A., 146

Golden Gate University, 3

Government of Eritrea. *See* Eritrea

Griffin, Colin, 33, 129

Habermas, Jürgen, 33, 127–128, 130, 140, 141, 144, 145, 146, 184, 185, 186–187, 188, 204, 205, 220, 233; on "convincing speech," 185, 186, 193

Habits of the Heart: Individualism and Commitment in American Life (Bellah et al.), 146, 157, 163

Hadamu, 242

Haile Selassie Secondary School, 81

Haile, Girmay, 6, 225, 226

Haile, Kaleab, 6, 7, 90, 101, 174, 175–178, 188–189, 197, 224

Hauser, Karen A., 5, 6, 8, 103, 152, 153, 155

health, 2, 18, 30, 44–45, 58, 75, 93, 105, 111, 116, 117, 129, 175, 177, 196, 197, 217, 254; education, 29, 70, 76, 77, 79, 90, 93, 229

Hearn, Frank, 125, 127, 220, 240, 257

Heidegger, Martin, 162

hermeneutics 4, 8, 12, 15, 16, 17, 18, 23, 33, 34, 67, 125, 126, 135, 140, 142, 144–146, 146, 149, 155–158, 220, 253, 260, 262; definition of, 33–34; purpose of, 251–252

"Hermeneutics and the Critique of Ideology" (Ricoeur), 142

Hermeneutics of African Philosophy, The (Serequeberhan), 252

Highfield, Paul, 5, 6, 74, 84, 93, 96, 99, 101–103, 155, 175, 195–197, 200, 221, 222, 226–227, 228, 229, 243, 256–257, 259

Hishkub, 92

historical conscious- ness, 67–68, 140, 146–147, 258

history, 119, 158–163, 251, 252, 253, 254, 256, 257; as hope, 158; as subject, 72, 76, 77, 89. *See also* educa- tion in Eritrea; Eritrea; narrative

Holland, Stuart, 52, 54, 87

Hoover Institute (Stanford Univer- sity), 8

hope, 21, 31, 34, 53, 158, 160

Horn of Africa, 2, 30, 48, 58, 59

Howley, Aimee, 151, 152

human sciences. *See* social science

ideal speech situation. *See* universal prag- matics

identity, 19, 20, 21, 32, 135, 158, 227, 231, 233–234, 238, 240; national, 34, 41, 103, 208, 258–259. *See also* Erikson, Erik H.

ideology, 127, 140–141, 142, 144, 146, 151, 161–162, 180, 231, 235; cri- tique of: *see* critical theory; as distortion, 140–141, 144, 145, 146, 233, 234, 259; as integration, 145, 147–149, 218, 232, 233–234, 238, 241–245. *See also* narrative; Erikson, Erik H.

illocution, 204–205

Institute of Italian Universities, 82

interpretation, 4, 12–17, 21, 32, 33, 125, 135, 140, 142, 144, 145, 148, 173, 185, 186, 251, 260–261; cross–cul- tural, 12, 14, 16–17, 145–146

Iraq, 52

Islam. *See* education in Eritrea; Eritrea, Muslim people in

Israel, 52, 58

Italian (language), 69, 75, 76, 77, 82

Italy. *See* Eritrea; Ethiopia

Iyob, Salome, 7, 72

James, Stanlie M., 155

Jani, 92

Jassir, Mohammedin, 6, 72, 174

Johnston, Sister Mary Thomas, 5, 6, 8, 85–86, 221, 222

Jones, Scott, 5, 6, 135–140

Kagnew military station, 46

Kalashnikov, 235

Kalish, Susan, 28, 34, 47

Kassa, Ras Arate, 82

kebeles, 50

Keneally, Thomas, 91, 260

Keren, 6, 47, 99

Kinet clubs, 84

Koran, 226

Krupat, Arnold, 71, 258

Kunama: people, 73–74; language, 188

Kuwait, 52

La Belle, Thomas J., 149–150, 151

land reform. *See* Eritrea

language, 17, 71, 131, 135, 137, 140, 141, 143, 163, 180, 182, 183, 186, 188–190, 204–205, 206. *See also* negotiation

Latin America, 118

Legesse, Asmaron, 253

legitimation, 19, 33, 125, 127–130, 143, 145, 146, 148–149, 159, 193, 205, 230–231, 232, 234, 241–245; and antiquity, 159; crisis, 22, 33, 122, 127, 130; of education, 9, 17, 22, 32, 189 241; of liberation movement, 34, 164, 181, 241, 254; of political leadership, 32, 34, 42, 119. *See also* narrative

Leirman, Walter, 113, 116, 120, 122

Lenin, V. I., 260

Leonard, Richard, 29, 93, 117

Lewin, Philip, 18, 32

Libya, 45

Lijam, Senait, 7, 174, 202, 217–218

literacy. *See* Eritrean People's Liberation Front; Eritrean People's Liberation Army; national literacy campaign

literacy and development, 111–113, 112, 115–120. *See also* national literacy campaign

local knowledge. *See* traditional knowledge

Luckmann, Thomas, 180

Madsen, Richard, 157

Mahmud, Saleh, 7, 87, 88, 190, 193, 203, 205, 206–207, 213–216, 218, 224–225, 244

Makane Hiwot (hospital), 187

Mali, 152

Mao Tse–tung, 260

Maoism, 117, 118

Marcos, Ayn Alem "Joe," 6, 7, 12, 89, 179–180, 181, 184, 194–195, 201, 206, 207–208, 209–210, 212–213, 223, 235–238, 241, 243, 244, 245, 258–259

Mareb River, 41

Maria Tselam, 72, 228–229

Mariam, Mengistu Haile, 41, 48, 49, 51, 52, 56

Markakis, John, 163–164

marriage, 18, 45, 72, 164, 191–192, 199, 215–216, 218; laws, 164, 257

Marxism, 3, 41, 49, 54, 143, 145; –Leninism, 51, 83

Massawa, 40, 44, 56, 57

Meki, Saleh, 8, 47, 261–262

memory, 4, 14, 15, 147, 157–158, 163, 173, 252

Mendefera, 6

Menelik, 40, 41, 161

Mesfun, Alula, 8, 87–88

Mesghinna, Wolde, 3, 8, 53, 70–71, 121, 122, 129, 151, 152, 158

Micael, Asfaha Wolde, 47

Middle East, 46, 53, 69, 164

midwifery, 93, 177

military: Ethiopian, 2, 27, 28, 41, 46–47, 48, 49, 50, 51, 54, 56, 82, 89, 90, 92, 96, 97, 153, 160, 161, 176, 177, 207, 219, 235–238, 239, 241, 243–244; Italian colonial, 44, 76, 77, 159; Portuguese, 40; Soviet, 50–51; United States, 46, 59

Mishler, Elliot G., 11

missionaries. *See* education

misunderstanding, 142, 143, 146

modernization, 9, 19, 20, 32, 34, 39, 135

Mogadishu, 59

Mozambique, 54

Muro, Asseny, 155

Mussolini, Benito, 42, 76

Nacfa, 92, 100

narrative, 8, 10–12, 17, 21–22, 34, 157, 181, 184, 197, 213, 232, 235, 253; and communities, 32–33, 34, 157–158, 240; and ethics, 22–23; and history, 146, 148, 158–162; and hope, 158; and ideology, 147–149, 232; and legitimation, 19, 22–23, 148, 149, 232; and promise, 19–21, 32, 34, 148, 213–217, 219; and self-understanding 18–22, 32–33, 34; and social transformation, 18, 32

national literacy campaign, 7, 29, 89–90, 94, 173, 253, 257; adult students in, 177, 178, 179, 180, 182, 196, 199, 202; beginning of, 89–90, 152, 175–180, 194–195; coercion of students, 70, 211–213; curriculum, 7, 90, 117–118, 176–179; dangers faced in, 2, 235–238; innovations of, 207–211; recruitment of students, 184, 194–195, 203, 205–206,

213–222; teachers of, 1, 5, 7, 12, 29, 89–90, 173, 177, 179, 180, 181, 191, 224–225, 253–254; teacher–student relationships in, 222–224, 235–244; teachers' commitment to, 183, 202, 206–207; teachers killed in, 11, 101, 206; teachers' learning process, 2, 90, 180, 182–183, 190–193, 205–206; teachers' participation in rural life, 29, 89–90, 94, 177, 190–193, 206–207; teacher training for, 177, 201–202, 224; and women, 154, 178, 202, 214–218, 254

National Union of Eritrean Students in North America, 2

National Union of Eritrean Women, 5, 6, 7, 92, 174, 217

nationalism, 158–162, 181, 227

Nefasit, 60

Negassi, Leteyesus, 7

negotiation, 8, 21, 34, 181, 183, 184–185, 196, 199, 213–222, 241; and language, 185, 199–200; and language of instruction, 225–229. See also language

Negussie, Birgit, 70

Niezen, R. W., 151

Nigeria, 54, 118, 147

nomads. See pastoralists

North America, 53, 164

Oakland (California), 52

oral culture, 70

Oromo: liberation movement, 56; people, 41, 59

Orthodox Christian Church, 45, 68, 69

Ottoman Empire, 40

Paice, Edward, 42

Painful Season and a Stubborn Hope, A (Tesfagiorgis), 7

Palestinian organizations, 52

Papstein, Robert, 90, 92, 154

parents' committees. *See* school committees

Parmelee, Jennifer, 158

pastoralists, 12, 30, 70, 89, 95, 101, 152, 153, 176, 197–199, 230–231, 258; settlement of, 18, 32, 231

Pateman, Roy, 28–29, 52, 53, 92 118, 134, 159, 255

Peace Corps, 73

peasants, 12, 28–29, 42, 50, 89, 94, 117, 153, 181, 183, 258

People's Assemblies, 92, 211–212, 227

Phillips, Sherry, 5, 6, 7, 73–74

philosophical hermeneutics. *See* hermeneutics

Plato, 184

play, 125–127, 145, 148–149, 220, 240

political educator. *See* Ricoeur, Paul

Polkinghorne, Donald E., 18, 32

power, 215–216, 218, 219, 220, 221

Power and Need in Africa (Wisner), 111

praxis, 19, 133, 149, 173, 180–183, 185, 189, 205, 210, 213, 216–217, 240, 254, 257. *See also* Schrag, Calvin O.

Prince Mekkonen Secondary School, 81

promise. *See* education in Eritrea; narrative

Provincial Office of Education. *See* Department of Education

Provisional Government of Eritrea. *See* Eritrea

Ramdas, Lalita, 154

rationality, 146, 220

Red Sea Secondary School, 81

Red Sea, 30, 39, 40, 46, 101, 214, 225

referendum on independence. *See* Eritrea

refugees. *See* Eritrea

Regional Centre for Human Rights and Development, 4, 6, 7, 174

Research and Information Center on Eritrea (RICE), 53

research, 1, 3, 4–8, 11, 12–17. *See also* conversation; dialogue

Revolution School. *See* Zero School

Revolutionary Ethiopian Women's Association, 49–50

Revolutionary Ethiopian Youth Association, 49

RICE. *See* Research and Information Center on Eritrea

Ricoeur, Paul, 13, 16, 18, 20, 21, 22, 23, 33, 121–122, 125, 126–127, 130–132, 134–135, 140, 142, 143, 144–146, 147–149, 156, 158, 204, 218, 233, 234, 240, 241, 260–261; on "the political educator," 23, 125, 127, 130–132, 134, 252

Riessman, Catherine Kohler, 11

Roy–Singh, Raja, 112

Sahel Province, 56, 88, 89, 182, 188, 200, 210, 237

Saho: people, 72; language, 188. *See also* Curriculum Development Institute

Said, Edward, 15–16

sanitary napkins, 86

sanitation, 18, 29, 79, 90, 175, 177

Santa Familia University. *See* University of Asmara

Sarris, Greg, 68

Saudi Arabia, 49, 58, 214, 226, 230

Schleiermacher, Friedrich, 142

school committees, 79, 92, 104–105, 227

Schrag, Calvin O., 133; on "communicative praxis," 180–181, 185, 203, 216, 218, 239

Science and Technology Education in Eritrea (Department of Education document), 68, 78, 80

science, 33, 69, 91, 112, 114, 150, 151, 197, 251; as subject, 118, 191

Selam Hotel, 61

Selassie, Haile, 41, 44, 45, 46, 47, 48, 52, 80, 81, 82, 163, 256

Selassie, Wubnesh W., 154

self–reliance. See Eritrea; Eritrean People's Liberation Front

Sembel Elementary School, 105

Semhar Province, 72, 214, 225

Senhit Province, 6, 72, 99, 174, 228, 237

Seraye Province, 6, 96, 174

Serequeberhan, Tsenay, 252, 254–255, 257

Sherman, Richard, 255

Shoa Province (Ethiopia), 40, 41, 82

Sironi, Bruna, 118

social change; see social transformation

Social Construction of Reality, The (Berger and Luckmann), 180

social science, 1, 4–5, 23, 33

social transformation, 1, 2, 30, 48, 74, 87, 113, 117, 120, 130, 149, 156, 175, 195–199, 256, 257. See also education; tradition

Solomon, Semere, 6, 96, 103–105, 175, 256

Solomuna refugee camp, 2

Somali kingdoms, 40

Somalia, 31, 45, 58, 59

Sorenson, John, 159, 161

South Africa, 54, 114

Soviet military. See military

Soviet Union, 3, 31, 46, 48–49, 50, 51, 260

Spencer, John, 47

Stalin, Joseph, 260

Stanford University. See Hoover Institute

Sudan, 28, 30, 49, 52, 56, 61, 89, 164, 178, 194; civil war in, 31, 59

Suez canal, 40

Sullivan, William N. , 157

Swedish mission schools, 75, 78

Swidler, Ann, 157

teacher training, 1, 6, 79, 100. See also national literacy campaign

Teacher Training Institute. See Department of Education

techne, 133

technocracy, 91, 112, 132

technology, 22, 31, 33, 114, 116, 121–122, 129, 132, 135, 143, 146, 150, 151

Tecle, Amare, 60

Tedros, Zecarias, 7, 190–193, 218–219, 222

Teklehaimanot, Berhane, 76, 78

terracing, 94

Tesfagiorgis, Abeba, 7, 174

Tesfamariam, Issayas, 8, 147, 164–165

Tessenei, 73, 97

Tewelde, Yacob, 6

Teweldemedhin, Isahac, 78

text, 4, 12, 14, 15, 17, 140, 144–145, 173, 181, 185; appropriation of, 32, 144–145; interpretation of, 12, 16–17, 126, 140, 145, 260

Thomas, Sister. *See* Johnston, Sister Mary Thomas

Tigray: liberation movement, 56; people, 40, 41; province, 30, 225;

Tigre: language, 88, 89, 188, 190, 192, 193, 226, 228; people, 60, 190–193, 228, 230;

Tigrinya: language, 79, 80, 81, 85, 88, 89, 163, 176, 182, 190, 192, 193, 201, 210–211, 226, 227, 229; people, 221

Tipton, Steven M., 157

tradition, 1, 8–9, 18–19, 20, 29, 33, 34, 39, 41, 125, 126, 131, 135, 139, 140, 145, 180, 186, 220, 224, 231, 252, 253, 254, 258; displacement of, 113; and education,

67–70, 74–75, 86, 195, 202; and legitimation, 119, 128, 144, 146, 163; and social transformation, 1, 23, 28, 30, 32–34, 71–72, 87, 144, 146, 157, 197, 230, 257

traditional knowledge, 9, 69–70, 94, 117, 129, 135, 183

Uccialli. *See* Wichale

understanding, 13–14, 17, 33, 34, 142, 146, 251; cross–cultural, 12, 14, 16–17. *See also* interpretation

Unionist Party. *See* Eritrea

UNESCO, 114, 116

United Nations, 1, 28, 46, 47, 59, 114, 115; Commission on Eritrea (1950), 45;

United States, 3, 31, 44, 46, 48, 51, 52, 59, 61, 129, 146, 157; aid to Eritrea, 52; Eritreans in, 53, 164

universal pragmatics, 141–142, 184, 186–188, 193, 204, 205. *See also* Habermas, Jürgen

University of Asmara, 1, 3, 4, 6, 7, 8, 72, 81–82, 83, 84, 85, 97, 182

University of Chicago, 121

University of San Francisco, 3

Urban Dweller's Association. *See* kebeles

Vanhoozer, Kevin J., 18

Vietnam war, 48, 113

Vittorio Emanual III School, 77

Ward, Christopher R., 149–150, 151

Wichale, Treaty of, 40

Wisner, Ben, 92–93, 111, 112, 116

Woldegiorgis, Andbrhan, 92

Woldemichael, Berhane, 96

Woldmichel, Solomon, 7, 71, 94, 97–99, 101, 201, 206, 219–220, 243

women, 5, 7–8, 18, 32, 73–74, 75, 86, 156, 175, 254; fighters, 53–54, 156; and land, 20. *See also* education; national literacy campaign

Worker's Control
  Committees
  (Ethiopia), 50
Workers Party of
  Ethiopia. *See*
  Ethiopia
World Bank, 112,
  115, 116
World War II, 39, 44,
  113, 115
Yemen, 226
Zakharieva, Mariana,
  151
Zenawi, Meles, 61
Zero School, 2, 12,
  29, 88–89, 92, 175,
  177, 201, 214, 221;
  and surrounding
  population,
  230–231
Zerom, Kiflemariam,
  8, 72, 83–84, 85
Zimbabwe, 115, 118